Fernando de Toro

Theatre Semiotics

Text and Staging in Modern Theatre

Translated from the Spanish by
John Lewis

Revised and Edited by
Carole Hubbard

University of Toronto Press
Toronto · Buffalo

First published in North America by
University of Toronto Press Incorporated 1995

© Vervuert Verlag, Frankfurt/M, 1995
Printed in Germany

ISBN 0-8020-0634-5 (cloth)
ISBN 0-8020-7589-4 (paper)

Toronto Studies in Semiotics

Editors: Marcel Danesi, Umberto Eco, Paul Perron, and Thomas Sebeok

Printed on acid-free paper

Canadian Cataloguing in Publication Data

Toro, Fernando de, 1950-
    Theatre semiotics : text and staging in modern theatre

(Toronto Studies in Semiotics)
Translation of: Semiótica del teatro : del texto a la puesta en escena.
Includes bibliographical references and index.
ISBN 0-8020-0634-5 (bound)   ISBN 0-8020-7589-4 (pbk.)

1. Theatre - Semiotics.   I.Hubbard, Carole.
II. Title.

PN2041.S45T6713 1995   792' .014   C94-930657-6

This book is a translation, expanded and updated, of *Semiótica del teatro: Del texto a la puesta en escena* (Buenos Aires: Editorial Galerna 1987). The translation was assisted by a translation grant from the Writing and Publication Section of the Canada Council.

To Mary, my true friend
To Alfonso, Rosalba, and Francisco,
my other true friends

CONTENTS

Acknowledgements xi

FOREWORD TO THE SPANISH EDITION - Marco De Marinis xiii

FOREWORD - Mario Valdés xv

PREFACE - Fernando de Toro 1

INTRODUCTION 3

CHAPTER I:
THEATRE DISCOURSE 5
   I.   The Notion of Discourse 5
   II. Theatre Discourse 8
      A)   Speaker/Hearer 8
      B)   Enunciative Situation/Utterance 11
      C)   Deixis/Anaphora 13
         1)   Enunciative Deixis 18
         2)   Spatial Deixis 19
         3)   Temporal Deixis 19
         4)   Social Deixis 21
         5)   Demonstrative Deixis 21
   III. Functions of Theatre Discourse 22
      A)   Functions of Language in Theatre 22
      B)   Functions of the Actor's Discourse 23
   IV. Specification of Theatre Discourse 24
   Notes 29

CHAPTER II:
TEXT, DRAMATIC TEXT, PERFORMANCE TEXT 35
   I.   Text 36
      A)   The Semiological View 36
      B)   The Classical View 39
   II. The Dramatic Text 43
      A)   Textual Function 43
      B)   Stage Function 46
   III. Performance Text 48
      A)   Production Text 48
         1)   Places of Indetermination 49
         2)   Performance Potential 50

		B)	Performance Text	52

        B) Performance Text 52
           1) Performance Codes 53
           2) Theatre Conventions 54
               a) General Conventions 55
               b) Particular Conventions 56
               c) Unique Conventions 56
    Notes 59

CHAPTER III:
THEATRE SEMIOTICS 63
    I. Semiosis 63
        A) The Notion of Semiotics 63
        B) The Various Versions of Sign 64
    II. The Nature of the Theatre Sign 68
        A) Signs of Signs 69
        B) The Mobility of the Theatre Sign 70
        C) Redundancy of the Theatre Sign 71
    III. The Icon, the Index, the Symbol According to Peirce 73
        A) The Icon 73
        B) The Index 74
        C) The Symbol 75
    IV. The Icon, the Index, and the Symbol at Work in Theatre ... 76
        A) Iconic Function 76
           1) The Icon as Code 76
           2) Visual Icon 77
               a) The Body 77
               b) Gestures 77
               c) Object/Mimetic Icon 78
           3) Verbal Icon 78
               a) Verbal Icon/Mimesis 78
               b) Verbal Icon/Action 79
        B) Indexical Function 79
           1) Diegetic Function 80
           2) Gestural Index 80
           3) Spatial Index 82
           4) Temporal Index 82
           5) Social Index 83
           6) Environmental Index 84
        C) Symbolic Function 84
           1) Visual Symbols 85
           2) Verbal Symbols 85
    V. Theatre Referentiality 86
        A) Referent/Reference 86
        B) Theatre Referentiality 87

	1)	Denegation	88
	2)	The Theatre Referent	89
		a) Stage Production	89
		b) Stage Production/Stage Production	89
		c) Stage Production/Exterior World	90
Notes			93

CHAPTER IV:
THEATRE RECEPTION ... 97
- I. Reception Theory ... 97
  - A) Places of Indetermination ... 98
  - B) Objectivization ... 98
  - C) Actualization ... 99
  - D) Concretization ... 99
  - E) Horizon of Expectation ... 102
- II. Theatre Reception ... 104
  - A) Mode of Production and Reception ... 104
  - B) Directorial Concretization ... 106
  - C) Spectatorial Concretization ... 108
  - D) Concretization Process ... 111
    - 1) From the Social Context to the Signified ... 111
      - a) Fictionalization ... 111
      - b) Ideologization of the Text ... 112
    - 2) From the Signifier to the Social Context ... 113
- III. New Perspectives ... 116
  - A) Object of Study ... 116
  - B) Levels of Receptive Activity ... 117
    - 1) Perception ... 117
    - 2) Interpretation ... 118
      - a) Pragmatic Interpretation ... 118
      - b) Semantic Interpretation ... 119
      - c) Semiotic Interpretation ... 119
    - 3) Emotive and Cognitive Reaction ... 119
    - 4) Evaluation ... 120
    - 5) Memory and Recollection ... 120
  - C) Methodology ... 121
    - 1) Selection of a Corpus ... 121
    - 2) Evaluation and Survey Methods ... 122
      - a) Questionnaires ... 122
      - b) Recording Reactions ... 122
- Notes ... 125

CHAPTER V:
TOWARDS AN ACTANTIAL MODEL FOR THEATRE 129
    I.   Background 129
    II. The Actantial Model 131
        A) Subject/Object 132
        B) Sender/Receiver 132
        C) Helper/Opponent 133
        D) Actants, Actors, Roles 136
        E) Sequences 138
            1) Micro-sequence 139
            2) Macro-sequence 139
            3) Super-sequence 139
    Notes 141

CHAPTER VI:
THEATRE HISTORY AND SEMIOTICS 143
    I.   General Background 143
    II. The Current State of Affairs in Historical Research 144
    III. Literary History in Latin America: One Example 150
        A) The Generational Method and Literary Currents 150
        B) Periodization 151
    IV. Theoretical Proposal 153
        A) Formal Level 153
        B) Contextual Level 158
    V. Methodology 161
    Notes 165

BIBLIOGRAPHY 171

Acknowledgements

This study, like all studies of its kind, owes much of its conception and preparation to various colleagues and friends. First of all, I would like to thank Patrice Pavis, Marco De Marinis and in a very special way, my brother, Alfonso de Toro, for his constant support and friendship, but especially for collaborating and sharing his knowledge and pioneer research in many areas, not to mention his comments and suggestions that guided me and were indispensable in preparing this book.

I would also like to thank my colleagues in the School of Comparative Literary Studies at Carleton University - Trevor Tolley, Francesco Loriggio, Hans-Georg Ruprecht and especially Robert Polzin - for their support and collaboration in my academic activities. They have made it possible for my work to continue to grow in a stimulating and constructive academic atmosphere.

I would not like to forget those who made other sorts of contributions: to my wife, Mary de Toro, my mother, Rosalba García, for their support and encouragement. To Kathleen Quinn and Janet Hay for their kindness in proof-reading the manuscript and galleys with infinite patience and especially for their methodical and accurate comments and suggestions. To Mario Valdés for having encouraged and motivated this translation even before the Spanish edition was published. To all of them, my most sincere thanks.

I must also thank in particular Carole Hubbard for having carefully and meticulously revised and prepared this translation for publication. I know how hard she worked in order to do justice to the original; to her my deepest and special thanks and gratitude.

I would like to take the opportunity to express my most sincere thanks to those who have supported my career and my research through the years, including the English publication of this book. Specifically, I refer to Professor Mario J. Valdés from the University of Toronto and Professor Wladimir Krysinski from the Université de Montréal. As well, I wish to thank the Social Sciences and Humanities Research Council of Canada for its continuous and generous support through all these years, and for providing me with the opportunity to research this book, thanks to a

Post-Doctoral Fellowship that allowed me to spend two years in Paris, an experience that proved essential in the writing of *Theatre Semiotics*.

In addition, I am grateful to the Canada Council which made possible, in the first place, the translation of *Semiótica del Teatro*. I would also like to take this opportunity to thank Carleton University; Dean of Arts, Stuart Adam; Dean of Graduate Studies and Research, John ApSimon for the generous grant that was awarded to me in order to carry out an in-depth revision of the original; former Dean of Arts, Janice Yalden; the Chair of the School of Comparative Literary Studies, Professor Robert Polzin; and my colleagues at the School of Comparative Literary Studies, for providing a constructive working environment. Finally, to my graduate students for their inspiration, ideas and for making every class a challenge and an exciting place to be. To them, my deepest gratitude.

Last but not least, I would like to thank Prof. Dr. Alfonso de Toro, Klaus Dieter Vervuert, and Dr. R. M. Schoeffel, for their encouragement and for having made possible the publication of this translation in Vervuert Verlag and the University of Toronto Press respectively.

Fernando de Toro
Carleton University

Foreword to the Spanish Edition

Fernando de Toro's book is one of the most important developments in the area of the systematization of the main themes and problems that a semiotics of theatre approach creates. This is one of the first complete studies of theatre semiotics (and it is the first to be written originally in Spanish). This study fills a void and is long overdue. It quite impressively succeeds in meeting its own dual objective: it not only contributes to theatre semiotics but also, and more to the point, to theory of Latin American theatre.

For obvious reasons, I will refer only briefly to the first aspect but not before pointing out how the author's geographical and cultural roots cannot help but facilitate his proposed theoretical project. His background contributes particularly well to the clarification of the social, political and historical dimensions of the artistic phenomenon. This is the most advanced and progressive component of Latin American culture and acts as the perfect antidote to the current scientific, formalist, in a word, ahistorical tendency in semiology.

Two of the main and most meritorious themes of this study are the chapters on reception and the basis for a history of theatre. The second important and very large theme is the extensive, balanced, original, exhaustive and appropriate update of pertinent problems (the specific nature of theatre discourse, the relationship between the dramatic text and the performance text, the semiosis process, the problem of the referent in theatre and the actantial analysis of character). Throughout this thorough analysis of current criticism (an incredibly vast and dissimilar group of texts, as the bibliography at the end of the book will testify) and thanks to the correct and 'creative' use of the adapted theoretical model (from Ubersfeld, Pavis, Hansen, Elam, etc.), de Toro successfully outlines current problems in a consistently clear manner.

Furthermore, Fernando de Toro also sheds light on previously unexplored points and proposes some interesting theoretical summaries: for example, his outline of intertextuality in theatre (which is an enrichment and synthesis of current typology) or his definition of the theoretical object as an intermediate between the dramatic text and the performance text that he calls the stage text and then the 'virtual performance text'. This is the result of the director's elaboration of the dramatic text which generally produces a material object similar to the *Regiebuch* or the script. In my opinion, the most interesting aspect of the notion of 'virtual performance text' is that it clarifies, once and for all, how the dramatic text becomes part of the theatre process and how it can be correctly understood through the use of theatre semiotics.

Marco De Marinis
Instituto di discipline della Comunicazione
Università di Bologna

Foreword

When readers of dramatic texts become the audience of a performance they enact a contrast and possible conflict between the world as represented on stage and the world as concretized in their reading. But, at a more profound level, they raise the possibility that the dramatic reality can be understood as a series of relationships within shifting parameters. In the case of reading, the variables are contained within the text/reader relationship which engages the historicity and full aesthetic repertoire of the reader as well as the formal constraints of the text. But with performance the variables on both sides multiply. The performance is the work of a director, actors, and all the components of stagecraft; and the spectator, who has also been a reader of the work in question, has an inner conflict between the previous concretization and the one affected by performance.

Understanding of theatre, both as text and performance, consequently, is the foremost challenge facing criticism. A theory which attempts to account for the variables and the transformations in reception must be a philosophically informed theory that brings together formal considerations with the problematics of reception. Fernando de Toro's *Theatre Semiotics* takes the much needed first step in this direction.

This book responds to the anti-formalism of radical scepticism that has effectively distanced semiotics from interpretation theory. In six tightly organized chapters, de Toro has laid out a cogent, informed argument for the place and the necessity of semiotics within the interpretive process of theatre, that most complex of artistic endeavours.

There is an explicit logical organization to the book that underscores de Toro's premise that rational explanation provides the most effective basis for communication and shared understanding. Fernando de Toro begins with an inquiry into theatre discourse as a point of departure. If meaning is produced at the level of discourse, the particular conditions and demands of the theatre produce the specific mode of discourse we designate as theatre discourse. Of special significance in de Toro's presentation of theatre discourse is the descriptive/logical development which moves from the notion of discourse to an analysis of the speaker, the situation of speaking, and what it is that is being talked about. It is on this ground that de Toro risks a generalization on the functions of theatre discourse.

In Chapter two de Toro takes up the concept of text and the dramatic text in relation to the performance text. He makes the case for theatre semiotics primarily on the strength of the analysis of discourse and text but, to his credit, de Toro does not stop with a merely expedient advocacy of semiotics. Chapter three is, in fact, the turning point in this book, for it is in the second half of the book that he demonstrates the strength of the method he has sketched out as one that is designed to engage theatre as process.

Chapter four, "Theatre Reception", has no equal in current theatre theory and criticism and can be positively compared to cinema theory and criticism of such prominent commentators as Dudley Andrew. This chapter can be examined as the beginning of a philosophically informed theory of theatre as experience. Chapter four is a likely essay to be carried in future collections of theatre theory and criticism. De Toro works with uncommon clarity through the complex problems of indeterminacy, concretization (Iser), horizon of expectations (Gadamer and Jauss), and then informs the debate with his wide knowledge of the modes of production and reception of theatre.

Chapters five and six are, in turn, a methodological and a historical excursion that firmly contextualizes the argument within teaching and research on theatre.

The dual forces of rigorous logical argument and fully informed, theoretical and historical assessment make this book, above all, a study of textuality and performance of theatre. The ideas and approaches of literary criticism have, on the whole, concentrated on the novel and stayed away from commentary on dramatic texts, theatre, and performance, recognizing the complexity of attempting to deal with its many variables. But the contemporary period of intense polemics between rational principles of interpretation and cultural paradigms of the production of meaning have not been profitable for the study of drama and theatre because of the marked bifurcation between a restrictive semiotics and reception theory. Beneath the surface of the controversies and mutual disregard amongst theorists and critics, there has been a persistent sense that researchers must take up both sides of drama, and study it as a formal composition and cultural artifact as well as the source of aesthetic experience. De Toro's book is a most welcome engagement of both sides.

The ideas of de Toro's semiotics are not, of course, the only possible illustrations of the conjunction of form and experience, but they are exemplary for their clarity of exposition.

The sense of this book can be expressed *in nuce* as the gradual expansion of the notion of performance in the singularity of the reader/spectator's imagination and collectively in the audience in the theatre.

Mario J. Valdés
University of Toronto

Preface

Theatre Semiotics was researched between 1982 and 1985 while I was a Fellow at the Université de Paris III. This was made possible by a Post-Doctoral Grant awarded to me by the Social Sciences and Humanities Research Council of Canada.

At the time, the field of theatre semiotics was relatively new. In fact, the very first articles and books only began to be published after 1975. And, even though the Czechoslovakian Structuralists had already worked in this field in the 1940s, their work was largely unknown to most theatre researchers during the early 1970s.

My interest in the field had two motivations: on the one hand, I wanted to do research in an area that was new and challenging, as the theatre had only been studied in a small way from a purely performative perspective and almost not at all from a semiotic perspective; secondly, I felt that it was important to introduce studies of this kind in Latin America, a continent where this field was totally unknown at the time. This is why I paid attention to so many theatre semioticians and why I decided to write the book in Spanish, knowing full well that *Semiótica del Teatro* would be largely ignored in the non-Spanish world.

In relation to the content of the book, I wanted to achieve two goals: one, to produce an organic work of theatre semiotics, a work that until then did not exist - in other words, a work that would deal with the most important and central topics of the discipline. Yet, at the same time, each chapter does not reduce itself solely to the presentation and discussion of the various theories regarding one subject; in each chapter I also contribute to and expand upon the topics discussed. Secondly, I searched for clarity. This is because one of the problems I always find with semiotics, in general, is its unnecessary jargonistic pedantry and total lack of examples in a field where the very object of study is a live one, and one that leaves almost no trace. Today, after almost ten years since the elaboration of this book, having gone through three editions and having received more than fifty reviews in seven languages, I strongly believe that those two objectives were accomplished.

When I was asked to translate this book into English I was rather reluctant to accept because today the research interests, at least in Europe, Canada and the United States of America, are not in Semiotics but in what is called Post-Structuralism and, more recently, Postmodernity. In fact, today this book has to be read in the context of the stage of development of the discipline at the time (1982-1985). Very little has happened in the field since then, and the discipline of Theatre Semiotics came and went with great speed. By the late 1980's the discipline had been exhausted and the best proof of this is that only three new books and very few articles have been published since 1987. This is not the place to explain why this happened but I can simply suggest that the whole semiotic and structuralist paradigm, which has been with us since the Russian Formalists, came tumbling down strenuously with the emergence of the Post-Structuralists and Deconstructionists. It seemed after a while that producing diagrams and arrows had been unnecessarily obtrusive and did not get us anywhere.

However, in spite of all the defects and shortcomings I see today in this book, I hope that it will serve as a useful tool to those who would like to know something about this discipline.

Fernando de Toro
Carleton University

INTRODUCTION

Numerous studies have appeared since the 1970s on the topic of theatre semiotics. Beginning with the studies of Anne Ubersfeld, Patrice Pavis, Marco De Marinis, Franco Ruffini, Alessandro Serpieri, Keir Elam, Andre Helbo and Eli Rozik, to name just a few, we can say that theatre semiotics has clearly begun to define itself. Of course, owing to the many views that exist on the theatre phenomenon, many problems have emerged, for example, whether theatre is verbal expression or whether it is a stage practice (set, characters, costumes, etc.). The semiological nature of the theatre object is complex and this complexity calls for a systematization of each of its levels. Its greatest complexity comes from the fact that, unlike other artistic practices, theatre is not comprised of a single signifying system but, rather, of a multitude of signifying systems that each have a dual function: as a literary practice and as a performance practice. At the same time, this complexity is continually growing because of the very nature of the theatre object: not only is the theatre object a *dramatic text*, it is also a *performance text*, with both a literary and a performance dimension. Theatre is composed not only of linguistic components but also of paralinguistic ones.

One question arises immediately when attempting a complete systematization of the theatre phenomenon: in what way does the practice of theatre differ from other artistic activities, whether they be performance or literary practices? Answering this question involves confronting the problem of the *specificity* of theatre discourse as a signifying practice. This is what I try to do in the first five chapters, for these chapters give an account of the signifying system of the theatre phenomenon. In these chapters, I examine theatre *discourse* as linguistic expression, as *text*, as *semiosis* (or production of meaning) and as *reception*. Character is viewed in this book as *actant* and *function*, not as ontological substance. The final chapter (VI) consists of a semiological reflection on the history of theatre.

These six areas provide the structure for this study, and as I have already pointed out, in the first five chapters the various levels of the stage phenomenon are discussed. We already know that this specificity is found at various levels which emerge from the pluri-codification of the stage practice. As well, we not only view these levels from the textual point of view (that is, viewing the dramatic text as a literary text) but also - and preferentially - from a stage perspective. Having stated this, neither the dramatic text nor the performance will be given privileged treatment; rather, both phenomena will have equal weight, for, in my opinion, it is together that they constitute the essence of the theatre object.

In the first chapter, "Theatre Discourse", the notions of discourse and theatre discourse will be studied from a semiological perspective: I will consider theatre articulation and linguistic production, how language functions in theatre and, to close the chapter, what differentiates theatre discourse from other forms of literary discourse and performance.

In the second chapter, the dramatic text/performance text problematic will be discussed and to do this, the relationship between the two will be explored as well as what differentiates a dramatic/performance text from other literary texts. In this chapter, then, the main goal is to delineate clearly and to separate the two types of text that constitute the theatre phenomenon.

In the third chapter, I will consider the process of theatre semiosis or the production of meaning. My goal is to establish how signification functions in theatre, that is, the semiological function as it relates to triadic sign production. This is fundamental in theatre, for it is in this process that theatre is most different from other signifying systems and artistic activities.

Theatre reception is essential to the theatre phenomenon. Thus, chapter four focuses on the *theatre relationship*, the exchange that goes on between the theatre public and the stage, the emitter and the receiver. This part of the study will be based on the work of the School of Constance (Jauss, Iser, Stempel, etc.) and on empirical studies carried out recently in Italy and Holland (De Marinis, Tan, Schoenmakers, etc.). Most recently, theatre semioticians have begun to consider this important area of theatre/stage and we hope to establish a model of the *theatre relationship* that is both theoretical and empirical.

The actantial model is the subject of the second-last chapter. In that chapter, an exhaustive explanation of the model is not given, nor is a new model provided; only a few additions are made to already existing models. Thus, the primary objective in this chapter is to effect a *mise au point* and to show how the model has evolved, along with its adaptations and additions. At the same time, the epistemological basis of this model will be outlined.

Finally, the sixth chapter deals with the ever difficult-problems of history and history of theatre. In this chapter, I discuss some of the central ideas and thoughts concerning the integration of literary theory, semiology and literary history. Finally, a model is proposed that could serve not only in the formulation of a history of theatre, but also of a general history of literature.

I hope these six chapters will contribute not only to current studies on theatre semiotics, but also to the theory of Latin American theatre, which is still in its birthing process. I also hope to provoke further scholarly debate and activity among my Latin American colleagues so as to attract the attention and scientific activity that Latin American theatre truly deserves, for up to now it has been considered a secondary artistic manifestation, at least by some critics. I believe, with others, that a great challenge lies before us and that we have already begun to confront it.

CHAPTER I

THEATRE DISCOURSE

> Auffi eft-il vrai que les difcours qui s'y font doivent être comme des Actions de ceux qu'on y fait paroître; car là *Parler*, c'eft *Agir*.
> D'Aubignac, *La Pratique du Théâtre*.

I. THE NOTION OF DISCOURSE

It is extremely important that we accurately define the notion of discourse from a linguistic point of view before considering theatre discourse, especially given the fact that this concept has diverse uses which are often contradictory and ambiguous.

In strict linguistic terms, discourse is *la langue* put into action. In an even stricter sense, discourse "refers to any utterance greater than the sentence, considered from the point of view of the rules for linking series of sentences".[1] A more comprehensive definition is the following one by L. Guespin: "discourse is the utterance considered from the point of view of the discursive mechanism which conditions it. Thus, if we consider a text from the point of view of its structure in language, we are dealing with an utterance; a linguistic study of the conditions of production of this text would be a discourse".[2] This definition incorporates an important element: the enunciation (*énonciation*) implicit in the conditions of production of a given discourse.[3] In this case, the strict linguistic view in which only the utterance and not the enunciation is considered analytically is abandoned. The utterance and enunciation are integral parts of discourse as communication,[4] for discourse is *la langue* expressed in its actual form. According to Emile Benveniste, discourse is "every enunciation presupposing a speaker and a listener, where the former intends to influence the latter in some manner".[5]

According to Benveniste, communication engendered by discourse falls into two universal categories of discourse: the person (*I/you*) space and time, and these submit discourse to a situation of determined enunciation. That is, discourse is always found engaged (*embrayé*) in a precise context of communication. The *I/you*, together with the category of time, implies that the utterance occurs and that it is always linked to a situation of concrete enunciation. In discourse, then, the utterance is *what is said* that proceeds from *la langue*, whereas the enunciation is the means and place through which the utterance comes into being. This is why "the enunciation is the individual act of putting language into use.... the very act of producing an utterance and not the text of the utterance".⁶ According to Benveniste, for the above individual act to occur, three formal enunciative processes must exist: a) the act of saying (*énoncer*), b) the situation of realization, and c) the instruments of realization.⁷ The central part of the first process consists of the appropriation of *la langue*, that is, the production of an utterance in which the speaker reveals himself or herself (*I*); in the second process, the central part is the incorporation of the receiver (*you*) into the referential aspect by means of the message the emitter is sending. For the message to take place, the following instruments come into play: 1) the *indices* or *deictics* (that is, the *I/you* relationship, is essential to communication); 2) the deictics of ostension (this, here) that delineate space and designate the object being referred to; 3) the verb tenses, especially the axial form of the present which coincides with the moment of enunciation - that is, the intersection of the event with discourse. This is why discourse is the only way of experiencing the *hic et nunc* and the only way of actualizing the present which is referring to the outside world.⁸

The speaker/listener relationship is central to the production of discourse, for the speaker's main objective is communication, the production of a message. But in order for this message to be transmitted, it needs an apparatus of precise functions that arise in three acts all occurring simultaneously in communication: a) the act of locution (or saying something) which in itself involves three acts: 1) the phonetic act (or sound sequence whose unity comprises the *phoneme*); 2) the phatic act (or the act of saying certain nouns or words, or a sentence, the minimal unit being the *pheme)*; 3) the rhetic act (or the act of producing meaning [naming] and reference [referring], the minimal unit being the *rheme*); b) the act of illocution (every act of language which tends towards or completes a designated action: this is a performative act); c) the act of perlocution (language functions which are not directly inscribed in the utterance but which have total dependence upon the utterance situation [the pragmatic situation] whose function it is to influence the listener: to attract, to frighten, etc.).⁹

J.L. Austin, the founder of speech act theory, points out that every act of perlocution makes use of paralinguistic means to produce and carry out the act of language. The importance of Austin's system lies in his notions of illocutive and perlocutive acts, the first of these being defined as a *performative* act or a performative utterance, whose performability must always occur in circumstances adequate for the realization and comprehension of the utterance - that is, a concrete situation of enunciation which also includes the perlocutive act or effect on the listener.¹⁰

These processes of enunciation and speech acts are described here because they are integral to the production of discourse, and therefore are equally important in our analysis of discourse. Both Benveniste and Austin are firm in their resolve that both the utterance and the enunciation are part of discourse, and thus the notion of enunciation needs to be incorporated into that of utterance. This broadening of the analysis of the discursive field is also recognized by such linguists as Oswald Ducrot, who worked for a long time on the concept of utterance. According to Ducrot:

> each act of enunciation is a unique event, involving a particular speaker located in a particular situation, while the utterance (= the sentence) stays, by definition, unchanged throughout the infinite number of acts of enunciation of which it could be the object. Constructing the notion of utterance is therefore necessarily making an abstraction of this infinity of uses, and it is nowhere more evident than in that the phrase *to introduce the enunciation in the utterance* is not a pure and simple absurdity.[11]

This is an acceptable position, for the production of an event (*token*) in the enunciation of the utterance constitutes the fundamental basis for the analysis of discourse.

In linking the enunciation to verb tenses (past/present), we find two different enunciative forms or levels that Benveniste calls *histoire* and *discours* (history and discourse).[12] The first case, that of historic enunciation, which is now limited to written language, is concerned with past events. According to Benveniste: "We will define the historical narrative as the mode of enunciation that excludes all linguistic 'autobiographic' forms".[13] As has already been explained, discourse, on the other hand, is the enunciation of a speaker and a listener in which the former attempts to influence the latter. Whereas the historic *enunciation* is limited to the written, the enunciation-discourse is not limited to spoken language because it also includes "the mass of writings which produce oral discourses or which borrow their ends: correspondence, memoires, theatre, didactic works, briefly, all the genres where someone addresses someone else, presents him/herself as a speaker and organizes what he/she says in the category of the person".[14]

The difference between these two types of enunciation is not found in written language, for historical enunciation has only recently been limited to written language. On the other hand, discourse can be both written and oral. For example, in the narrative, one passes from one temporal system to another quite frequently. Nevertheless, the fundamental distinction between the two kinds of enunciation lies in the fact that, whereas historic utterance is distinguished by *tales, events, the past*, discursive utterance exists only in the present, in the *hic et nunc*. Thus, whereas both the utterance and the enunciation are given in a different space and time in the first instance (in the narrative), in the second case (in theatre), they converge.

The historical discursive utterance is a key area in theatre semiotics, for it allows us to identify the type of utterance in the theatre and then to distinguish it from the narrative and poetic utterance. That is, the *discursive specificity* of the theatre utterance may then be formulated. At the basis of these two types of utterance is the *attitude* of the speaker before the expressed object and the listener. This brings us to the concepts of *opacity* and *transparency* which have to do with the *distance* between the speaker and his or her discourse. In historical discourse, it is the transparency of language which stands out, for this type of discourse generally seeks objectivity, and the subject of the utterance tends to distance himself or herself from the utterance to achieve this effect. In theatre or poetry, on the other hand, it is the opacity of language which is more obvious, in that the subject of the utterance and the utterance itself coexist in time and space. The way these coincide, however, is different: in theatre discourse there is a strong referential nature, while in poetry the nature of the discourse is non-referential. One should also include the concept of *tension* which exists in the relationship between speaker and listener. This relationship varies from one enunciation to another.[15]

Based on these definitions of discourse and the components they include, I may now be able to suggest a more complete definition of discourse. It is the mobilization of *la langue* by an enunciating subject who incorporates an addressee. Discourse always occurs in a concrete enunciative situation and its final meaning is influenced by the production conditions that characterize this situation.

II. THEATRE DISCOURSE

The analysis of theatre discourse has always been a source of preoccupation for many specialists in the field.[16] Such researchers as Patrice Pavis, Anne Ubersfeld or Keir Elam consider relationships such as those between speaker and listener, utterance and enunciation, deixis and anaphora, and performability and representativity, to be essential to theatre discourse. Their studies are concerned with one or the other of the many aspects of theatre discourse; but they do not attempt a comprehensive and systematic articulation of the components of theatre discourse, nor do they provide a clear definition or description of theatre discourse. In other words, one should ask: what *enunciation* is specific to theatre? For example, Anne Ubersfeld points out that theatre discourse is "the ensemble of linguistic signs produced by a theatrical work".[17] But what group of signs are we dealing with? How are these signs organized? Patrice Pavis affirms that: "What makes the specificity of theatre discourse is the particular nature of its enunciation, the modal play that the stage may impose upon it".[18] But what is the particular nature of the theatre enunciation? I will now try to answer these questions and then propose a definition of theatre discourse.

A) *Speaker/Hearer*

One of the fundamental elements of theatre discourse is the relationship between speaker and listener; that is, the structure of dialogue without which theatre would not exist. This relationship is much more complex than in other forms of literary discourse simply because one is dealing with a form of discourse which somehow shares elements from both *literary* and performance texts. Communication (and this term is to be interpreted in the strict sense, despite what G. Mounin has said on the topic)[19] in theatre does not occur in a rectilinear circuit, as it does in the basic code of everyday communication;[20] rather, it works in a similar way, but with a doubling of the emitters/receivers and the signs/messages. The theatre communication model, according to Ubersfeld, is the following: 1) an informative discourse (*discours rapporteur*) whose sender is the author/scriptor;[21] 2) a related discourse (*discours rapporté*) whose sender is the character.[22] These two types of discourse work in two types of language situations in the theatre: the *theatre* or *stage situation*, whose emitters could be all those who make up the theatre *performance* - author, scriptor, actors, scenographers, director, etc. - and who are concerned with the production of the concrete enunciative conditions. There is also the *performed situation* created by the speaker-listener relationship which produces the conditions for the imaginary *enunciation*. These two forms of discourse (*rapporteur, rapporté*) may be subdivided in the following diagram of the theatre communication process:

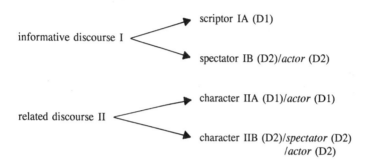

In my opinion, this model established by Ubersfeld (and to which I have added *actor* in IB-D2 and IIA-D1, and *actor* and *spectator* in IIB-D2) is insufficient for explaining the whole theatre communication process. The two additional categories incorporated into the model embrace two important zones that are not considered by Ubersfeld. The model is to be understood in the following way: the informative discourse comes from the author/scriptor and is destined to the public; or, in other words, a dramatic text will be read by, or performed for, a given public. Thus, the scriptor has to be the sender (D1) and the public the receiver (D2). The relationship which forms between the scriptor and the spectator is essential because the spectator implicitly receives a command (see, hear, etc.). But, at the same time, by means of the didascalia which may or may not be present in the text, the actor also receives a command to act and to say this or that.[23] In the stage text, however, some form of didascalia must be present in order to be incorporated into the actor's knowledge. One must not forget that: "The didascalic textual layer is characteristically at the same time both a message and an indication of the contextual conditions of another message".[24] In the related discourse, the speaker-listener relationship is in the form of dialogue between two characters (*I/you-you/I*). That is, what is said is a message between two participants in a concrete situation (D1-D2/D2-D1). But this message is also directed to the audience (D2), for the performance is obviously enacted for the audience. It is in this type of communication that Ubersfeld sees the unique character of theatre discourse: "The fundamental trait of theatre discourse is to be understandable only as a series of orders given with a view to staging a production, a representation, to being addressed to the addressee-mediators who are charged with transmitting it to an addressee-audience".[25] Although I am in agreement with the fact that this type of communication is specific to theatre, I do not believe that this particular form of discourse contains theatre specificity; rather, it contains only a trace of this specificity.

The dual discursive articulation of theatre is one of the characteristics of its specific definition. The scriptor's discourse does not appear in the dramatic or performance text in any explicit way, for it is mediated by the actor(s). Theatre discourse, then, appears to be a discourse without a subject insofar as there is no *I* articulating the narrative, given that the narrative is composed of a dialogue between characters, a series of *I*s or a fragmented, dispersed *I*. In fact, there is a multiple subject, a series of enunciative subjects who together constitute the story. Nevertheless, the *mark* or *trace* of the scriptor's discourse is felt on various levels: a) in the distribution of the characters' responses; b) in the structure of the performance text; c) in the ideological charge of the text in question; and d) in the didascalias. As well, the scriptor's discourse is a discourse determined by an era, by conventions as much social (the *general cultural text*) as they are theatrical (*performance codes*).[26] In the end, the discursive production of the scriptor is influenced by current contextual practices.

The dramatic text is one which is inscribed in a social formation[27] and in a specific historical moment, but the contemporary stage production of a text (which is simply a contextualized reading of that text - for example, of a text by Corneille or Lope de Vega) may alter and re-articulate the original *discursive formation*. This is done either to *modernize* a text which is culturally and ideologically alien, or because the director wishes to create a different *reading*[28] or concretization of this text. This is why the term *scriptor* is preferable: it includes both author and director.

The discourse of the character/actor (which is in fact the scriptor's discourse attributed to various enunciative subjects) and the various communicative functions (referential, cognitive, emotive, phatic) have a fundamental characteristic: the characters/actors are instrumental in the referential illusion because they present a discourse that creates its own enunciative conditions. But this is only a simulacrum, an artifice, for the enunciative situation is already determined by the context or director. This is a truly paradoxical situation, for on the one hand, theatre discourse seems to speak truthfully about the world (because it simulates the creation of an enunciative situation and because the actor's discourse is a real act); but, on the other hand, the actor carries out a *denegation*,[29] for the characters express a (fictive) discourse belonging to someone else (Hamlet or Segismundo), and they live, embody and imitate the lives of this someone else. At the same time, the actor/character's discourse is only a part of the total discourse of the performance - the linguistic and paralinguistic (gestures, corporal movement) part; thus, this is just one part of theatre. This is why the dramatic text only becomes theatre when it is fully materialized on the stage. In a word, the dramatic text is just one part - an essential one, no doubt - of the performance text.

These comments outline theatre discourse as it compares to other discursive practices, for example to narrative or poetry. In poetry there is a speaker/voice, in narrative there is a narrator, and in the theatre there is a subject of enunciation. In these forms of discourse we do not encounter the dual discursivity of theatre discourse. The relationship is direct, between the narrator/speaker and the reader. Furthermore, both narrative and poetic texts are complete and self-sufficient, for they both include the signified and the signifier, whereas the dramatic text is incomplete, for its content and even its signifier do not acquire a final realization until the performance.[30] On the other hand, none of these different forms of discourse have the definitive character theatre has: the illusion of creating one's own enunciative conditions. In the narrative, it is the narrator who creates and fabricates the enunciative conditions of the characters; in poetry, there seems to exist an enunciative void - words without a contextualized referent. Finally, whereas in both narrative and poetry the narrator/speaker is the source of meaning, in theatre the source of meaning is located in the actors, the scriptor, the scenographers, etc. Thus, the informative discourse/related discourse relationship is, according to Ubersfeld, "a whole within a whole".[31]

B) *Enunciative Situation/Utterance*

The theatre enunciation is perhaps the most determinant aspect of the specificity of theatre. Theatre discourse is what makes theatre so distinct from other literary discursive practices. Central to this kind of enunciation is the fact that, in the theatre, *to speak is to act* and *to act is to speak*. This is so for several reasons: first of all, a performance creates an enunciative situation which mimes a real situation; in other words, the actors/characters always speak in a concrete situation, fabricated by themselves and imitating the dialogic structure. If this were not the case (and herein lies a significant difference from other discursive practices), the theatre message would be incomprehensible. Ubersfeld states: "The 'signification' of an utterance in the theatre, taken apart from the situation of communication, is simply nothing: only this situation, which permits the conditions of enunciation to be established, gives the utterance its *meaning*".[32] This is why the dramatic text depends more upon the enunciative conditions than any other textual form.

In the reading process (which is insufficient in theatre), the enunciative situation is given in the didascalia, and the reader has to imagine these enunciative conditions, as he or she would when reading a novel. But more often than not, as we know, these enunciative conditions are determined by the director in the performance text. Only in the performance do dialogue and theatrical communication acquire full meaning, for in the performance they are *embrayés* (or shifted into a precise context). What makes communication possible and transparent in this context are the various forms of deictics. There are several exemplary cases: *Où sont les neiges d'antan?* by Tadeusz Kantor (Théâtre CRICOT 2, Centre Pompidou, Paris, 1982); *Écrans noirs* by P. Friloux-Schilansky (Théâtre d'en Face, Centre Pompidou, Paris, 1983); *Correspondance* (Théâtre de l'Aquarium, Cartoucherie de Vincennes, Paris, 1982); *Le dernier Maquis* by Armand Gatti (Atelier de Création Populaire, Centre Pompidou, Paris, 1985). In all of these cases, it is the contextualization of the discourse which makes the situation comprehensible. This is the opposite of the cinematic or real enunciative situation; in theatre, the situation is understood through the message.

Secondly, "the character is at the same time the actant of the utterance of the play ... and the verbal actant of the enunciation".[33] That is, the character constitutes and is constituted by the world represented in the discourse of the play, which, in turn, generates action. This feature is crucial in theatre: whereas the dramatic text (or other texts) presents the *word* of the text, the stage presents the *doing*. Thus, what Patrice Pavis calls *discursive performance*[34] is simply the convergence of *speaking* and *doing* on the stage. This is what constitutes a performative situation, for there is no mediation between *speaking* and *doing*. The situation is illocutory, for the actor/character acts without announcing his/her acting: they do not say "I say that I am now acting". One of the best examples is *Paso de dos* by Eduardo Pavlovsky.

A third important point is the interrelation between denial and reality. The concrete, stage enunciative conditions are superimposed on the fictitious enunciative situation, or, more precisely, on the world represented in a given text; but the stage conditions are no less fictitious in their content than the world represented in the text. Thus, *to stage is to stage language*, to put a language act *in situ*. It is the nature or design of the stage which determines how theatre discourse will function.

At this point, it would be pertinent to distinguish between the enunciative situation of the dramatic text and that of the performance text. The difference lies in the enunciative conditions of a given situation. In the dramatic text, there is a partial enunciative situation where characters participate in a dialogue and where the context is sometimes rendered more explicit by use of didascalias. Nevertheless, the enunciative conditions are not given. All the extra-linguistic elements - the intonation, the gesticulation, the space in which the talking occurs, the proxemic, and even the *theatre relation*,[35] are all part of the enunciative conditions in which the speech act takes place. The enunciative situation of a dramatic text therefore only provides a potentially staged matrix whose enunciative conditions will be produced by the performance text. The imaginative dimension provided by the reader while reading the dramatic text is not necessary, at least at this level, in the physical and concrete situation of the stage. According to Saraiva, these extra-linguistic elements or *supports*[36] are what distinguishes theatre discourse from other forms of literary and performance discourse. Theatre discourse is not only a form of "literary" discourse and a specific type of performance manifestation; moreover, these *supports* which mediate between the utterance and the sender make the communication and understanding of the message possible.

At first glance, then, it would seem that the enunciative situation in theatre is identical to that of everyday life.[37] However, one should distinguish among what Saraiva calls the *simple message*, the *absolute message*, and the *oratory message*. In theatre there exists a combination of the simple message (a message which depends on the exterior supports of the enunciative situation) and the oratory message (a message which has its own supports). Theatre discourse incorporates its own supports which proceed from fiction. But at the same time these supports refer to real exterior supports which constitute the simple message and which are provided by the performance text. A good example comes from *Hamlet* in which there is a significant amount of *deictization* and *anaphorization* of the discourse. The difference between the simple message of theatre and the real message of everyday life is clarified in the following quote by Saraiva: "The latter presupposes a situation which pre-exists itself and which gives it its meaning; whereas in the dramatic play the situation comes only after the message, and is created by it".[38] In the simple message, the situation is already there and the message is simply the result of that very situation. For example, if a character says "close the door" (which would be the *posé*, according to the terminology of Oswald Ducrot), this would imply that someone else is in the room, that the door is open and that this order will be carried out (the *présupposé*, the presupposed, according to Ducrot).[39] On the other hand, in the dramatic text, or rather, in the theatre enunciative situation, there is no situation - it is created by the message (discourse) by means of the deictics, anaphora, gesturality, etc. In this way, the situation is understood through the *message,* whereas in the previous case, the message is understood through the *situation.* The dialectical relation that is established here is in a sense a referent that becomes a sign, and a sign that becomes a referent.[40] No doubt, from a formal point of view, there exists an identity common to both the enunciative situation of everyday life and that of theatre, in that in both situations the referents of the message are not *represented* but rather *presented*. For instance, in a sentence such as, "bring me a coffee", both situations imply a real consumer, in the real world and on the stage. On the stage, however, the referent *refers* within the stage area, but this referent is a *reproduction* (a replica) of an exterior referent.[41] In this manner: "There exist for the spectator two things, one being the referent of that which is, by supposition, identical to it. The articulation between the two is assured by the *Mimique*".[42] Thus, the *reproduction* or *mime representation* creates an unreal identity but, paradoxically, this is transformed into something real through the simple fact that it mimes a real exterior situation. Anne Ubersfeld is correct when she says: "theatre discourse is therefore the *mime of an utterance in the world* and of what it says about itself and about the world".[43]

C) *Deixis/Anaphora*

Theatre discourse, just like any other form of discourse, implies the presence of a sender and a receiver of the message, a communicative situation in a precise context, and its occurrence as a speech act performed in the present. The contextualization of discourse, in both the dramatic text and in the performance text, is carried out by means of the deixis and anaphora that impregnate the speech act. The use of deictics and anaphora is an inherent part of the speech act and its function is very important in the communication of the message and in the determination of the verb tenses,[44] as is the case in many plays by Gambaro, in particular *Puesta en claro*.

Most agree that theatre deixis is decisive in this type of discursive practice.[45] One of the most exhaustive studies on this subject was by Alessandro Serpieri and his research group. They point out that "all linguistic and semiotic functions in drama emerge from the deictic orientation of the utterance towards its context, so that what Jakobson terms the 'shifter' (*embrayeurs* - the empty verbal context) becomes the constitutive unit of dramatic representation in general".[46] Because of the central role of deixis and anaphora, it is necessary to systematize the various types of deixis and anaphora found in theatre discourse. The first step is to define these two central concepts. According to John Lyons: "By deixis is meant the location and identification of persons, objects, events, processes and activities being talked about, or referred to, in relation to the spatiotemporal context created and sustained by the act of utterance and the participation in it, typically, of a single speaker and at least one addressee".[47] In this manner, demonstrative pronouns and adjectives, time and place adverbs, and personal pronouns are all deixis.

Anaphora, on the other hand, implies reference to the preceding context (the antecedent) and it functions as a substitution for something that occurred previous to that time frame. According to Lyons, however, the anaphoric reference may function in two ways: a) "the pronoun refers to its antecedent.... Here the term 'refer' can be traced back to the Latin *referre*, which was used to translate the Greek ... and, in this context, meant something like 'bring back', 'recall' or 'repeat'"; b) "we can say that an anaphoric pronoun refers to what its antecedent refers to ... or that it refers to the referent of the antecedent expression with which it is correlated".[48]

Deixis is fundamental in theatre discourse and it is one of the components that separates theatre from all other forms of literary discourse. This is due to the fact that, above and beyond the dual articulation of normal language (1. morpheme; 2. phoneme, that is, the locutory act), theatre possesses a third articulation. As in everyday communication, deixis links the locutory act to a pragmatic context.[49] Without this articulation, the theatre dialogue would be incomprehensible.[50] Nevertheless, the deictic workings of theatre discourse are different from everyday discourse in the fact that

> in the latter the deictic dimension does not need to be inscribed semantically within the verbal fabric of discourse itself, remaining a pure and simple *index*, while in the former the indexical dimension is semanticized, *becomes iconic* (being inscribed, with a surplus of information, within the verbal-pragmatic fabric) and *becomes symbolic* (entering into the paradigmatic axes of a text-action which, far from retaining the fragmentary or 'spontaneous' character of a collection of everyday utterances, appears as an organic and 'fictitious' structure).[51]

This is due to something I have already mentioned - the fact that whereas in everyday speech the pragmatic situation or context already exists, in theatre the situation is created by the characters' discourse. In the spatial and temporal contextualization of theatre, there exists an informational 'overload' in order to produce a *présupposé* that will make the *posé* comprehensible.

Pragmatic discourse, which is no more than *la langue in situ*, operates by means of different kinds of axes and anaphora. It is important to take note of these and to show how they work, especially given the terminological variety that exists and that can often be confusing. Both the deixis and the anaphora have three axes that, according to Serpieri, operate within the stage: a) *the anaphoric axis*, whose function is to refer to elements that precede the enunciative situation; b) the *narrative or dynamic axis*, whose function is to refer to the sequences of the plot; c) the *deictic axis*, whose reference is internal to the very enunciative act.⁵²

These three axes determine three distinct types of anaphora that have been named in different ways but that point to the same respective linguistic realities: the *extra-referential anaphora* (Serpieri) or *exaphoric anaphora* (Elam), the *intra-referential anaphora* (Fernando de Toro), and the *infra-referential* (Serpieri) or *endophoric anaphora* (Elam).⁵³ The function of these extra-referential anaphora is either to refer to reality preceding the *in situ* discourse or to refer to an exterior discourse. As an example, we have *Los invasores* by the Chilean playwright Egon Wolff:

> PIETA: [*Stopping him at the bottom of the stairs.*] Tell me ... Did you see those strange people wandering around the streets too, while we were coming home?
> MEYER: Strange people?
> PIETA: Yes ... Like shadows, jumping among the shrubs.
> MEYER: Oh, do you mean the ragged ones from the garbage dump from the other side of the river?
> PIETA: It was them?
> MEYER: They cross now and then to go rummaging in our garbage cans ... The police haven't been able to stop them from crossing to these parts, at night ...
> PIETA: I could have sworn I saw two of them climbing up to Andreani's balcony, like thieves in the night.⁵⁴

This is the opening scene of the play. It is characteristic of the whole play, beginning *in medias res*. The first thing one observes in both the dramatic and performance text are the characters in the middle of a dialogue. Any reference made to any event or reality previous to this situation is done by means of extra-referential anaphora. In the course of the dialogue, events may occur outside of the stage, and they too are referred to by means of this type of anaphora. This sort of anaphora is also recurrent in *Mother Courage and her Children* by Bertolt Brecht:

> YVETTE: [*Comes panting in*] They'll do it for two hundred if you make it snappy - these things change from one minute to the next. I'd better take One Eye to my colonel at once. He confessed he had the cash box, they put the thumb-screws on him. But he threw it in the river when he noticed them coming up behind him. So it's gone. Shall I run and get the money from my colonel?⁵⁵

The function of the inter-referential anaphora is to refer to the internal sequences of the dramatic/performance text; that is, it links the various segments of the action through discourse, and in this way, functions as a *narrative* and *dynamic* element that allows action to evolve. A good example of this is found in *Heroica de Buenos Aires* by the Argentine writer Osvaldo Dragún:

> NEGRO: Forgive me ... I believed we were friends ... So many times we shared a little fire in the winter! Is that not being friends?
>
> MARIA: Come on, Negro! ... Do you know what that is? That is being alone, Negro, freezing to death and looking for someone to tell who you are when you die and they come to take you away and put you with the roaches! I don't have friends. I have children ... who are like I was myself.
>
> (..)
>
> MARIA: [*Completely changed now*] Are you going too?
>
> (..)
>
> NEGRO: Yes. I'm going too.
>
> MARIA: [*Looks at him. Pauses, desperate*] Negro ... How did you do it? Tell me, please ... how did you do it? For years I've dragged around this cartload of worthless junk ... and I've never been able to save a cent! I must have made a mistake in something! You tell me how you did it! After all, we've always been friends, right ...[56]

These two scenes, separated by two acts, are connected and give a new direction to the diegetic component, which is central to the progression of the action. One can say the same with respect to the opening scene of *Hamlet*, the extra-referential anaphora which will later serve as an intra-referential anaphora:

> Ghost: ... Sleeping within my orchard,
> My custom always of the afternoon,
> Upon my secure hour thy uncle stole,
> With juice of cursed hebona in a vial,
> And in the porches of my ears did pour
> The leprous distillment, whose effect
> Holds such an enmity with blood of man
> That swift as quicksilver it courses through
> The natural gates and alleys of the body ...
> Thus was I, sleeping, by a brother's hand
> Of life, of crown, of queen, at once dispatch'd
>
> (..)
>
> Lucianus: Thoughts black, hands apt, drugs fit, and time agreeing,
> [Confederate] season, else no creature seeing,
> Thou mixture rank, of midnight weeds collected,
> With Hecat's ban thrice blasted, thrice [infected],
> Thy natural magic and dire property
> On wholesome life usurps immediately. [*Pours the poison in his ears*].[57]

This second scene, like the previous one (when Hamlet plans the assassination of the Duke) would be incomprehensible without the intra-referentiality and it is this that allows the action to take a new direction: revengeance facing the proof of a crime.

The infra-referential or endophoric anaphora is a reference to the discourse that immediately precedes actual dialogue. Its function is to connect utterances, to give theatre its tension, dynamism and continuity. In this way, this type of anaphora creates the impression of theatre discourse developing and being created as it takes place on the stage. Harold Pinter uses this most effectively in his plays, which are known for the dynamism of their dialogue. For example, *The Caretaker*:

ASTON:		You could be ... caretaker here, if you liked.
DAVIES:		What?
ASTON:		You could ... look after the place, if you liked ... you know, the stairs and the landing, the front steps, keep an eye on it. Polish the bells.
DAVIES:		Bells?
ASTON:		I'll be fixing a few, down by the front door. Brass.
DAVIES:		Well, I ... I never done caretaking before, you know ... I mean to say ... I never ... what I mean to say is I never been a caretaker before. [*Pause*].
ASTON:		How do you feel about being one, then?
DAVIES:		Well, I reckon ... Well, I'd have to know ... you know ...
ASTON:		What sort of ...
DAVIES:		Yes, what sort of ... you know ... [*Pause*].[58]

The anaphoric co-reference also promotes the appearance of continuity in the universe created by the theatre discourse. According to Keir Elam,"it maintains the stability of the object once introduced. As such, it is subordinate to the deixis proper, which ostends the object directly and introduces it as dramatic referent".[59]

This brings us to another important point that should be discussed with respect to theatre anaphora: the appearance of *reality* it produces, despite the fictive nature of theatre discourse. This appearance is possible because of what Andrea Bonomi calls *object of discourse*, that is, real or fictitious entities that are the subjects of discussion.[60] The very fact that one refers to these entities gives them, in a sense, a 'real' existence. It is precisely these *objects of discourse* that allow fiction to pass as 'real'. Fiction does not have a real referent in the world, only a material referent on the stage and in the enunciative situation that evokes them. In this way, these referents exist solely in the universe of the discourse.[61] Thus, the dramatic referents, according to Elam, "are objects of this kind: they are created for the duration of the drama and exist for as long as they are mentioned, ostended or otherwise referred to in the dialogue".[62] There are many examples of this in theatre, from the time of the Greeks to the present, from medieval *autos* to the highly codified *Commedia dell' Arte*, not to mention *Die heilige Johanna der Schlachthöfe* by Bertolt Brecht, *Lear* by Edward Bond or *Rhinocéros* by Ionesco.

The anaphora works only when intimately linked to the deixis, for the deixis allows for the entry of entities into the universe of the discourse and it is these that the dialogue can refer to in the course of the play.

As we have already seen in the beginning of this section, in general, deixis has an ostentative, redundant function, and this ostentation is made possible through different types of deixis. In theatre, there is a generic type of deixis: *verbal deixis*. This can be subdivided in the following manner: 1) deixis originating from the discourse or enunciative deixis, 2) spatial deixis, 3) temporal deixis, 4) social deixis, 5) demonstrative deixis. These subdivisions exist as much in the dramatic text as in the performance text.[63]

1) Enunciative Deixis

This type of discourse is central to theatre discourse, for all discursive activity is articulated from the deictics *I/you* which imply the integration of all the rest of the deixis involved in understanding the utterances. This inter-relationship is always performative: when a character says: "I swear", he/she performs both a locutory act and an illocutory act. That is, there is coincidence between the word act and the action implied by this act. This is why, as Serpieri points out, dialogue, and dialogue alone, constitutes the basic situation of theatre, and it is the act of dialogue that actually turns a stage into a stage. This is the staging of the language acts of the *I/you*.[64] When I say that in theatre only the *I* and the *you* exist, this is because there exists a constant shifting between *I* and *you*, *you* and *I*, and the *he/she* has no place there, for the third person is neither a speaker nor a listener and hence plays no role, even when alluded to in the discourse of the *I/you*. The grammatical person in theatre, according to Saraiva, "is not a dramatic character, but a character of the narrative. It is found not at the level of staging, however we may see it as if looking through a window which has been superimposed on it".[65]

It is important to emphasize that in theatre the *I* acts as in other pure literary discourses. Besides being deictic, however, the body of the actor also provides support. In the enunciative act, the actor produces discourse that is supported by both his/her voice and body. Thus, "the relay of the body exempts the discourse from indicating the enunciative process textually (the character does not say 'I say that it is nice' but rather 'it is nice'").[66] One cannot insist enough on this type of discourse deictically engaged in a contextual situation (a pragmatic situation), nor on the difference between this type of discourse and the narrative or poetic discourse in which deixis functions differently. The double dimension of the *I*, the discursive (linguistic) and the physical (body/voice) dimensions are what makes theatre discourse a non-literary form of discourse, or even an 'impure' literary discourse. The presence - in the text or on the stage - of the *I/you* is what allows us to say that theatre is a *stage practice* and not a literary practice.

The theatre dialogue assumed by the deictics of the *I/you* creates a *social practice*, but this practice is in fact a pure model of everyday communication. If one compares a theatre dialogue to a real dialogue (and even to a cinema script), the differences are obvious with respect to the syntactic order, the informative intensity, the illocutive force and the timing of the cues. All these factors are remodeled, stripped down in theatre discourse so as to render the message intelligible, and that is why we said previously that theatre discourse has an extra informational charge and a semantization of elements unnecessary in everyday dialogue. In theatre discourse, locutory, illocutory and perlocutory acts do exist, but in a different form.

I have argued that the *I/you* deitics constitute the basic situation of theatre, the very performability, the word made into action, and that this implies and involves the other forms of deixis. But if this is the case, what happens in a monologue where there is no physical addressee? The enunciative situation of monologue is the same as for the deictics of the *I/you*, for monologue is simply an interiorized dialogue between an *I-speaker* and an *I-listener* that is more closely determined by deictics than in normal dialogue. There is an excellent example in *Macías* by the Chilean author, Sergio Marras. One quote should suffice to show what I mean:

> As a people/town we have stayed empty/vacant/unoccupied and history must continue. We must surpass ourselves to fill it with meaning like to many other towns. *Some fill me with whispers, with gossips! Other provoke a moral hatred in me! All oblige me to grasp/sieze the ax/torch in my own hands!* Yes, it is certainly Macías. He has been indifferent to no one. Many took up the ax with you, against their own brothers. Some turned against you in the middle of the slaughter/massacre. Others assumed the role of your martyrs. We were all your servants. This/It is clear. You and we have always been the same thing. We are all responsible for your existence. *Do not allow me to die, therefore. You are much more to blame.*[67]

In this paragraph we can see the play between the *I-speaker* and the *I-listener*. At the beginning, it is the *I-listener*, the other, the judge who judges Macías for his political crimes and then it is the *I-speaker* (written in bold type) Macías, who defends himself against these accusations. The deictics *us/them* indicate the listener and the I (*me*) indicates Macías.

2) Spatial Deixis and   3) Temporal Deixis

The relationship between the *I* and the *you*, as I have already pointed out, is always present in a given pragmatic enunciative situation, which could be called the *dramatic communicative context*. This context has been defined by Keir Elam in the following way: a) "the situation in which a given exchange takes place, that is, the set of persons and objects present, their physical circumstances, the supposed time and place of their encounter, etc.;" b) "the communicative context proper, usually known as the *context-of-utterance*, comprising the relationship set up between speaker, listener and discourse in the immediate here-and-now".[68] This global definition of the dramatic context implies a spatial and temporal deixis that sets discourse in a precise *hic et nunc*. One could say that the very relationship of the *I* and *you*, especially on the stage, already creates a spatialization (*I/you*) and a temporalization (*I/you-they*) because it is directed to the spectators. But this spatialization/temporalization is only at the level of the concrete communication act occurring *on the stage* before the spectators. In order for a theatre spatialization/ temporalization to occur, the participants in the dialogue have to refer to time and space in their dialogue. That is, in many cases, and in particular when space and time are not represented, or rather, presented, the actual discourse may create this space and time. The use of the verbal spatial/temporal deixis can depend on two factors:

a) the type of dramatic text one is dealing with - modern texts, for example, tend to use them profusely, especially when *the word*, that is, discourse, contrasts strongly with what is being performed. This is the case in *Waiting for Godot* by Samuel Beckett:

> ESTRAGON: (*Very insidious*) But what Saturday? And is it Saturday? Is it not rather Sunday? (*Pause*) Or Monday. (*Pause*) Or Friday?
> VLADIMIR: (*Looking wildly about him, as though the date was inscribed in the landscape*) It's not possible!
> ESTRAGON: On Thursday?
> VLADIMIR: What'll we do?
> ESTRAGON: If he came yesterday and we weren't here you may be sure he won't come again today.
> VLADIMIR: But you say we were here yesterday.[69]

On the other hand, spatialization and temporalization of older texts tends to be done in an iconical and indexical manner. This does not mean that these texts do not have spatial and temporal didascalia in the characters' discourse.

b) the performance text can for various reasons disregard what is being presented on the stage and make use of discourse to set the space and time. The performances of Ancient texts (Greek and Roman), unlike those, for example, of the Naturalist era of the nineteenth century, made use of the deictic dimension of discourse to set space and time. The spatial and temporal adverbs (*here, now*) permeate all forms of theatre from this era. In this respect, theatre discourse is unique: its language, as Serpieri points out, "is permeated by deictic expressions to a degree quite unknown in other literary genres, above all because the theater exists on *the axis of the present* in a specific spatial situation".[70] Both spatial and temporal deixis are essential in understanding theatre discourse because they result in the inscription of discourse into a situation of communication and in a precise dramatic context.

The temporal deixis works both by means of time adverbs and verbs, which in discourse assume the same deictic function. Theatre, unlike the narrative, always occurs in a *hic et nunc*: the events are presented as if they were happening for the first time (even though they may be events from a remote past: for example, *Antony and Cleopatra* by Shakespeare, *Galileo Galilei* by Brecht, *Los libertadores* by the Chilean playwright Isidora Aguirre, *Un requiem para el Padre las Casas* by the Colombian Enrique Buenventura, etc.). It is the actual deictic verbal function that creates the simultaneous presence of utterance and enunciation in theatre.

4) Social Deixis

This is simply the class position of the characters. For example, in plays like *Save* by Edward Bond, or in *Hechos consumados* by the Chilean Juan Radrigán, both authors use language, costumes and gesture, three elements that characterize the social position of the character, in a unique way.

Save

LEN:	I used a'car, know what?
FRED:	'Ear what? - 'E's like a flippin' riddle.
LEN:	You an' 'er.
FRED:	Me an' 'oo?
LEN:	On the bash.
FRED:	Do what?
LEN:	Straight up.
FRED:	Chriss.[71]

Hechos consumados

EMILIO:	(*Pointing*) Look.
MARTA:	So, how long did I sleep?
EMILIO:	I found you about one o'clock in the morning, and you've just woken up: you figure it out.
MARTA:	And you looked after me all this time?
EMILIO:	(*Getting up*) What was I to do. At least it didn't start to rain; the night was ugly.
MARTA:	(*Looking*) But now it's lovely, right?
EMILIO:	Lovely? Don't you see that it's a filthy, worthless day? Now it's raining. Seems the water's getting into your brains.[72]

In the stage productions of these works (*Save*: Maison des Arts de Créteil, Paris, 1985; *Hechos consumados*, Café Esperanto, Montréal, 1982), discourse was accompanied by highly codified gestures from various social contexts, and the costumes complemented the deictic function of the discourse. Every play posits one form or another of social deictization that is essential to the contextualization of the message. In fact, the brechtian *Gestus* is very close to this type of deixis.[73]

5) Demonstrative Deixis

The function of demonstrative and ostentative deixis (this, that, etc.) is dual in theatre: a) there is an *indexical* function that relates the utterance to the referent, in a tautological but necessary way, if the discourse is to be understood. When a character refers to an object or to persons *present* on the stage, it is by means of demonstrative adjectives and pronouns that point to the ostentated person or object. Without this informative redundancy, discourse would be ambiguous. Thus, deixis serves as an informative and ostentative guide; b) there is an *indexical representative* function that allows for absent objects or persons (in a textual or a performative way) to be referred to, and hence allows for their incorporation into the discourse and events of the work. In this way, demonstrative deixis functions as *representation*. The use of this form of deixis in theatre is always varied, and especially the representative deixis, which is generally determined by a stage practice that depends on material determinants (means of production, theatre space, etc.) or type of theatre being performed.

III. FUNCTIONS OF THEATRE DISCOURSE

In this section two important aspects of theatre discourse will be examined. On the one hand, I will consider the function of language in theatre: that is, the specific function of language as it relates to theatre mimesis. On the other hand, I will examine the function of the actor's discourse, a type of discourse that is always incomplete and that constitutes only one portion of language in theatre.

A) *The Functions of Language in Theatre*

A capital component of theatre discourse is its *representative* function, that is, the way representation is done in theatre. At this juncture, the process of semiosis will not be considered (about this matter, see chapter III); rather, I will simply discuss a few of the mechanisms involved in the representation of language in theatre. However, I must first determine exactly what sort of universe is being represented in theatre, so as to examine the mechanisms involved in its representation. According to Roman Ingarden, the represented universe is made up of: a) *objective realities*: objects, human beings, processes displayed to the audience by the actors, the set, or what has been called *aperception*; b) objective realities represented by means of their simple presence on the stage and/or by means of the spoken word; c) the objective realities represented by the spoken word.[74] Although in general agreement with Ingarden, I do not feel that it is necessary to divide the represented reality into three groups (with the second divided into two groups), for in fact these are two distinct forms of representation: a) representation through the presence of objects on the stage; b) representation by means of the spoken word when the objects are absent.

The latter occurs by means of two concrete functions of language. First, there is the function of representation where words refer to objects that are on stage. In this case, the word has a supportive function, a role secondary to the more important, exhibitionist role that the object plays on the stage. This language function deictically guarantees the relationship between utterance and object. It is the means by which objects of the stage space are related to what is said in the character's discourse.

Second, there is the function of representation where words refer to objects absent from the stage. (It matters little that these objects may not be in the dramatic text or that they have been eliminated in the stage production). This function gives these objects validity and connects the objects off-stage to those on-stage by means of allusion (for example, a character's reference to past events or to something seen by the characters but that does not appear on the stage). We can say that the difference between both functions is that the first operates by means of deixis, whereas the latter operates by means of anaphora.

Besides these two functions, one can include a third that also refers to objective realities but that is different because they are not material. This is the *expressive function*. This function has to do with the expression of the character's internal realities or experiences when these are expressed by means of discourse or movement. According to Ingarden: "This process of expression is accomplished thanks to the demonstrative qualities (*Manifestationsqualitäten*) of the tone of the discourse and takes place in the global expressive function which exerts itself through gestures and the mimicry of the speaker".[75]

Ingarden establishes two further functions. In my opinion, however, the communication functions (*Mitteilung*) and the *persuasive functions* are not part of the represented universe; in other words, these functions do not represent as the others do. Furthermore, these two functions are already included within the representative and expressive function, for both communicate or attempt to persuade, depending on the enunciative situation and the performance context. For example, besides the communicative function, the expressive function can also have a persuasive function.[76]

B) *Functions of the Actor's Discourse*

These functions are assumed by the actor. The distinction (character/actor) may or may not be formal, depending on whether one is referring to the dramatic text or to the performance text. If it is the latter, the character-actor distinction is a purely formal one, for on the stage the distinction disappears. If one is considering the dramatic text, however, one is dealing with the character's discourse. Whatever way one regards this distinction, it is useless to discuss other functions which really only appear in the various *dramatic contexts* of the performance. According to Ubersfeld, there are four functions in the actor's discourse: a) the telling of a story (fabula); b) the indication of the imaginary conditions of enunciation; c) the assumption of a fiction discourse; d) the demonstration of a *stage performance*.[77]

In my opinion, the first function, the telling of a story, is shared by both the actor and the character and is not the property of just the actor, as Ubersfeld suggests. The actor-character tells a story in two ways. On the one hand, this is done through the dialogue or discourse that evolves bit by bit within the overall discursive process of theatre discourse. What the characters communicate, express or describe gradually forms a dialogue mosaic that acquires its full significance at the end of the representation-reading. The characters' discourse, which is only one part of the overall discourse that constitutes the staging of the play, has an important role in the *narration* of the story. On the other hand, the character-actor is a *lexeme* within a story, that is, a structural element of the dramatic syntax that acts as an actant-actor of a *subject in process*.[78] The character-actor's acting and the actantial-actorial function of the drama constitute fragments of a story. This is how discourse combines with the actantial function to form a productive act that constitutes itself in the story.

In order to transmit this story to the spectator in a comprehensible manner, the actor must indicate the conditions of *imaginary enunciation* of his/her discourse. These conditions are imaginative insofar as the actor's discourse is fictive and insofar as the world the actor creates in the character he/she represents and what he/she says is fictive. But at the same time, *the act of the word is a real act* because the actor is a living discourse-creating being. The conditions of enunciation, however, are determined by the text or the staging of the text. Whatever the case, the conditions of enunciation are linked to fiction. The function of the actor is to complete the incomplete discourse of the dramatic text, this being complete only when staged in relation to a situation of concrete/fictive enunciation. As was pointed out already, the actor presents the conditions of enunciation through his/her physical presence which allows the discourse to be transmitted to an individual as well as to the deixis and anaphora that place the actor in a concrete situation.

The final function of the actor's discourse is the demonstration of a *stage performance*. In this case, it is not solely discourse that has priority: gesticularity, kinesics and proxemics also play important roles. It is truly the actor's entire body that links discourse and mimesis, discourse and the audience. The physical presence of the actor is fundamental in theatre: "The actor is everything in the theatre. We can do without everything in the representation, except [the actor]".[79] What characterizes the stage performance is its duality. On the one hand, its function is to create a sign, that is, to be transformed into a character, an emitter of diverse signs - a system of signs constructed by means of the *theatre process*. On the other hand, in this process of semanticization of the actor, there is always a part of the process which is never semanticized, the part that makes it obvious to the audience that an actor is in front of them. In the first case, the actor is integrated into the fiction (as a character) while in the second case, the actor carries out a performance destined to present the fiction by means of his/her concrete and physical presence. This dual articulation of theatre discourse, as both mimesis and activity of the actor, constitutes the two basic axes of all theatre discourse. They are present in every form of theatre and differentiate this discourse from other forms.

IV. SPECIFICATION OF THEATRE DISCOURSE

The components of theatre discourse that we have considered thus far - speaker, listener, enunciation, utterance, deixis, anaphora, the functions of language in theatre and the functions of the actor's discourse - all provide a basis on which to establish the linguistic specificity of theatre discourse.

In my opinion, this specificity lies in the particular nature of theatre discourse. In order to determine this specificity, two different yet complementary levels will be examined: on the one hand, the concepts of *histoire* and *discours* as defined by Emile Benveniste,[80] and on the other, the enunciative situation and the deictics that are part of this situation. If we define *discours* as a *text* that includes deictics (that is, a deixis that links the utterance to the moment of enunciation), and *histoire* as any text that lacks deictics for the enunciative situation (Sit ∈, see table II), and if we accept that the linguistic basis for discourse is the present tense, the first and second person and that the basis for *histoire* is the preterite and the third person, then we can situate theatre discourse within the category of *discours*. This is because one is dealing with a text whose reference occurs with relation to the enunciative situation (Sit ∈). On the other hand, in texts that fall under the category of *histoire*, such as the narrative, the text refers to itself. In this case (and in keeping with the terminology of Jenny Simonin-Grumbach),[81] this will be referred to as the utterance situation (Sit E). According to Simonin-Grumbach, "it is no longer a question of the presence or the absence of *shifters* on the surface, but of the fact that the determinations refer back to the enunciative situation (extra-linguistic) in one case, while in the other, they refer to the text itself".[82]

A clarification is necessary here: when I speak of theatre discourse, I do not distinguish between oral and written discourse. This distinction applies only to narrative or poetry, for in my opinion, theatre discourse is a form of oral discourse, even in its written form. This is so because the written form reproduces the dialogue structure and the dialogue presents itself in an enunciative situation that is *present simultaneous* to the subject's utterance, while in the narrative the enunciative situation has to be verbalized (explicated). One could argue that the didascalia elements refer to the enunciative situation (sit ∈), but one must take into account the fact that the stage directions come from various sources: a) they are produced by the character's discourse informing or naming other characters, etc.; b) by the stage objects when these are understood on their iconical, indexical or symbolic level;[83] c) by the didascalia that are inscribed in the text by the author/script writer. This last type of didascalia disappears in the staging (this being the enunciative situation that is always implicit) because it is absorbed by the enunciative situation and by the actor playing his/her role.

I must also point out, in full agreement with Ubersfeld, that theatre is not to be considered solely as a literary genre, but rather, as a stage practice.[84] It is a stage practice in that the speaker-listener relationship is fundamental and constitutive of the process and that time and place are both present in theatre discourse. This is also supported by T. Todorov, when he says:

> The signification of each utterance is constituted in part by the meaning of its process of enunciation. From the point of view of the subject of the enunciation, evey sentence, every utterance is at the same time action, that is, the action of articulating that utterance. There is, therefore, no utterance that is not performative in the sense Austin gives that word.[85]

Todorov is correct, but it is important to note that he is referring to the narrative in which, despite the performability of the utterances, there can never be a Sit $\in$, only a verbalized Sit E. The following formula will be helpful in specifying theatre discourse.[86] Two types of discourse can be established: a) oral texts - including theatre - in which the utterances refer to the enunciative situation (Sit $\in$); b) written texts that also refer to the enunciative situation but in which at least one part of the Sit $\in$ is verbalized as the utterance situation (Sit E). In the first case, I will use the following formulae: Sit $\in$ = Sit E, the time (T) of the $\in$ = the time (T) of E of the Subject (S). All of these elements are common to both S and to the addressee S'. It is here that one finds the linguistic specificity of theatre's unique form of enunciation and its radical difference from other discursive practices. In a second type of discourse, the formula differs, depending on whether a poetic or narrative discourse is involved; in the narrative, the Sit $\in$ $\neq$ Sit E, $T \neq$ E T of S, and none of the elements are common between S and S'. In the poetic discourse there is no actual Sit $\in$ or Sit E, but rather an abstract Sit $\in$* and Sit E* that does not refer to anything (S*), for in poetry there are no events and T gives way to an abstract time (T*), to a non-time with respect to the Sit $\in$.[87]

One example will suffice to demonstrate these two types of discursive articulation: if we take the utterance, "What heat!", this appears differently with respect to the Sit $\in$. In theatre the Sit $\in$ is implicit and the utterance is found to be deictically engaged by implication. It is the actual context-occurrence that gives it its meaning, for there is no reference to the S, and yet the presence of the *I/you* must exist along with the context. On the other hand, for such an utterance to be understood in the narrative, it has to be verbalized in relation to the Sit $\in$ in the form of Sit E, mediated by the narrative voice. Whereas in the theatre the simultaneous presence of discourse and event is emphasized, in the narrative the discursive act is separated from the event. In poetic discourse, there is no simultaneous presence whatsoever because there are no real events, only a non-referential utterance.

Another important aspect of theatre discourse is that in theatre, the present has real value in the discourse. Theatre is the discourse of *hic et nunc*, forever in the present. Even when events take place in the past, they present themselves in the present, in the form of performative action. This is so because in theatre, discourse *is* action and action *is* discourse. In the narrative, if one is to consider the events as real, these events have to be in the past. This is where the illusion of 'objectivity' comes from in the narrative. In theatre, however, there is always a sort of 'subjectivity', for despite the physical presence of the actors and real objects on the stage, a process of denial occurs: theatre is a referential illusion. Theatre always states that *we are in the theatre* and that one is dealing with a *reality transformed into a sign*, with a referential simulacrum or a sign that is being transformed into reality.[88] This is what is special about the present tense in theatre.

This distinction that Simonin-Grumbach establishes with respect to this problem is important: the value of the present tense lies in its reference to the time of the utterance and it is this axial tense that differentiates what happens before from what happens afterwards. In the narrative, Simonin-Grumbach adds, "the relations of order cannot be marked ... since the value of the base time is its reference to the moment of the event itself".[89] That is, one event follows on another, even when its structure is in the *sujet*.[90] The linguistic time is inherent in theatre discourse, whereas in the narrative, time is chronological. Benveniste points out that: "What is singular to linguistic time is that it is organically linked to the exercise of speech, that it is defined and ordered as a function of the discourse. This time has its centre - a generative and axial centre - in the *present* of the immediacy of speech".[91] There is coincidence of discourse and event, for every enunciative act breaks from this axis, the moment of the discourse. For example, in theatre the utterance "today" is a spatio-temporal co-reference; in the narrative, on the other hand, one must consider this utterance in relation to the mesurative, directive or stative conditions, that is, to the chronological time of the calendar.[92]

In summary, the specificity of theatre discourse can be found in the articulation Sit $\in$ = Sit E. What is important about this articulation is the fact that theatre discourse can only be understood when related to a Sit $\in$ that is shifted into a precise occurrence-context. That is why this form of discourse always expresses what is on the stage or related to it in some way. At the same time, this form of discourse is a *discursive activity* that creates its own conditions of enunciation which are attached to the stage referent. It is also the discourse *par excellence* of the *hic et nunc* and, therefore, it is necessarily permeated with deictics incorporated into the Sit $\in$. Theatre deixis only acquires its full meaning within discursive performability, the way signs are set up and in the evolution and organization of this signifying world. This is why theatre discourse should be considered an oral discourse, since it can only operate within the space established by the stage. It is fitting that I end this chapter with another quote by D'Aubignac: "In a word, in the Theatre, the discourses are the accessories to the Action, albeit all of Tragedy in the Representation consists of nothing but discourses".[93] A very revealing quote, for it answers the main question of this chapter on the specific nature of theatre discourse: in theatre there exists a performative reality, or, in other words, discourse engenders action, and action is discourse. In theatre, the spoken word is intimately linked to the activity of theatre.

Table I

ANAPHORA
anaphoric axis / exophoric axis (before the enunciative situation)
narrative or dynamic axis / intrareferential anaphora (refers to diegetic sequences)
deictic axis / endophoric anaphora (internal to the enunciation)

DEIXIS
enunciative deixis (I/you)
spatial deixis (here/there)
temporal deixis (today/yesterday)
social deixis (ideolect)
demonstrative deixis (this/that)

Table II

theatre discourse	narrative discourse	poetic discourse
shifted/implicit	shifted/explicit (verbalization)	not explicit/nor implicit
Sit $\in$ V Sit E	Sit $\cap$ Sit E	Sit $\in$* $\mathbb{V}$ Sit E*
oral	written	written
stage practice	reading activity	reading activity
Sit $\in$ = Sit E	Sit $\in$ $\neq$ Sit E	Sit $\in$* $\circ$ Sit E*
$T \in$ = T E $\longrightarrow$ S	$T \in$ $\neq$ T E $\longrightarrow$ S	$T \in$ * $\circ$ T E* $\longrightarrow$ S*
Sit $\in$ = Sit E > S + S' : Sit $\in$ (S + S')	Sit $\in$ $\neq$ Sit E < S + S' : Sit $\in$ (S - S')	Sit $\in$* $\circ$ Sit E* $\not>$ S + S' : Sit $\in$ * (S / S')

Sit $\in$*	= enunciative situation without a reference		$\circ$	= abstract space and time
Sit $\in$	= enunciative situation		V	= implicit shifter
Sit E	= utterance situation		$\cap$	= explicit shifter
$T \in$	= time of enunciation		$\mathbb{V}$	= neither implicit nor explicit
T E	= time of utterance		>	= common basis for S and S'
T*	= abstract time		<	= no common basis for S and S'
S	= subject of the enunciation		$\not>$	= absence of any common basis
S*	= abstract subject		S'	= addressee of the enunciation
-	= I and not-you		+	= I/you
=	= equal to		/	= no concrete I or you
			$\neq$	= not equal to

ENDNOTES
CHAPTER I

1. J. Dubois, M. Giacomo, L. Guespin, C. and J.B. Marcellesi, J.P.Mével, *Dictionnaire de linguistique* (Paris: Librairie Larousse, 1973), p. 156 (our translation).

2. "Problématique des travaux sur le discours politique", *Langage,* 23 (septembre 1971), 10 (our translation).

3. *Ibid.*, p. 10. Concerning the problematic of discourse analysis and its production, see: Bernard Conein, Jean Jacques Coutrine, Françoise Gadet, Jean Marie Marandin and Michel Pêcheux, *Matérialités discursives* (Lille: Presses Universitaires de Lille, 1981); Michel Pêcheux, *Les vérités de La Palice* (Paris: François Maspero, 1975); Jean Claude Gardin, *Les analyses de discours* (Neuchâtel, Switzerland: Delachau et Niestlé, S.A., 1974); Pierre Bourdieu, *Ce que parler veut dire* (Paris: Librairie Arthème Fayard, 1982); Regine Robin, *Histoire et linguistique* (Paris: Librairie Armand Colin, 1973).

4. Emile Benveniste, "L'Appareil formel de l'énonciation", in *Problèmes de linguistique générale, II* (Paris: Editions Gallimard, 1974), pp. 79-88.

5. "Les relations de temps dans le verbe français", in *Problèmes de linguistique générale, I* (Paris: Editions Gallimard, 1966), p. 242 (our translation).

6. "L'appareil formel de l'énonciation", in *Problèmes de linguistique générale, II,* p. 80 (our translation). See also A.J. Saraiva, "Message et littérature", *Poétique,* 17 (1974), 1-13. In this study, there is an interesting formalization of what precedes the *énonciation,* which Savaira calls 'support'; he also touches on theatre discourse from the point of view of *simple discourse.*

7. "L'Appareil formel de l'énonciation", in *Problèmes de linguistique générale, II,* p. 81.

8. On this point Benveniste adds the following: "man has no other way to live the 'now' and to make it real than to realize it through the insertion of discourse into the world". *Ibid.,* p. 83 (our translation).

9. J.L. Austin, *How to Do Things with Words.* 2nd edition (Cambridge, Mass.: Harvard University Press, 1975), pp. 6, 12, 94-198, 107-120.

10. *Ibid.,* pp. 99, 110, 118, 121, etc.

11. "Structuralisme, énonciation et sémantique", *Poétique,* 33 (février 1978), 108 (our translation).

12. "Les relations de temps dans le verbe français", in *Problèmes de linguistique générale, I,* p. 238.

13. *Ibid.,* p. 239 (our translation).

14. *Ibid.,* p. 242 (our translation). This difference that Benveniste establishes with respect to past time is concerned with the past in French, but the distinction between *histoire* and *discours* is universally valid.

15. Concerning the concepts of distance, modalisation, tension and transparency/opacity, see Louis Courdesses, "Blum et Thorez en mai 1936: analyse d'énoncés", *Langue française,* (février 1971), 25.

16. For example, Patrice Pavis, *Problèmes de sémiologie théâtrale* (Montréal: Presses de l'Université du Québec, 1976) and *Voix et images de la scène* (Lille: Presses Universitaires de Lille, 1982); Anne Ubersfeld, *Lire le théâtre 2.* Postscript to the fourth edition. (Paris: Editions Sociales, 1982); Keir Elam, *The Semiotics of Theatre and Drama* (London and New York: Methuen, 1980); Marco De Marinis, *Semiotica del teatro* (Milano: Studi Bompiani, 1982). These are just a few of the better known studies.

17. *Lire le théâtre,* p. 225 (our translation).

18. *Voix et images de la scène,* p. 41 (our translation).

19. Georges Mounin subordinates communication to the intention of communicating, which would qualify theatre as a non-communicative act, as if in theatre there were no communication. As well, Mounin departs from the restrictive notion of communication, in which communication can only occur between two participants in a dialogue whose answers/questions and the right to speak would define the communicative act. But it is clear that theatre communicates in various ways that we cannot really touch on at this point. *Introduction à la sémiologie* (Paris: Editions de Minuit, 1970), p. 68. See also: Alessandro Serpieri, *et. al.*, *Come comunica il teatro: dal testo alla scena* (Milano: Il Formichiere, 1978).

20. The model of rectilinear communication alluded to is, for example, that of Jakobson:

Context
referential

Sender...................*Message*................*Addressee*
Emotive   Poetic   Cognitive

Contact
Phatic

Code
Metalinguistic

Each communicative function is accompanied by another series of functions particular to it. The message goes from the sender to the receiver and is mediated by the functions which can be found in the centre and which assure the proper transmission of the message. *Essais de linguistique générale* (Paris: Editions de Minuit, 1963), pp. 213-220.

21. The term scriptor (*escriptor*) is meant to include not only the author of the dramatic text but also the director and the stage participants who do the work of writing or rewriting the dramatic text as the virtual performance text. See chapter II, section III.

22. *Lire le théâtre*, p. 229. See also chapter VII of *L'école du spectateur. Lire le théâtre 2* (Paris: Editions Sociales, 1981), pp. 303-328.

23. By didascalia I mean not only the stage directions from the dramatic text but also all forms of information contained in the dialogue, for example the description of some event, state of mind, etc., including names mentioned which identify each speaker/listener.

24. Anne Ubersfeld, *Lire le théâtre*, p. 231 (our translation). If we think of *Hamlet*, for example, one can see that it is often the very discourse of the characters that works as didascalia, establishing the enunciative and the performative conditions: this is the case in the vision at the beginning of the work when the Queen refers to the insanity of Ophelia. See Marco De Marinis, "Vers une pragmatique de la communication théâtrale", *Versus*, 30 (September-December 1981), 71-86.

25. *Lire le théâtre*, p. 235 (our translation).

26. For more on these points, see chapter II.

27. I understand *social formation* in the sense Marx used it (*ökonimische Gesellschaftsformation*). For more on this term, see *Grundrisse*.

28. By *reading* I mean interpretation, decodification, concretization and realization of a dramatic text in the form of a virtual performance text and a performance text. See chapters II and IV for more details.

29. *Denegation* accounts for the double nature of theatre: it exists as a real and concrete fact on the stage (there are actors, objects, words) but at the same time all of this is negated, for all that is found on the stage is a sign of a sign, a referential simulacrum. Theatre tells us, 'I am a lie but I am also truth'.

30. It is clear that the reader's imagination plays a central role in the reading, especially in a novel. What I hope to illustrate is that the elements that allow for this imaginative representation, the *actualization/concretization* of the linguistic strata, etc., of a novel are given within the strata. For more on the topic see Wolfgang Iser, *The Act of Reading. A Theory of Aesthetic Response* (Baltimore and London: The Johns Hopkins University Press, 1978) and *The Implied Reader* (Baltimore and London: The Johns Hopkins University Press, 1974); Umberto Eco, *The Role of the Reader* (Bloomington, Indiana: Indiana University Press, 1984). See also chapter IV of this book.

31. *Lire le théâtre*, p. 229 (our translation).

32. *Ibid.*, p. 227 (our translation).

33. Patrice Pavis, *Voix et images de la scène*, p. 39 (our translation).

34. *Ibid.*, p. 227.

35. This concept concerns the relationships among all of the producers of a given performance and between the stage and the audience. For more on this point see the entries on *relation scène-salle* and *relation théâtrale* in *Dictionnaire du théâtre* (Paris: Editions Sociales, 1980) by Patrice Pavis. See also chapter IV of this book.

36. "Message et littérature", 6. On dialogue and the enunciative situation, consult Jiří Veltrusky, "Construction of Semantic Contexts", in *Semiotics of Art. Prague School Contributions*, edited by Ladislav Matejka and Erwin R. Titunik (Cambridge, Mass. and London, England: The MIT Press, 1976), pp. 134-144; "Dramatic Text as a Component of Theatre", *Ibid.*, pp. 94-117 and "Basic Features of Dramatic Dialogue", *Ibid.*, pp. 128-133; Jan Mukařovský, *Word and Verbal Art*, translated and edited by John Burbank and Peter Steiner, forword by René Wellek (New Haven and London: Yale University Press, 1977); and the excellent article by Erika Fischer-Lichte, "The Dramatic Dialogue - Oral or Literary Communication"? in *Semiotics of Drama and Theatre*, edited by Herta Schmidt and Aloysius Van Kesteren (The Hague: John Benjamins, 1984), pp. 137-173.

37. If we tape a conversation, a dialogue between two or more people in real life (or in a film) and then compare it to a similar situation in the theatre, we will observe the great difference that exists between these two dialogues.

38. "Message et littérature", 5 (our translation).

39. "Présupposés et sous-entendus", *Langue française*, 4 (février 1969), 36.

40. Patrice Pavis, *Voix et images de la scène*, p. 16.

41. For more on the theatre referent, see section V, chapter III.

42. A.J. Saraiva, "Message et littérature", 6 (our translation).

43. *Lire le théâtre*, p. 290 (our translation). When I quote from this edition (1982), I will indicate the year. Otherwise, it is always the first edition.

44. For more on deixis, refer to John Lyons, *Semantics 2* (London, New York, Melbourne, Cambridge: Cambridge University Press, 1979), pp. 636-646.

45. See studies by Keir Elam, *The Semiotics of Theatre and Drama*; Anne Ubersfeld, *Lire le théâtre* and *L'école du spectateur*; Patrice Pavis, *Problèmes de sémiologie théâtrale*; "Théorie du théâtre et sémiologie: sphère de l'objet et sphère de l'homme", *Semiotica*, XVI, 1 (1976), 45-86; and "Représentation, mise en scène, mise en signe", *The Canadian Journal of Research in Semiotics*, IV, 1 (Fall 1976), 63-86; Alessandro Serpieri, Keir Elam, Paola Guilli Publiatti, Tomaso Kemeny and Romana Rutelli, "Toward a Segmentation of the Dramatic Text", *Poetics Today*, II, 3 (Spring 1981), 163-200.

46. Quoted by Keir Elam in *The Semiotics of Theatre and Drama*, p. 139. See also the above article by Alessandro Serpieri, *et al.*, "Toward a Segmentation of the Dramatic Text", 163-200.

47. *Semantics 2*, p. 637.

48. *Ibid.*, p. 660.

49. On theatre pragmatics, see Anne Ubersfeld, *Lire le théâtre*. (1982), pp. 227-294.

50. An excellent example is found in the study of Alessandro Serpieri, *et al.*, "Toward a Segmentation of the Dramatic Text", 165, and in Keir Elam, *The Semiotics of Theatre and Drama*, pp. 179-180. See also Marco De Marinis, "Vers une pragmatique de la communication théâtrale", 71-86.

51. Alessandro Serpieri, *et al.*, "Toward a Segmentation of the Dramatic Text", 165-166.

52. *Ibid.*, pp. 168-169.

53. Jindrich Honzl calls the extra-referential anaphora *"fantastic oriented deixis*, because of the fact that it specifies a dramatic action that is carried out solely in the imagination of the spectator". "The Hierarchy of Dramatic Devices", in *Semiotics of Art*, p. 124.

54. *El teatro hispanoamericano contemporáneo*. 2nd edition. Edited by Carlos Solórzano (Mexico: Fondo de Cultura Económica, 1975), p. 132.

55. Bertolt Brecht, *Mother Courage and her Children*. (London: Eyre Methuen, 1962), p. 38.

56. (Buenos Aires: Editorial Astral, 1967), pp. 30 and 90 respectively (our translation).

57. William Shakespeare, *Hamlet. The Riverside Shakespeare*. (Boston: Houghton Mifflin Company, 1974), Act I, Scene V, pp. 1149-1150 and Act III, Scene II, p. 1164, respectively.

58. (London: Eyre Methuen, 1979), p. 51.

59. *The Semiotics of Theatre and Drama*, pp. 152-153.

60. *Universi di discorso* (Milano: Feltrinelli, 1979).

61. For more on referentiality in theatre, see chapter III of this book.

62. *The Semiotics of Theatre and Drama*, p. 150.

63. For a complete classification of deixis and anaphora, see table I at the end of chapter I.

64. "Toward a Segmentation of the Dramatic Text", 169-171. See also Anne Ubersfeld, *Lire le théâtre* (1982), chapters VI and VII; and *L'école du spectateur*, chapter IV. Also, Keir Elam, *The Semiotics of Theatre and Drama*, chapter V, pp. 35-207.

65. "Message et littérature", 5 (our translation).

66. Patrice Pavis, *Voix et images de la scène*, p. 38 (our translation).

67. (Santiago, Chile: Las Ediciones del Ornitorrinco, 1984), p. 82 (our translation).

68. *The Semiotics of Theatre and Drama*, p. 137.

69. (New York: Grove Press, 1954), p. 11.

70. "Toward a Segmentation of the Dramatic Text", 167.

71. (London: Eyre Methuen, 1977), p. 63.

72. In *Teatro de Juan Radrigán. 11 obras* (Santiago, Chile and Minnesota: CENECA and University of Minnesota, 1984), p. 227 (our translation).

73. See the section on sign-indices in chapter III of this book.

74. "Les fonctions du langage au théâtre", *Poétique*, 8 (1971), 532-534.

75. *Ibid.*, p. 535 (our translation).

76. See Anne Ubersfeld, *Lire le théâtre*, chapter I, pp. 13-49.

77. *L'école du spectateur*, pp. 165-238.

78. Regarding this concept, see Julia Kristeva, "Le sujet en procès", *Tel Quel*, 52 (1972), 12-30, and 53 (1973), 17-38. On the character as actant, see chapter V of this book and chapter II of *Lire le théâtre* by Anne Ubersfeld as well as chapter II of my book *Brecht en el teatro hispanoamericano contemporáneo* (Buenos Aires: Editorial Galerna, 1987).

79. Anne Ubersfeld, *L'école du spectateur*, pp. 165 (our translation).

80. "Les relations de temps dans le verbe français", in *Problèmes de linguistigue générale, I*, pp. 237-250.

81. "Pour une typologie des discours", in *Langue, discours, société. Pour Emile Benveniste*, under the direction of Julia Kristeva, Jean-Claude Milner, Nicolas Ruwet (Paris: Editions du Seuil, 1975), pp. 85-121.

82. *Ibid.*, p. 87 (our translation).

83. See chapter III of this book.

84. See *Lire le théâtre* and *L'école du spectateur*.

85. *Littérature et signification* (Paris: Librairie Larousse, 1967), p. 27 (our translation).

86. See table II at the end of this chapter.

87. For more details and a general view of these formulae, see table II at the end of this chapter.

88. This is the process of denial: it is in the affirmation of the theatrality of the representation. On denial, see the article by Anne Ubersfeld, "Notes sur la dénégation théâtrale", in *La relation théâtrale*, texts compiled by Régis Durand (Lille: Presses Universitaires de Lille, 1980), pp. 11-25. See also chapter I of *Lire le théâtre*, pp. 13-49.

89. "Pour une typologie du discours", p. 94 (our translation).

90. We use the concept of *sujet* in the sense given to it by the Russian Formalists, that is, as artistic organization of the discourse that can be non-linear. For more on this see, "La théorie de la 'méthode formelle'" by Boris Eikhenbaum, in *Théorie de la littérature*, texts by the Russian Formalists collected, presented and translated by Tzvetan Todorov, preface by Roman Jakobson (Paris: Editions du Seuil, 1965), p. 48.

91. "La langue et l'expérience humaine", in *Problèmes de linguistique générale, II*, p. 73 (our translation).

92. *Ibid.*, pp. 70-72.

93. *La pratique du théâtre*. Nachdruck der dreibändigen Ausgabe Amsterdam 1715 mit einer einleitenden Abhandlung von Hans-Jörg Neuschäfer (Genève: Slatkine Reprints, 1971), p. 260 (our translation).

CHAPTER II

TEXT, DRAMATIC TEXT, PERFORMANCE TEXT

> Script has *become* performance, by pursuing a line of potentiality that had previously been only implicit, and therefore hidden, but which is now actualized in such a way as to seem inevitable.
> Richard Hornby, *Script Into Performance*.

For decades now there has been a debate on whether or not theatre, or more specifically, the dramatic text, is a *literary genre* or a stage practice. Already in 1941, Jiři Veltrusky indicated that: "The unending quarrel about the nature of drama, whether it is a literary genre or a theatrical piece, is perfectly futile. One does not exclude the other".[1] In itself, the dispute may be futile, as Veltrusky puts it. The origin of the debate, however, has well-determined causes. In my opinion, the problematic, or rather, origin of the dispute between theatre *practitioners*, *performers*, *critics*, and *theoreticians* comes from the confusion pertaining to the theatre *object*, which has generally been approached in two different ways. If the *theatre object* is to be understood as a signifying practice, then it presents itself differently for the director (and his/her associates: actors, scenographers, decorators, costume designers, etc.) than it does for the critic or the semiotician. In the first case, the *dramatic text*, if indeed one exists, is an almost plastic object that the director shapes, adapts, adopts, changes. In fact, one could say that this is a sculptive type of activity. The director's task is to shape, to resolve space and time problems, meaning concretization, proxemic and kinesic problems, the *theatre relation*, ideological problems, etc. - that is, everything directly involved with stage practice. In the second case, the dramatic text is treated as an object of *literary* study and the objective is then to explain the historical aspects, to interpret the text in different ways, including the identification of its structure and various formal elements. Finally, the task of the theatre semiotician resides mainly in the description of the process of the production of meaning, in the explanation of how something is said in theatre, as much in the dramatic text as in the performance text.[2] My job here is to see how the various codes are organized and how meaning is produced. The purely dramaturgic aspects of theatre are central to this chapter: that is, the production of signs by the actor, space, and the whole of the performance. In semiological work pertaining to theatre the text is seen as just one more component of the theatre phenomenon. Thus, theatre semiotics presents itself differently when faced with the theatre object. The point is not to discuss whether theatre is literature, or whether theatre is purely a stage practice; rather, theatre should be approached as a whole. For us, the dramatic text is a fundamental, unavoidable, material reality. When faced with this text two attitudes are possible: either to treat it as a dramatic text, forgetting that the reality of this text has always been dual (literary/performance), or, rather, to treat it as another component of the theatre performance, integrated into the stage practice. These levels are all legitimate and in no way exclusive. Nevertheless, it appears that the most fruitful work that can be done with respect to theatre is in semiotics, for semiotics accounts for the dual nature of theatre. Other than serving to confirm theatre's duality, the polemic which has arisen around this question is most futile.

If one is to refer to the dramatic text and the performance text, one should first consider the actual notion of text so as to define, however briefly, what constitutes a text. This, in turn, will allow for a more accurate definition of dramatic text and performance text. There do indeed exist various versions of the meaning of text, and, at times, everything seems to pass for text.[3]

There are different ways of defining text. One method, put forth by Roland Barthes, Jacques Derrida, Philippe Solleres, Tzvetan Todorov and especially Julia Kristeva, may be called the semiological view. Paul Ricoeur's definition, on the other hand, exemplifies the classical view.

I. TEXT

A) *The Semiological View*

The semiological view defines the text as *productivity* and thus the text is considered as "implementation in writing of the relation sender-receiver, writing-reading, like [the relation] of two productivities that intersect and in so doing create a space".[4] At the basis of the concept of *productivity* is the fact that the text *makes a work out of language*, but at the same time, the text is *worked on* by other texts because every text is the assimilation and transformation of many texts; that is, inside every text an *intertextuality* exists and functions.

The concept of productivity implies all sorts of readings, combinations, and infinite interpretations. Consequently, the semiotician perceives the text as a dynamic-infinite entity, as a reproducer of language. But this infinity has a finite-contingent quality due to the dual nature of the text: that is, the opposition between *pheno-text* and *geno-text*. In the first case (pheno-text), *significance* (that is, the multitude of operations language performs in a given area) is phenomenalized, made *visible* in the signifying structure. This *pheno-text* is generated by a *geno-text*, the place of structuration of the *pheno-text*. This may be expressed in another way: the pheno-text is the verbal (or written) phenomenon as it would present itself in the structure of a concrete utterance; the geno-text, then, is the text that undertakes the logical steps inherent in the constitution of the subject of the utterance.[5] This is why the geno-text is the place of structuration of the pheno-text. Kristeva locates the textual specificity in the dialectic between both components of the texts. In other words, it lies in "the fact that it is a translation of the geno-text in the pheno-text, decipherable in the reading by the opening of pheno-text to the geno-text".[6]

I have already stated that the infinite number of possible combinations of the geno-text has a contingent goal (the pheno-text); this is because the pheno-text is found *in* the geno-text and its manifestation is a slice of the *geno-text*. This is due to the fact that the geno-text, which generates the pheno-text, is the actual *significance* (infinity of possibilities open to language) and thus the text is the *writing which contains significance*. In summary, the geno-text constitutes the infinite number of possibilities of textualization and the pheno-text *is one of these textualizations*.

The notion of *intertext* or *intertextuality* is fundamental to the understanding and function of a text. Generally speaking, we can say that *every* text is an intertext in that other texts exist on various levels within the text: there are fragments of other texts, texts from current or past cultural trends, from other cultures, or from non-literary or non-artistic practices.[7] The intertext is the *social* or inter-social part of culture. As such, it functions in an accumulative manner: "It is all the language, old and contemporary, which comes to the text, not by means of a traceable filtration, of a voluntary imitation, but by means of a dissemination - an image which assures the text the status, not of a *reproduction*, but of a *productivity*".[8]

At the same time, the notion of *ideologeme* is intimately linked to the notion of intertext. This notion subsumes different ideologies. In a text or textual practice, the ideologeme is present in the utterances it assimilates and which refer to other textual practices or to other texts. According to Kristeva, ideologeme is "the common function which links a concrete structure (let's say the novel) to the other structures (let's say the discourse of science) in an intertextual space. I shall define the ideologeme of a text through its relations with other texts".[9] In fact, the ideologeme is comparable to the *locus* or *loci* of ancient rhetoric, in that the *loci* were veritable repositories of the most complete and efficient ideas that could be found, and were used especially in the *questio finita*. In this way, one can consider the *ideologeme* as a *topical ideological* maxim that confers authority and coherence and has the same function as the Aristotelian *topos koinos/locus commune*. Thus, intertextuality and ideologeme are tightly linked, for an intertext posits a series of ideologemes. The ideologeme is naturally understood as something more complete and less punctual or pointed than a *locus* and its specificity resides in the fact that it allows the text to be articulated in the intertext.

The very notion of intertextuality can be better defined and further subdivided if distinctions are made among the different ways an intertext works. These intertextual *practices*, according to Lucien Dällenbach, include the following: *general intertextuality*, or the intertextual relationships between texts and different authors; *limited intertextuality*, that is, the intertextual relationships between the texts of the same author; *external intertextuality*, the relationship of one text to another; *internal intertextuality*, the relationship of a text with itself; and finally, *autotextuality* or *mise en abîme*.[10] These distinctions of forms of intertexuality are useful, for they give a more accurate view of how the intertext works. Nevertheless, it is important to point out that these categories work in an interrelated way: for example, both general and limited intertextuality constitute external intertextuality. Furthermore, autotextuality is internal intertextuality. The reason for separating internal intertextuality and autotextuality is the fact that all forms of intertexuality are autotextuality. It is possible to have a text that refers to other texts and to parts of itself.

These categories are not terribly useful for dealing with the various characteristics of the dramatic text, for in theatre, and especially in modern and contemporary theatre, dramatic texts from other eras or from other contemporary authors are often used in a new way. One only has to think of *Man and Superman* by Bernard Shaw, *Heroica de Buenos Aires* by Osvaldo Dragún, *Lear* by Edward Bond, or *Die Mütter* by Bertolt Brecht. This form of intertextuality is purely literary, but there are also historical forms of intertextuality or intertext. This intertextuality can be with reference to form or to content. For example, as a basis for its text, a dramatic text can refer to a historical event found in historical texts. This is the case in *Galileo Galilei* and *Die Tage der Commune* by Brecht, *Santa Juana de América* by Andrés Lizárraga, *Revelo 1929* by Jorge Goldenberg, *Lauturo* by Isidora Aguirre, *La denuncia* by Enrique Buenventura, etc. In this way, intertextuality can be divided into two generic areas: either *historic intertextuality* or fictionalized historical intertexts, such as those just mentioned, or *literary intertextuality* or fictitious intertexts that have been recoded. An example of each of these cases will suffice to explain what is meant by this.

Lautaro by Isidora Aguirre is based on the figure of an Araucano leader and his fight for the land. Aguirre took a real historical figure and his fight against the Spanish and then fictionalized and dramatized these elements. The text posits a dual referentiality, for it is directed to both the past and the present. One could say the same for Brecht's *Galileo Galilei* in which there is an immense amount of referentiality concerning the decisions that scientists must take with respect to nuclear war. In general, this type of intertextuality is always dual - past and present - although it does not have to be, as is the case in the trilogy *Coronas* by Rudolfo Usigli.

The second case (literary intertextuality) consists of the re-fictionalization/codification of an existing fictive text. Take for example *Antigone* by Jean Anouilh or *Lear* by Edward Bond, their intertexts being *Antigone* by Sophocles and *King Lear* by Shakespeare. In both these types of intertextuality, the intertext serves as a referential mark. But the treatment of the *fabula* and the message put forth are distinct.

These two types of intertextuality are not the only ones, however; they are only the generic types. We may also encounter fragmentary intertextuality, that is, not a precise historical event which is fictionalized, but perhaps the event itself without the facts, as in for example *Die heilige Johanna der Schlachthöfe* by Brecht or *Purgatoire Ingolstadt* by Marieluise Fleisser (Théâtre de la Commune, Paris, 1982).

The adaption of a novel is also in the area of literary intertextuality, and the novel usually only plays the role of providing a name and the fabula, as in the case of the play based on the Mario Benedetti novel, *Primavera con una esquina rota* (Teatro ICTUS, Santiago de Chile, 1984). Or the intertext might consist of fictive fragments from other texts. Finally, I should add that every dramatic (or performance) text presents every kind of intertextuality from the social and cultural sector: news, television, newspapers, etc.

Within these two generic intertextualities exist the general, limited, external and internal forms of intertextuality, as well as autotextuality. In my opinion, external intertextuality is redundant and tautological, for general and limited intertextuality are necessarily external. The following is a possible outline of intertextuality:

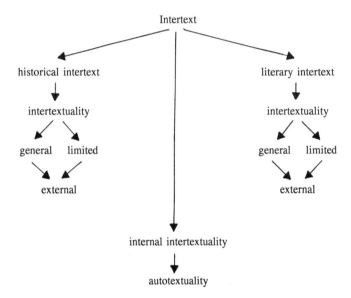

B) *The Classical View*

When confronted with the question, 'what is a text?', Roland Barthes answers from a classical perspective (and then semiological):

> It is the phenomenal surface of the literary work; it is the texture/fabric of words engaged in the work and arranged in such a way as to impose a stable and as much as possible unique meaning. ... it is, in the work, that which elicits the guarantee of the written thing, by which it draws together the functions of safeguard: on the one hand, the stability, the permanence of the inscription, destined/intended to correct the fragility and imprecision of memory; and on the other, the legality/law of the lettre, unimpeachable/unchallengeable, indelible, one thinks, in the sense that the author of the work has intentionally deposited it there.[11]

In his perspective, the text is conceived simply as discourse rendered permanent through writing, without having the characteristic of *productivity* that is part of the semiological perspective. The text, however, is both permanence and productivity: it is because of this very permanence, or if one prefers, the *writing deposited in significance,* that productivity can exist, for productivity is nothing more than the effects of language plus the space where the producer and consumer of the text meet. This is why, in my opinion, the text is the productive phenomenal surface; that is, it is the inscription of discourse in writing.

What I am doing here, in fact, is making a clear and obvious distinction between *text* and *discourse*: on the one hand, the text is the *noema* or the inscribed part of the discourse; on the other hand, the inscribed part is not the actual act or occurrence of language but rather the *meaning* of the act of language. While discourse has an enunciative apparatus (the enunciative situation, the enunciative context, the intention or perlocutive act, etc.) that refers to this situation and *anchors* meaning, the text has no enunciative situation. That is, the authorial intention, text meaning, context, etc., do not coincide; rather, there is a division or separation between the producer of this discourse and the product as it relates to the receiver. In oral discourse, however, what is intended and what is signified coincide; the signifier and the signified of the speaker and discourse are one, as they relate to the listener. In this way, the text *liberates* meaning from the bondage of the emitter or scriptor. Thus, once again, there is productivity of the text, for this liberation or textual opening productively involves the receiver/producer who re-works the language of the text. The absence of referential ostentation in the text creates a fundamental difference; this is not *in* the text but is created in the reading.

According to Paul Ricoeur, the referential aspect plays an important and fundamental role with respect to the text: "For me, this is the referent of all literature; no longer the *Umwelt* of the ostensive references of dialogue, but the *Welt* projected by the nonostensive references of every text that we have read, understood, and loved".[12] Following Ricoeur's example, one may establish the following distinctions between discourse and text:

	Discourse		*Text*
1)	always occurs temporarily and in the present: instance of the discourse;	1)	inscribes meaning: outside all temporality;
2)	instance of autoreferential discourse: presence of an enunciating subject;	2)	concealment and distance with respect to the subject (author) and his/her communicative intentions;
3)	the discourse always refers to something real or fictive (describes, expresses or represents a world);	3)	lacks ostentative references;

4) presence of an emitter/receiver (exchange of messages), speakers;	4) directed to a universal public; absence of speakers;
5) emphasis on perlocutory acts.	5) absence of perlocutory acts.[13]

With respect to the *producer-receiver* relationship in discourse and in the text, the following homology can be established: the reader replaces the addressee, the writing replaces the speaking, and the text replaces discourse since it registers it; that is, "what comes to writing is the discourse in so far as intention ... that liberation of writing which puts it in the place of speech is the birth of the text".[14] At the same time, a productive process occurs in the receiver or reader of a text as he/she imposes an interpretation terminating the reading process.[15] What is important is the reading *process* which is affected first of all by the actual text and secondly by tradition (this being understood as the accumulation of previous readings and interpretations of this text). In this way, the textual task of the reader, the way he/she appropriates meaning, is very different from the discursive task of the listener: they are two different ways of acquiring meaning.[16]

As a conclusion to these comments, I would like to introduce a concept that will certainly be useful when considering dramatic text and performance text: the notion of *pre-text*. This notion was first used by Jean Bellemin-Noël, who defines it as "the ensemble constituted by the drafts, the manuscripts, the proofs, the 'variants', seen from the angle of *that which materially precedes* a work when it is treated as a *text* and *with which it may constitute a system*".[17] There are two important things to point out here: first, the pre-text constitutes the text previous to the text, (the terminated phenomenal of the pre-text); second, the pre-text is *in* the text and is a fundamental part of the text.

At this point, I feel it important to broaden this notion by assigning other functions to it. With respect to theatre, or any other type of textual or artistic practice, a pre-text precedes the productive act and provides the creative codes particular to a given practice. From the moment a writer begins the process of creating a work of theatre, he/she has to submit to a certain number of operations that are proper to the discourse being initiated; whether these are called operations, rules, conventions, or codes of different *genres* does not really matter. The important fact is that the pre-text exists as an operative mark and as a resource for a given system. If one considers theatre, one will observe that the pre-text imposes a certain practice which must include certain fundamental characteristics if it is to be dramatic: characters, dialogue, enunciative situation, some form of internal and external division, a certain use of the language, etc. These components, in fact, are found in the pre-text. If one were to compare an ancient text with a modern one, one would see that the difference is very small in terms of the main components that exist in both of them. This is because the basic theatre code has not changed; what has changed is the internal articulation of language, the use of language, or the represented world. Briefly, while the way of representing the world has changed, the basic components are the same.

No doubt, there is a dialectic between the pre-text and the text, in that the text incorporates new elements in the pre-text, without necessarily canceling them. In some eras or types of dramatic text certain components of the pre-text are favoured, whereas in others they are not used or have a secondary role. One could argue that the pre-text, as I have said, is the *theatre code*, but I believe that it *includes* the theatre code, or rather, theatre codes. In this case, code has a more restricted meaning than pre-text. While the pre-text is a sort of *reservoir*, a code is precise and takes elements from the pre-text.

This notion may be useful as defined here, especially when considering the historiographic work in theatre. No doubt, we have moved a considerable distance from the notion as defined by Bellemin-Noël, but its signifier is always useful when we use or incorporate the signified, as I have done, within a new field of analysis.

This discussion of text would not be complete without the notion of *places of indetermination* (*Unbestimmtheitsstellen*) coined by Roman Ingarden with respect to literary work.[18] In every text, and especially in the literary (and dramatic) text, there exist places of indetermination which are a sort of informational vacuum. That is, the presented objects are not determined by the text. In part this is due to the fact that the literary work, like all artistic work, is a *schematic structure*, and its schematic nature only allows for a limited number of descriptions, leaving quite a lot undetermined. This is precisely the function of what Ingarden called *concretization*, that is, the process of making up for or complementing the determination of the objects in the text. The *concretization*, as with *objectivization* and *actualization*, complements the text; at the same time, in the text-reader-spectator dialectic, the text is created in this triple process of objectivization/concretization/actualization.[19] The point here is simply to remark that the places of indetermination *are part* of the text. I shall return to this point later.[20]

Discussing the notion of text and the notions that go along with it (intertext, ideologeme, pre-text) was an attempt at elaborating the notion of dramatic text. I believe that much of what has been said in the previous pages will be seen to be part of the dramatic text. Thus, I can now begin to develop new perspectives with the basic notions I have just established.

II. THE DRAMATIC TEXT

A) *Textual Function*

One of the most shared and well known ideas on the dramatic text is that of Roman Ingarden, who claims that this text is composed of a) a main text made up of the dialogue and the characters and b) a secondary text - the didascalia and the stage directions.[21] This view is also shared by Anne Ubersfeld, although she also adds a series of other points to the discussion on dramatic text. Although this understanding of dramatic text is insufficient, it does provide a valid and necessary point: it is a dual or bifaceted text. First, this text is characterized by and structured according to the dialogue of the characters, but this dialogue is destined to be heard more than read; second, this text is full of stage directions that I shall call didascalia. The didascalia are more than simply stage directions, for there are texts that do not even have these. The didascalia include every element of information that has to do with the *theatricality* of the text[22] and can proceed either from the actual stage directions or from the dialogue of the characters.[23] This dual nature of the dramatic text - as written text and as text to be performed - is at the basis of the information provided by Ingarden and Ubersfeld.

The first thing that should be clarified is that we began with the idea of the dramatic text itself as an object of study, which need not be compared to the performance text, which constitutes *another* object of study. Instead of comparing one text to another, I believe it would be more useful to link these two realities together.[24] With this in mind, I shall now outline, on the theoretical level, the forms of organization of the dramatic text as proposed by Steen Jansen: a) the theoretical form of the *dramatic text* and b) the theoretical form of the *dramatic work*. Jansen defines the first form as "the structured whole comprising the elements which the dramatic author arranges and must use and from among which the reader recognizes this or that text as a dramatic text". He defines the second as "the structured ensemble of means which serve to unify the elements of the theoretical form of the dramatic *text* in such a way as to form a coherent whole".[25]

Theoretically, the dramatic text can be viewed on two levels: a) the textual level, which includes successive units of cues and didascalia, and b) the stage level, which includes the non-successive units such as the characters, the set, etc. Both levels form a whole in which the cue is controlled by a character and, thus, there is a relationship of selection between characters and cues. In the first case, there is a presence-permanence situated in both the dramatic text and the performance text in that both share the same cues and characters. In the second case, the way the set is done by the stage management (*la régie*) is selective because the decor can be done in different ways in different stage productions. In this way, the didascalia become a virtual element because of the way they develop in the performance text. These four categories are definitive for all dramatic texts; that is, their presence is obligatory if a text is to be called a dramatic text. The above can be systematized in the following diagram:

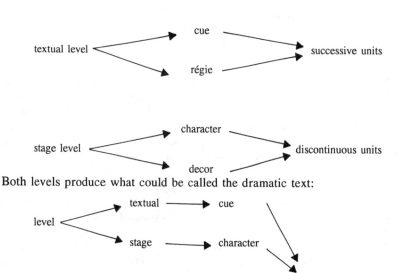

Both levels produce what could be called the dramatic text:

These four categories of the dramatic text are organized into *situations*, with situation being understood as "the result of a division of the textual plane into parts which correspond to completed groups of the stage plane".[26] According to Jansen, the concept of situation is fundamental, for it organizes the elements of the text and also determines the form of the *dramatic work*.[27] The situation is the minimal unit of the dramatic work providing coherence to the textual elements. It is also the smallest part of a text capable of becoming a work.[28] Each work is composed of one or more situations. What is key here is the theoretical form of the dramatic work establishing a model of the relationships between situations. In my view, a description of the situations can occur on two levels: on the paradigmatic level, that is, in the analysis of components that integrate each particular situation; and on the syntagmatic level, that is, in the relationship between one situation and another. The second level is of particular importance, for the *mode* of relating can result in two distinct types of dramatic form: a structuration with scenes (for example, the epic theatre) and another with acts (*Aristotelian* theatre).[29] The first case presents a relationship of selection and the second, of combination (if these are to be understood as dependence/interdependence). One may also say here that these relationships occur either in succession or in a group. A succession is to be understood as a *chain* of situations that are structurally linked, but whose structure does not work according to any logical/causal process. By group I mean a *system* whose structure is logical/causal.

The *dramatic form* can be represented in the following way:

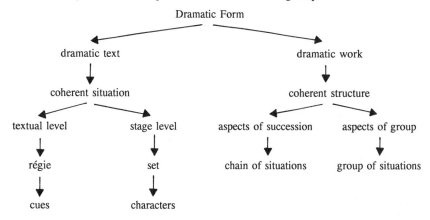

Jansen's model requires some clarification, for the distinction between text and dramatic work is not clear. The *dramatic form* is proposed as an abstraction whose objective it is to include the fundamental traits of every drama capable of being articulated in a dramatic text/work. The *dramatic text* is proposed as an incomplete or fragmentary part of the *dramatic form*, and the *dramatic work* as a complete component. The work is found *in* the dramatic text that constitutes the whole. This distinction is not of much use, however, since the dramatic text can in fact be present in its complete form, if one reformulates the model as follows:

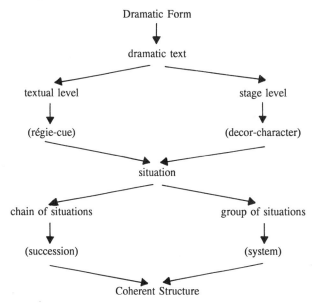

The dramatic text is comprised of a textual level and a stage level (with its respective elements) which are organized into situations that can be articulated differently (as a chain/as a group), forming a coherent structure.

B) *Stage Function*

In the preceding section, I established the organization and function of the text in its textual aspect without considering the performative and stage aspects. In this section, I shall consider the text as a *stage practice*; that is, I shall consider the potential the text has of being produced. Whereas, in the preceding section, I observed one type of organization, in this section, I will observe another one, which is more specific to the dramatic text. In doing so, I shall refer to the concept of linguistic sign as proposed by Hjemslev in order to avoid the traditional polarization between the dramatic ('literary') text and the performance text.

Every dramatic text presupposes some form of completion since every playwright works from a pre-text imposed on him/her by theatre tradition and by newer theatre practices. One should begin, then, with the presupposition that, in the dramatic text, there exist matrices of representativity or theatricality which make the staging possible - that is, the idea that there exists no dichotomy between text, dramatic text and its stage production, and that the text, in one way or another, is present in the performance, especially in the cues and characters within a coherent structure of primarily verbal theatrical elements (scenography, gestes, set, etc.). The dramatic text-performance relationship can be formalized in the following manner:

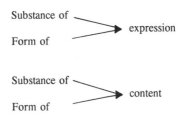

For example, the substance of expression of a given text consists of the various concrete performances of the text - not only those done on the stage, but also the radiophonic, cinematographic performances, etc. The form of expression consists of the elements and structure of the text and they are shared by the various concrete presentations. The substance of content consists of the various interpretations that have been done over time. Finally, the form of content refers to the fact that in the end a given text has one content, that is, a coherence that will not allow the text to be altered. Two points are of importance here: the form of expression and the form of content. These two components are present in the stage production and remain the same, independent of the various productions and concretizations the text might undergo. In no way whatsoever do they alter the levels of form of expression and of content. In fact, if this does happen, then another text or an adaption has been created. For example, *Lear* by Edward Bond is not the Shakespeare text, although they contain common elements. Bond's *Lear* is a new form of expression and content.

The relationship, then, between, dramatic text and performance text resides in the fact that both share the same form of expression and form of content. There is a transcodification from the dramatic text to the performance text. What happens is that the performance text *adds* to, or rather, actualizes and concretizes the places of indetermination in the dramatic text - these places that are *in* the dramatic text. The task of the director resides precisely in the process of *filling in* these places and in making them appear in the stage production. For example Vitez's production of *Hamlet* (Chaillot, Paris, 1983)[30] is done in a large, empty space and only the voices and bodies of the characters fill and modify this space. At times, for example, in the scene where Hamlet kills Duncan, a curtain crosses the stage from one end to the other, isolating the 'living' space. The spatial and temporal systematization is done in the manner just described, and at no time are realist components used. The same can be said for the productions of Shakespeare's *Richard the Second* or *The Twelfth Night* done by Ariane Mnouchkine (Théâtre du Soleil, Cartoucherie de Vincennes, 1982-1983) or the stage production *La terrible mais inachevée histoire de Norodom Sihanouk, roi de Cambodge* (Théâtre du Soleil, Cartoucherie de Vincennes, 1985-1986),[31] in which an empty space is also used and all acting occurs through the character's *gestures* or, in some cases, backdrops to express time, feelings, etc. There are no stage directions concerning the movement and enunciative positions of the characters. All of this is the director's job and she often depends on didascalia from the actual dialogue of the characters, or on precedents set from previous productions. What constitutes a stage production, then, is the material presentation of what was previously in the written form and hence the costumes, set, etc. are integrated into the performance text (they are presupposed or implied in the dramatic text). The dramatic text is 'full of holes' (*troué*) according to Ubersfeld, and this is what gives it its duality.[32]

The dramatic text provides the verbal component and the performance potential (virtuality) for the performance text which contextualizes language by removing the ambiguity of the semantic component.[33] In this way, what we call the performance text is the sum of all the components of the dramatic text: word/story and performative virtuality. The discourse in the text is the transformation of both text into staging (social and discursive) and staging into text.[34] This does not mean that there is an exact coincidence between dramatic text and performance text, but rather a relationship of necessary reciprocity. What changes in going from one text to the other is the substance of the expression.[35] This duality of the dramatic text, as I have already indicated, is due to the dual articulation of language, or to be more precise, the contextualization of speech acts. The dramatic text is inscribed on the stage as performance text, or in other words, the stage is textualized. The literary code/stage code process of transcodification may be systematized in the following model proposed by Alessandro Serpieri and based on Hjelmslev's connotative semiotic model.[36]

Stage potential of the text
Performative inscription given by the author

Metalanguage of realization
Performative transcodification inscription

The first system, ERC (expression/relation/content), proposes an expression, E, which is potentially inscribed in the text by the author before any performance. At the same time, the director transcodifies this expression into a second system, ERC, thus proposing a concrete production, C. The transcodification process (staging of the linguistic component) is then projected in relation to the system which is at its base. That is to say, language is translated into a poetic code (theatre language) that is a rhetorical translation (rhetorical code) of a cultural system. In conclusion, theatre language proceeds from a socio-cultural code, and this is why I speak of translation and not of transcodification. This only happens in the transition from dramatic texts (a mono-code) to the stage space where other codes exist (costumes, the set, lighting, etc.).

III. PERFORMANCE TEXT

The intention here is not to do a detailed study of the notion of performance text. This has already been done in a magnificent study by Marco De Marinis.[37] My objective here is to consider what constitutes the performance text as it relates to the dramatic text. It is important to consider the elements that link the dramatic text and the performance text. At this stage, all one may say is that the performance text is a performance, a stage production in the complete sense.

A) *Production Text*

Anne Ubersfeld points out that the mediating factor between the dramatic text (DT) and the performance text (PT) is the production text (PRT).[38] This production text functions in a dual manner: on the one hand, it works in relation to the dramatic text, a relationship which may be represented in the following manner:

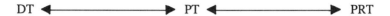

The relationship is one of reciprocity: the PT is simply the contextualization of all the enunciative situations, the concretization of space, time, rhythm, movement, the text's ideology, proxemics, kinesics, contextualization of the utterance/enunciation situations. One might say that the PT is the process of *inscription* of the dramatic text's potential. This is not a process of *transcription*, but rather, *inscription*, for the DT and the PT do not coincide. On the one hand, the places of indetermination are being filled, and on the other, the staging potential is being inscribed.

1) Places of Indetermination

The PT is the text that *concretizes* and *actualizes* the enunciative situation and the utterances of the DT. It makes this situation unique; for example, it determines how this or that sentence is said, with what tone, rhythm, the meaning of a given situation, what feelings are involved in this or that situation or utterance. In fact, this is true dramaturgical work, for the way that things are *said and done* requires an understanding of the feelings and ideological position of the characters who speak *from concrete discursive positions*. In other words, the PT has to render these positions explicit if the meaning is to emerge in the clearest possible way. The places of indetermination unfold mainly in conjunction with discourse; this implies effort with/from the actor who is the superficial manifestation of the DT's potential discourse. It is the actor who actualizes and achieves discourse, based on the concretization worked out between him/her and the director. The following model summarizes these practices:

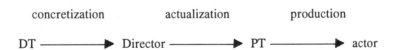

The evolution of this process results in the modulation of the word (rhythm, tone, timbre) in the PT. This discursive process implies *construction* of fabula and fiction with its referents, for discourse is referential. That is, the PT has as first referent the DT, but it also has a historical referent (fictive/real) and a concrete referent on the actual stage. Discourse also involves temporalization and spatialization and thus, the incorporation of the theatre object that functions on-stage as a multi-levelled referent.[39] One point must be emphasized: the PT eliminates a considerable part of the schematicism (and the places of indetermination) of the DT. This is its fundamental role - to make the potential of the DT obvious in a concrete way. Whereas the role of the DT is one of *writing* from precise theatre codes, the role of the PT is dual: on the one hand, there is a process of writing, or perhaps re-writing, of the DT for the PT. That is, the text as sign is staged. On the other hand, and as a consequence of the above, there is a concrete process of staging discourse or staging language, the physical manifestation of the DT *transformed* into PT.

2) **Performance Potential**

This physical manifestation is also present in the performance - in the scenographic potential (stage and space) that includes the theatre object (the set), the actor's movement, and gestures (choreography, proxemics, kinesics).[40] The precise role of the PT is to create a *virtual performance text* (VPT). A fundamental difference between the role of the VPT and the DT is that the director and actor work with something given by the DT: the dialogue and didascalia that may refer to the production of the enunciative situation. For example, didascalia might say *Gets up abruptly and says to x...*. In this case the director has to create, invent a space, even when the didascalia are explicit and abundant (as in naturalist theatre); he/she has to find diverse elements for the temporalization and support them with a set and then situate the producers of the stage discourse - the actors. Not only does the director have to indicate where the actors should be, their various movements within the stage, the entries and exits, etc., but he or she also has to create a gesturality contiguous with the discourse as well as precise kinesics and proxemics during the characters' dialogue. For example, when Tartuffe confronts the accusations of Elmira in the presence of Orgon, one asks: 'What is Tartuffe like? Is he near or far from Orgon? What are his gestes like? His physical demeanor? How far away are Elmire and Orgon?' All these questions are part of the process of the VPT as it relates to the potential of the DT. Thus, the VPT inscribes what is *absent* (only potential) from the DT. The convergence of potential performance elements with the places of indetermination produces this virtual performance text, virtual in that it is almost a performance. The performance text, then, would be the product of the previous interaction between the DT and the PT, or rather, the VPT. Also, in theatre where there is no previous text (experimental groups, collective creations, happenings, etc.), there does exist some form of stage textualization or VPT that may, although only as a rough sketch, provide a possible attempt at a PT. If this does not exist, then we are dealing with a type of theatre that leaves no traces, since it is created and consumed in the very moment of production of the performance. Obviously, this is an extreme case, for, generally speaking, most do theatre work with some form of a VPT. Thus, the VPT is the inscription (translation and transcodification) of the DT as a stage *material, concrete* entity by means of the aforementioned process. The following diagram provides a model of this process:

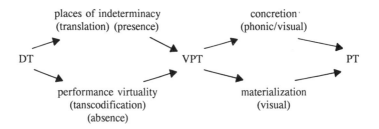

Before I speak of the performance text, however, the theatre *record* (log) needs to be discussed. The purpose here is not to propose a new way of doing this, simply because this falls outside my area of competence and also because it is very difficult to propose a universal type of note-taking.[41] Indeed, the actual VPT process consists of a form of note-taking in such a way as to decide on the linguistic dimension (in all its dimensions, rhythm timbre, modulation, etc.) as well as the way the performance's stage potential is to materialize (movement, set, scenography, etc.). A problem that cannot be ignored since it also concerns the PT is the following: because *this* text *is* performative (it is a performance) and thus instantaneous, its traces are sometimes difficult to reconstruct.

The note-taking of the DT is the job of the director, whereas the note-taking of the PT is the job of the theatre semiotician. In the first instance, the director's work done on the DT results in the production of the VPT that for the director *is the production* of a PT; in the second case, this PT produced by the director has to be recorded. These are, therefore, two different modes of *note-taking*, each one with its own specific object of *reconstruction*. How the recording is done in the first case varies and in the majority of cases is very individual.[42] Despite this diversity, however, the fact is that at least some form of note-taking is inevitable, for it is the director's and stage manager's guide. It is well known that Brecht, for example, worked with hundreds of photographs to create or choose the appropriate *Gestus* for a situation or the entire work. Nowadays, the VPT is often videotaped to correct it or make it more elaborate; others simply put notes on the script in the clearest way for themselves. In some cases, each actor receives his or her part with the director's comments already on them and the actor can add further notes to these.

The task of the theatre semiotician is to record/describe the theatre performance. This is difficult to do for the performance can last for hours and is repeated for days and weeks and thus the same production can vary greatly. But to describe properly the performance text, it is important to define precisely what I mean by PT and the elements that make it up.

B) *Performance Text*

A discussion of the VPT has shown us how the PT is a unique product: it is the *performance* of the DT without the mediation of the VPT. This is a paradox since the PT is the product of the VPT, but the VPT is found *in situ* in the PT and it then disappears without leaving any obvious trace in the performance; that is, in the stage production, we see only the PT. Following Marco De Marinis' definition, the performance texts are those "units of theatrical manifestation which are the performances, taken in their aspect of complex signifying 'processes', both verbal and non-verbal".[43] If it is the case that the DT is staged, then it also true that the stage is textualized. The theatre performance is textualized in that a series of common codes function on-stage and thus are disseminated in various *performances as texts*. The particular nature of the PT resides in the fact that, when compared to other dimensions of theatre, there is a heterogeneity of codes, a complexity over and above the dual absence of the performance object: "a first time as 'scientific' object ... and a second time as material, 'pre-scientific' object".[44]

The heterogeneity of codes does not simply mean a plurality of codes or the simultaneous presence of diverse codes or sub-codes. A clarification is needed here on what is meant by code, for there are various ways of defining the term code - at least five, according to Eliseo Veron: a) code as synonym of *la langue*, that is, as an ensemble of rules necessary for producing the message or speech (generally, the following equivalences are made: code-*la langue*, message-speech, at least from a linguistic perspective); b) in the area of theory of information, code designates the ensemble of transformations that make it possible to pass from one system of signs (for example, morse) to another (*la langue*); c) as a synonym of 'ensemble of *contraintes*' that defines the nature of the signifier of a given system; d) in the area of semiotics, it is a repertoire of units (signs) common to the users and that is used for communication; e) finally, code can refer to a social practice, that is, the ensemble of institutional norms that make up the way social systems function.[45] Code as used here has three meanings: it is a social code, the ensemble of rules or the repertoire of signs. At the basis of these different ideas, however, there is a common fundamental element: a code is invariably a group of rules that regulate a message, whether this be linguistic or of some other nature (gesticular, musical, etc.). Whereas verbal text is monocoded, the performance text is pluricoded, not only because it includes various types of codes, but also because it has distinct substances of expression (visual, gesticular, auditive). The theatre performance text, however, is characterized as being pluricoded.

Codes function in the theatre performance in two ways: simultaneously (paradigmatically) or linearly (syntagmatically) and both produce theatre signification. The signs that the spectator receives from the various codes on the stage are received in a simultaneous manner, yet they proceed syntagmatically to form signification. If, like De Marinis, I consider the PT as a *macrotext* (or a *text of a text*), then this text would be made up of a series of partial performance texts (PPT) that would constitute unique expressive material (music, costumes, gestes, dance, etc.). At the same time, these texts from the PT appear in contexts - at least two, according to De Marinis: a) the special or *performance context* that consists of the *conditions* of production and reception of the PT (this is the concrete performance practice, which, as we will see further on, has its own rules and ways of proceeding); b) the general or *cultural context* that is made up of the ensemble of cultural texts, whether they be from the theatre (mime, scenographical, dramaturgical, etc.), or from outside theatre (from literature, pictographic, rhetorical, philosophical, etc.) and these belong to the synchrony of the PT. That is, they are the socio-cultural surroundings of the PT. In fact, these texts are *intertexts*. Also, both the theatre texts and extra-theatre texts form the *general cultural text* (GCT). The articulation of these two contexts is fundamental in understanding every PT, for in the first case (*performance context*), the elements for understanding the PT are provided *in situ*, and in the second case (*cultural context*), the referents of this text are inserted into the GCT. Any analysis of performance should necessarily consider both contexts if it is to be competent.[46] It is only in the PT that both contexts are found, for in the DT the performance context is absent as performance, as enunciative situation and as production of this situation. That is, in terms of the stage, they are not present.

1) Performance Codes

Formulating these two codes brings us to the distinction of different processes involved in performance codes and theatre conventions. I shall begin with the performance codes (PC).

What is a performance code? According to De Marinis, a performance code "*is that convention which*, in the performance, *makes it possible to link determined contents to determined elements of one or more expressive systems*".[47] For example, the gesticular code is the convention by which gestes in a performance come to signify something. At the same time, a performance code is not specific to the theatre performance, since we also find it in other artistic practices and in everyday life. What makes the theatre performance different is the use of these performance codes (that are also components of the GCT) in a special and specific manner; that is, there is an adoption-adaption of codes such as linguistic, proxemic, etc., that are actually cultural codes because they belong to a given culture. De Marinis establishes the following relationship between performance and cultural codes:

> *the performance codes are the result of the usage, more or less particular and specific, in the performance, of non-specific cultural codes....* The distance between an *extra-performance code* (as we will call the cultural code *before* its use in the performance - for example a code of an everyday gesture) and the *performance code* (the gestures of the actor in a performance) varies notably according to performances, 'genres', authors, periods, etc.[48]

Thus, we have the following situation: when they are used in a performance, the cultural or extra-performance codes (that are part of the GCT) become performance codes. They will differentiate according to the type of performance, era, culture, etc. The difference between one or the other of these types of code is the following: an extra-performance or cultural code is a 'natural' code, in that individuals and groups learn them as they would their own language and this code is part of their GCT. When the PT absorbs one of these codes, however, it is transformed into a performance code in two ways: either by means of a super-codification which indicates the code is artificial and has to be learned, or simply by means of the fact that it is there on the stage with its artistic/aesthetic or purely pragmatic function.[49] For example, the linguistic and gesticular codes may be super-codified as in such theatre forms as Nô or Kabuki or Katakali in which the fabula is propelled by the geste. But this also happens in the productions of Mnouchkine and Kantor.[50] The language of certain contemporary playwrights - for example, Edward Bond in *Save* - is the result of extreme codification of a linguistic code. In fact, the PT *makes reference* to this code, or rather, as *referential illusion*, it *mimes* the code. This is exactly where naturalist and realist theatre placed emphasis, trying in this way to *reproduce* perfectly so there would be no distinction between the performed codes and the spectators' code. The following diagram illustrates this relationship:

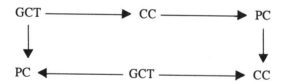

The GCT determines the cultural codes (CC) and these are integrated into the performance as performance codes (PC). But at the same time, the PC are part of the CC determined by the GCT that motivates the productions of the PC.

This model helps us to see the relationship between the CC and PC, but it is still unclear as to how these codes are transformed, or what process of transformation occurs in going from a CC or extra-performance code to a PC. *Theatre conventions*, the second category of codes, might help in this area.

2) Theatre Conventions

What are theatre conventions? According to Marco De Marinis, "it is a question of 'technical' codes which, unlike 'naturalized' cultural codes, require a particular apprenticeship and conscious decoding".[51] Three points about this definition are important. The *technical* aspect of theatre codes depends on a variety of factors: in other words, the type of theatre that is being considered implies that codes are being used differently. For example, the codes used in epic theatre are not the same as those in the theatre of the absurd or the theatre of cruelty. At the same time, each form of theatre produces its own code, and thus the naturalist-realist theatre of the nineteenth century has codes that are different from those of contemporary theatre. The way a play is performed, the way actors act, *the type of stage production* - in a word, the construction of the PT - varies from one era to another and also within the same era. This means that the codification the director and actors choose has to be well learned by the spectators doing the de-codification. These last two points are important. For example, a Western spectator unfamiliar with the codes of Japanese Nô or Kabuki theatre will not be able to de-codify the staged code. Ariane Mnouchkine's Théâtre du Soleil uses Kabuki and Nô codes, among others, in their productions of *The Twelfth Night* and *Richard the Second* by Shakespeare (Théâtre Du Soleil, Cartoucherie de Vincennes, 1982-83). These codes are not known by all of the spectators. However, because the highly codified gestes are accompanied by Shakespearean discourse the codes are partially, though not fully, understandable. That is, they are not received as they would be by a spectator with experience of these codes, costumes, make-up, and gestes. These three theatre components - the theatre code, the learning process/codification and knowledge/decodification - are the components that define theatre conventions.

There are, however, three kinds of theatre conventions: the general, the particular and the unique. This categorization of conventions that De Marinis has proposed is extremely useful, not only because it accounts for the mode of existence of these conventions, but also because they may be useful in the area of theatre history, as we shall see when I refer to the relationship between these three types of conventions.[52]

a) General Conventions

General conventions have to do with the *rules* of theatre production in the achievement of fiction. From the moment the spectator enters into the theatre, he/she knows that a series of conventions distinct from social conventions must be accepted, for a stage production does not provide an exact replica of exterior reality and is not the world exactly as the spectator knows it. The spectator knows that the human being on the stage is not Hamlet or Segismundo, but rather an actor whose name is known from the program or from previous productions; the spectator knows the time and space of the utterance (of the DT) is not the same as that of the enunciation (of the PT) and that the objects on the stage are simply a referential illusion (the furniture in a play by Lope de Vega is not really from the seventeenth century, or the set in Vitez's *Hamlet* (Chaillot, Paris, 1983) is not really a palace with an interior, exterior, etc.).

The general nature of these conventions does not mean that they cannot also be specific. That is, they are not confined to some technical definition. They are general in that there are no unique forms for each theatre production. Each production, depending on the era, type of theatre, etc., will use different conventions to create *theatricality, to become fiction*. In this way, one may say that there are as many conventions as there are productions. But they are specific to theatre (and thus, technical) because they are more specific than other performance codes and because they belong exclusively to the performance arts and to stage production. As soon as the spectator enters the theatre, the specificity of the general conventions starts to function, in the sense that the production makes use of a fairly restricted variety of forms of representation - to suggest rain, noise, an outstretched hand, an umbrella, or something else. Naturally, when I speak of general conventions, I am speaking only of Western ones, for as soon as we go to another continent, to the Middle or Far East, for example, these conventions change. Grotowski was someone who pushed theatre to its limits, as far as general conventions were concerned, and therefore his theatre ceased being theatre and became a something between a *happening* and a real event.[53]

b) Particular Conventions

Whereas general conventions are common to *all* the performance and production arts (cinema, television, painting, mime), particular conventions are specific to theatre in that they are technical codes of a precise theatre practice (absurdist, expressionist, etc.) or of a given author (Brecht, Pinter, Beckett) or genre (*Commedia dell'Arte*, comedy, tragi-comedy, satire)[54] or era or even region (for example, *teatro rioplatense*). In this case, these codes are hyper- or hypo-codified. The difference between these conventions and general conventions is not so much at the qualitative level as at the quantitative level, for these conventions have to do with an even smaller number of PT. At the same time, they are fairly rigid conventions, for example, those from *Commedia dell'Arte*, Japanese Nô, Brecht's distancing effect (*Verfremdungseffekt*), the *Happening*, etc. Both general and particular conventions are 's-codes', technical code-systems that are external and exist previous to the PT that presents them.

c) Unique Conventions

Unique conventions, on the other hand, are those that emerge from a given performance, that are present *ex novo*, and that can only be understood through that particular message and performance context. They can often be confusing and ambiguous due to their novelty and originality. This is one of the effects of the constitution or reestablishment of a new code. On this point, De Marinis states that "respect for the conventions of the first and second types generally leads to a *standardization* of the performance, the 'singular' conventions augment the *aesthetic originality* and *ambiguity*, this being understood as a deviation from the norms external to and pre-existing the performance".[55] This is a *performance ideolect.*[56]

The unique conventions may also become particular conventions: in fact, all particular conventions (and general conventions) were unique conventions at the time of their introduction. One only has to think of the case of Brecht, Beckett, etc.

There is another important difference characterizing the general, particular and unique conventions: the first two undergo a code alteration or transformation so as to produce general and particular performance codes from non-theatre situations from cultural codes, whereas unique conventions function, as De Marinis has pointed out, as *an institution of codes* which, through their *ex novo* nature, create unique codes.

In conclusion, I would like to explain the relationship that exists between the General Cultural Text (GCT), the theatre conventions (TCon) and the performance codes (PC). The following model proposed by De Marinis will clarify this relationship.[57]

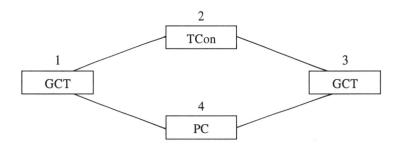

1) The PC of the PT result from the transformation brought about by the effect of TCon on the extra-performance cultural codes and thus the PC are determined by the TCon;
2) The extra-textual cultural codes exist before the PT and the PT's conventions and thus they have a determining/motivating function on the TCon, in that they are part of the GCT1;
3) In this way, the extra-textual cultural codes function as determinants/motivators and determinees/motivees;
4) The PT, as we saw in 1) are the codes of the transformed GCT by the TCon, and also have an effect on the GCT - that is, on other texts that make up the GCT, altering or influencing other artistic practices.

As a conclusion to these remarks on the PT, I should say that the dramatic text is only one component of the level of expression of the PT and not *the* level of expression as argued by Alessandro Serpieri. This is because it provides only one structure and this is in the dialogue form; the rest is the job of the PT. Therefore, the transcodification of the PT occurs from the DT and from the GCT. In fact, Serpieri recognizes this fact but still prefers the dramatic text. Nevertheless, this text is part of the GCT, its codes are in a latent state and only the PT brings them to the level of manifestation.[58]

In order to account for the extra-textual elements or cultural codes, Serpieri establishes a connotative scale in four phases:[59]

4	SIGNIFIER		SIGNIFIED
3	signifier	signified	
2	se	so	
1	se | so		

The first level (1) constitutes what I call GCT, the second what Serpieri calls *poetic code*, which in fact refers to a mix of PC and TCon (generals, particulars and singulars); the third level is the DT determined by the poetic code (antitext), and the last level is the staging or PT or "*texto escénico*" according to Serpieri. Nevertheless, I believe that De Marinis' theoretic proposition is without a doubt the most comprehensive and the best account of the problematic of DT/PT.

The PT, which is the specifically *theatrical* manifestation of the DT, implies *ipso facto* the problem of the production of meaning or semiosis, that is, how the stage is semiotized, and what mechanisms are valid for this process.

ENDNOTES
CHAPTER II

1. "Dramatic Text as a Component of Theatre", in *Semiotics of Art. Prague School Contributions*, edited by Ladislav Matejka and Erwin R. Titunik (Cambridge, Mass. and London, England: The MIT Press, 1976), p. 95.

2. We will see in more detail the notion of *performance text* in the next few pages; for now, let us say that the *performance text* is the convergence and materialization of cultural codes transformed into performance codes, and then in the case of theatre, transformed into theatre codes or conventions.

3. For more on the notion of the *performance text*, see below the section on "The performance text", and as well, Marco De Marinis, "Le spectacle comme texte", in *Sémiologie et théâtre* (Lyon: Université de Lyon II, CERTEC, 1980), pp. 195-258 and *Semiotica del teatro* (Milano: Studi Bompiani, 1982).

4. Oswald Ducrot and Tzvetan Todorov, *Dictionnaire encyclopédique des sciences du langage* (Paris: Editions du Seuil, 1972), p. 443 (our translation). On productivity and text, Kristeva says the following: "we define the text as a *trans-linguistic* apparatus which redistributes the order of language by bringing into relation a communicative speech aimed at direct information with different types of previous or synchronic utterances. The text is thus a *productivity*, which means: 1. its relation to the language in which it is situated is redistributive (destructive-constructive), consequently it is accessible across logical and mathematical categories rather than purely linguistic categories, 2. it is a permutation of texts, an inter-textuality: in the space of one text several utterances taken from other texts cross and are neutralized". "Problèmes de la structuration du texte", in *Théorie d'ensemble* (Paris: Editions du Seuil, 1968), p. 299 (our translation).

5. See Roland Barthes, "Texte (Théorie du)", in *Encyclopedia Universalis*, vol. 15 (Paris: Encyclopedia Universalis, Editeur, 1968), p. 1015.

6. *Semiotikè* (Paris: Editions du Seuil, 1969), p. 280 (our translation).

7. The notion of practice is used in the Barthesian sense, meaning that "the signification is produced, not at the level of an abstraction (language), as Saussure had postulated, but rather at the will of an operation, a work in which the debate of the contest of the subject and the Other and the social context are invested at the same time and in a single movement", in *Encyclopedia Universalis*, p. 1015 (our translation).

8. *Ibid.*, p. 1015 (our translation). Kristeva adds: "*intertextuality* (is) that textual interaction which is produced inside a single text". "Problèmes de la structuration du texte", p. 311 (our translation). See also the excellent resumés and exposition of the notion of intertext by Hans-George Ruprecht in "Intertextualité", *Texte*, 2 (1983), 13-22, also "Intertextuality", in *Intertextuality*, edited by Heinrich F. Plett (Berlin and New York: Walter de Gruyter, 1991), pp. 60-77; and for an evolutionary view of the concept see Marc Angenot, "L'intertextualité: enquête sur l'émergence et la diffusion d'un champ notionnel", *Revue des sciences humaines*, LX, 189 (janvier-mars 1983), 121-135 and "Intertextualité, interdiscursivité, discours social", *Texte*, 2 (1983), 101-112.

9. "Problèmes de la structuration du texte", p. 312 (our translation). See also Marc Angenot, "Présupposé, topos, idéologème", *Etudes françaises*, XIII, 1-2 (1977), 11-34.

10. "Intertexte et autotexte", *Poétique*, VII, 25 (1976), 282-296.

11. "Texte (Théorie du)", p. 1013 (our translation). See also: Jean Bellemin-Noël, *Le texte et l'avant-texte* (Paris: Librairie Larousse, 1972).

12. "The Model of the Text: Meaningful Action Considered as a Text", *New Literary History*, I, 1 (Autumn 1973), 96. In this same article, Ricoeur characterizes the text from a perspective that is hermeneutic: the inscription of meaning, its dissociation from the mental intention of the author, the manifestation of non-ostentative references and the universality of its messages. For Ricoeur, these four factors constitute the objectivity of the text. *Ibid.*, p. 105.

13. *Ibid.*, p. 92.

14. Paul Ricoeur, "Qu'est-ce qu'un texte?", in *Hermeneutik und Dialektik* (Tübingen: J.C. Mohr, 1970), p. 183 (our translation).

15. On this point, Ricoeur adds: "By appropriation, I understand the following: the interpretation of a text is achieved through the self-interpretation of a subject who thereafter understands him/herself better or differently, or even begins to understand him/herself". The reading "completes the discourse of the text in a dimension similar to that of speech". *Ibid.*, pp. 194-195 and 195 respectively (our translation).

16. See Hans-Robert Jauss, "Literary History as a Challenge to Literary Theory", *New Literary History*, II, 1 (Autumn 1970), 7-38 and *Pour une estéthique de la réception*, translated from the German by Claude Maillard, preface be Jean Starobinski. (Paris: Editions Gallimard, 1978).

17. *Le texte et l'avant texte*, p. 15 (our translation).

18. See *The Cognition of the Literary Work of Art*, translated by Ruth Ann Crowley and Kenneth R. Olson (Evanston: Northwestern University Press, 1973) and *The Literary Work of Art*, translated with an introduction by George G. Grabowicz (Evanston: Northwestern University Press, 1973).

19. See Roman Ingarden, *The Cognition of the Literary Work of Art*, p. 50.

20. See chapter IV.

21. On didascalia, see Anne Ubersfeld, *Lire le théâtre* (Paris: Editions Sociales, 1977), pp. 13-57.

22. The concept of *theatricality* attempts to define the specific nature of theatre, in the same way as the concept of *literariness* in literature introduced by the Russian Formalists. See T. Todorov, *Théorie de la littérature*, texts by the Russian Formalists compiled, presented and translated by T. Todorov, preface by Roman Jakobson (Paris: Editions du Seuil, 1965), especially pp. 31-75; and *Russian Formalism: History - Doctrine* (The Hague and Paris: Mouton, 1969) by Victor Erlich. For more on the concept of *theatricality* see Patrice Pavis, *Dictionnaire du Théâtre* (Paris: Editions Sociales, 1980), pp. 409-410. Additionally, Roland Barthes points out that theatricality "is theatre minus the text, it is a depth of signs and sensations which is built upon the stage from the written summary, it is that sort of ecumenical perception of sensual artifices, gestures, sounds, distances, substances, lights, which submerge the text under the plenitude of its exterior language". *Essais critiques* (Paris: Editions du Seuil, 1964), pp. 41-42 (our translation).

23. A good example of what I have been discussing may be found in *Hamlet*:

>   Ophelia: My lord, as I was sewing in my closet,
>   Lord Hamlet, with his doublet all unbrac'd,
>   No hat upon his head, his stockins fouled,
>   Ungart'red, and down-gyved to his ankle,
>   Pale as his shirt, his knees knocking each other,
>   And with a look so piteous in purport
>   As if he had been loosed out of hell
>   To speak of horrors - he comes before me.

William Shakespeare, *Hamlet. The Riverside Shakespeare* (Boston: Houghton Mifflin Company, 1974), Act II, Scene I, p. 1152.

24. This is exactly what Tim Fitzpatrick does in his excellent article "Playscript Analysis, Performance Analysis: Towards a Theoretical Model", *Gestos*, 2 (noviembre 1986), 13-28.

25. "Esquisse d'une théorie de la forme dramatique", *Langages*, 12 (décembre 1968), 73-74 (our translation). See also "Qu'est-ce qu'une situation dramatique"?, *Orbis Litterarum*, XXVII (1973), 253-292.

26. *Ibid.*, p. 77 (our translation).

27. With respect to another view of the dramatic situation (actantial perspective) see Etienne Souriau, *Les deux cent mille situations dramatiques* (Paris: Flammarion Editeur, 1950), and chapter V of this book.

28. See the interesting book by Juan Villegas, *Interpretación y análisis del texto dramático* (Ottawa: Girol Books, 1982).

29. On the notion of *Aristotelian* theatre, see Fernando de Toro, *Brecht en el teatro hispanoamericano contemporáneo* (Buenos Aires: Editorial Galerna, 1987), pp. 13-17 and 35-36.

30. Regarding the stage productions of Antoine Vitez, see Anne-Françoise Banhanou, *et al.*, *Vitez: toutes les mises en scène* (Paris: Jean-Cyrville Godefroy, 1981) and Antoine Vitez and Emile Copfermann, *De Chaillot à Chaillot* (Paris: Hachette, 1981).

31. We could say the same of the recent stage production of Victor Hugo's *Lucrecia Borgia* done by Vitez (Chaillot, Paris, 1985). Perhaps one of the most extraordinary and exemplary cases of the use of space can be found in Ariane Mnouchkine's productions, for example *Henri IV* and *Travaux d'amour perdu* (Théâtre du Soleil, Cartoucherie de Vincennes, 1983-84). Mnouchkine is truly a master of space: few directors today have a similar view of space, where the actor's body and discourse are truly the elements that fill this space.

32. *Lire le théâtre*, pp. 13-24.

33. Jiří Veltrusky points out how dialogue - the words used in theatre - always includes not only the material situation, that is, the combination of things that are around the speakers, but also the speakers themselves, their intentions, knowledge pertinent to the dialogue, their mutual relationships, the tensions existing between them, etc.; in a word, what we could call the psychological situation. "Basic Features of Dramatic Dialogue", in *Semiotics of Art. Prague School Contributions*, p. 128. See also, Keir Elam, *The Semiotics of Theatre and Drama* (London and New York: Methuen, 1980), pp. 178-210 and Jean Alter, "From Text to Performance", *Poetics Today*, II, 3 (Spring 1981), 113-139.

34. Patrice Pavis, *Voix et images de la scène* (Lille: Presses Universitaires de Lille, 1982), p. 32.

35. Jean Alter develops several concepts having to do with the relationship that he calls the total text (TT) and staged text (T) to which he adds the literary text (LT). These concepts, however, do not really add much to what Ubersfeld, De Marinis, Pavis, Serpieri or Elam had established. The text would be total in a way that De Marinis calls performance text, at least in the manner Alter proposes it. "From Text to Performance", 117.

36. "Toward a Segmentation of the Dramatic Text", *Poetics Today*, II, 3 (Spring 1981), 166.

37. *Semiótica del teatro*.

38. *Lire le théâtre*, pp. 15-25. The quote of Ubersfeld is as follows: "work on the text also presupposes the transformation *into text*, by the theatre practitioner, of non-linguistic signs, by a sort of reciprocity. From there the presence, beside the author's text (in theory printed or typed) which we call T, of another, *staging* text which we call T', both in opposition to P, the representation: T + T' = P". *Ibid.*, p. 24 (our translation).

39. For more on the theatre object, see Anne Ubersfeld, *Lire le théâtre*, pp. 194-202; *L'école du spectateur. Lire le théâtre 2* (Paris: Editions Sociales, 1981), pp. 125-164. Also, Maryvonne Saison, "Les objets dans la création théâtrale", *Revue de metaphysique et morale*, LXXIX, 1 (janvier-mars 1974), 253-268.

40. See Evelyne Ertel, "Vers une analyse sémiologique de le représentation", *Travail théâtral*, 32-33 (1979), 164-172. Also, Patrice Pavis, "Représentation, mise en scène, mise en signe", *The Canadian Journal of Research in Semiotics*, IV, 1 (Fall 1976), 63-66 and "Théorie du théâtre et sémiologie; sphère de l'objet et sphère de l'homme", *Semiotica*, XVI, 1 (1976), 45-86.

41. In his excellent article on theatre notes, Patrice Pavis shows the difficulty in systematizing note-taking. However, his own suggestions are of an abstract order and he does not really propose a usable system for those working in theatre. See "Réflexions sur la notation de la répréntation théâtrale", in *Voix et images de la scène*, pp. 145-170.

42. One only has to look at the great diversity of the cases in the *Modellbuch* by Brecht.

43. "Le spectacle comme texte", p. 197 (our translation).

44. *Ibid.*, p. 202 (our translation).

45. "Pertinence (idéologique) du 'code'", *Degrés*, deuxième année, 7-8 (juillet-octobre 1974), b-b13. Umberto Eco claims that codes "provide the rules which *generate* signs as concrete occurrences in communicative intercourse" and that the sign "establishes the correlation of an expression plane (in its purely formal and systematic aspect) with a content plane (in its purely formal and systematic aspect)". *A Theory of Semiotics* (Bloomington and London: Indiana University Press, 1976), pp. 49 and 50, respectively. See also the *Dictionnaire du théâtre* by Patrice Pavis and the *Dictionnaire encyclopédique des sciences du langage*, by Oswald Ducrot and T. Todorov.

46. See Marco De Marinis, "Le spectacle comme texte", pp. 230-231.

47. *Ibid.*, p. 215 (our translation).

48. *Ibid.*, p. 224 (our translation).

49. On the notions of sub-codification and super-codification, see Umberto Eco, *A Theory of Semiotics*, pp. 129-136 and also his article, "Semiotics of Theatrical Performance", *The Drama Review*, XXI, 1 (March 1977), 107-117.

50. For example, *1789, 1793*, and *L'âge d'or*, collective productions by the Théâtre du Soleil, or *La Classe Morte, Wielepole, Où sont les neiges d'antan?* by Tadeusz Kantor. For more on Mnouchkine's work see: "Deux créations collectives du Théâtre du Soleil: *1973* et *L'age d'or*", by Catherine Mounier in *Les voies de la création théâtrale*, vol. V (Paris: Editions du Centre National de Recherche Scientifique, 1977), pp. 121-278; Ariane Mnouchkine "Différent le Théâtre du Soleil", *Travail Théâtral*, special issue (février 1976). See Denis Bablet, *T. Kantor. Les voies de la création théâtrale*, vol. XI (Paris: Editions du Centre National de la Recherche Scientifique, 1983), which is completely dedicated to Kantor. Also, Kantor's *Le théâtre de la mort*, texts compiled and presented by Denis Bablet (Lausanne: Editions L'Age d'Homme, 1977).

51. "Le spectacle comme texte", p. 229 (our translation).

52. *Ibid.*, pp. 224-231.

53. Grotowski provides a good example both in his theatre practice and in his theoretical writings. *Towards a Poor Theatre* (New York: Simon and Schuster, 1968). See also, *The Director and the Stage* (London: Methuen, 1983) by Edward Braun.

54. On the problem of the concepts of tragedy, comedy, etc., see the excellent article by Alfonso de Toro, "Observaciones para una definición de los términos 'tragoedia','comoedia', y 'tragicomedia' en los dramas de honor de Calderón", in *Texto-Mensaje-Recipiente* (Tübingen: Gunter Narr Verlag, 1988), pp. 101-132.

55. "Le spectacle comme texte", p. 229 (our translation).

56. *Ibid.*, p. 229.

57. *Ibid.*, p. 232.

58. According to Serpieri: "It can be claimed, therefore, that *the written text is at the center of a framework of connotative semiotics* which on the one hand produces the transcodification of its stage potential (*staging of the linguistic level*) and on the other is projected against the background of the system underlying it (*the translation into language of an institutional poetic code that is in turn a rhetorical translation of a typologico-cultural system*)". "Toward a Segmentation of the Dramatic Text", 171.

59. *Ibid.*, p. 171.

CHAPTER III

THEATRE SEMIOTICS

> Qu'est-ce que le théâtre? Une espèce de machine cybernétique. Au repos, cette machine est cachée derrière un rideau. Mais dès qu'on la découvre, elle se met à envoyer à votre adresse un certain nombre de messages ... on a donc affaire à une véritable polyphonie informationnelle, et c'est cela, la théâtralité: *une épaisseur de signes*.
> Roland Barthes, *Essais critiques*.

Among the performance arts, theatre has a place of privilege because of its production of signs, the variety of which originates primarily from its diverse signification systems. There have been different attempts at isolating these. One of the first attempts was by Tadeusz Kowzan[1] who formulated thirteen sign systems that function in a performance. This interesting study, however, did not succeed in fully systematizing the production of meaning in theatre, and in fact it completely ignored the problem of how meaning is produced on the stage. This list of signs or systems of signification established a medium for the production of meaning but in none of the cases did it discuss meaning production. To do this, one has to go further and establish the sort of sign(s) that functions in the theatre performance. The problem of *semiosis* and the systematic study of this phenomenon is fundamental for the understanding of how the intricate goings-on of a performance operate.

I. SEMIOSIS

A) *The Notion of Semiosis*

Humanity's relationship with the world, nature and other human beings is *mediated* by signs. Signs serve to describe nature and to communicate with other men: the communicative act, that is, *the production of signs*, is what we generally mean by semiosis.

This ancient notion comes from Greek medicine where it meant, and still means, *symptom*. From the point of view of communication, semiosis involves at least three elements: a sign-vehicle or signifier, a *designatum* or that to which the sign or signified refers, and an interpreter that interprets this signifier and perceives it as a sign. This idea is the basis of the notion developed by Charles S. Peirce, the first to formulate a typology of systems of signs: "by 'semiosis' I mean ... an action, or influence, which is, or involves, a cooperation of *three* subjects, such as a sign, its object, and its interpretant ...".[2] This triadic conceptualization of semiosis and of the sign is very similar to the proposal put forth by Charles Morris for whom: "The process in which something functions as a sign may be called *semiosis* ...".[3] Morris formulates his proposal using three elements: the mediators or sign-vehicles that he calls *designata*, the effect produced on the interpreter or interpretants, and the agents or interpreters.

This notion of semiosis that comes from logic (Peirce) and from linguistics (Morris) has been incorporated into theatre theory with hardly any change. For example, according to Patrice Pavis, semiosis in theatre is intimately linked to Peirce's triadic system, since "the theory of semiosis tied to icons, indices and symbols would be an attempt to explain the appearance of signification".[4] Umberto Eco adds another dimension to theatre semiosis in stating that the way signs function in theatre constitutes what he calls the *square of semiosis*, that is, the displacement of the theatre sign considered as real (object), then transformed into a sign so that it may refer to another object.[5] For example, an actor on the stage representing a beggar is taken as a real beggar, but later is transformed into a sign, because he/she imitates/mimes the real beggar and thus refers to extra-theatre reality.

These notions come together in the sign, the object the sign denotes and the meaning the sign acquires in being interpreted by someone. Semiosis, however, varies from one signifying practice to another, for sign systems do not function equally, even though they retain the same structure for the production of meaning (sign/object/meaning). In this sense, theatre differs fundamentally from any of the 'literary' and even performance practices, for in theatre there are other concrete references besides language (the actor, object, etc.). The multitude of systems (for example costumes, decor, etc.) have their own way of signifying. This complexity and heterogeneity of systems requires that the specific nature of the theatre sign be examined. That is, it is important to define what constitutes this sign and how it works. In order to do this, however, the general concept of sign should first be clarified.

B) *The Various Versions of Sign*

In this section I will not be reformulating the well-known ideas of Saussure and Hjelmslev. Rather, these and other versions of the notion of sign will simply be referred to when discussing the theatre sign.

The most useful idea for my purposes is the integration of the object or referent into the communication process and the production of meaning. This understanding of the sign does not come from linguistics but from philosophy and logic. These disciplines have had the most to do with the nature of the relationship between the sign and the object. This relationship is particularly important for theatre, since in theatre, unlike literary discourse, objects do have a real existence, a real presence, although in the end it only takes the form of the presence of the voice and body of the actor. It is natural, then, that 'literary' semiology should favour the Saussurian or Hjelmslevian linguistic view, for in literary discourse one is dealing with a *substance of expression* (linguistic), whereas in theatre this substance is at least dual in nature (visual and auditive), if not multiple - if one takes into account the diverse material dimensions of the visual substance (lighting, set, costumes, gestures) and of the auditive substance (voice, tone, rhythm, timbre, noises, music).

In the phenomenology of Edward Husserl, there is a clearly defined notion of the triadic sign in what he calls *the expressed*, which in my opinion is nothing more than the globality of the sign with its three components. According to Husserl, in every expression (in every sign) there is:

    1) something shown (signifier);
    2) something signified (signified);
    3) something named (object: referent).[6]

A proposal very similar to this was put forward by C.K. Ogden and I.A. Richards. Their reading of Peirce was quite definitive on this point. The famous sign triangle also incorporates the notion of the triadic sign. What is important for Ogden and Richards is "the nature of the correspondence between word and fact ..." since this relation constitutes "the highest problem of the science of meaning".[7] The importance of the triangle resides in the difference between reference and referent (I will return to this problem further on):

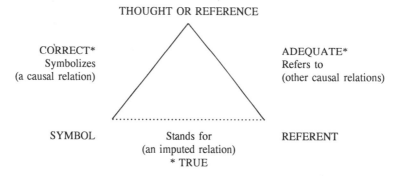

The symbol refers to a reference or to a thought which then refers to a referent or object (and not necessarily the real object). The relationship between the symbol and the reference is one of causality: words in a language have a meaning. At the same time, the reference and the referent also maintain a relationship of causality, but it is always determined by the contextualization of the reference. For example, if we use the sign *granada* (the Spanish word), it has various references (for the Spanish speaker): a bomb, a city in Spain, a fruit. The referent to which these references refer depends purely on the utterance and the enunciative situation. With a capital letter, the referent is the city in Spain; with lower case, along with the appropriate enuciative situation, it is either the fruit or the bomb. The relation between the symbol and the referent is arbitrary and is indirectly mediated by the reference. (Morris's understanding of the sign as mentioned above in relation to semiosis is also triadic). However, the most useful view of the sign for the study of theatre is undoubtedly Peirce's view, and this is why I have left it to the last.

For Peirce, a sign is "Anything which determines something else (its *interpretant*) to refer to an object to which itself refers (its *object*) in the same way, the interpretant becoming in turn a sign, and so on *ad infinitum*".[8] In this definition, there are a number of points that should be highlighted. The triadic relationship is important, not only because Peirce integrates the sign of the object to which the sign refers to, but also because every triadic relationship implies a constant reference between the components of the sign (*representament, object, interpretant*) which are themselves also signs. That is, *granada* does not refer to the object, but to another sign that is its interpretant: the city, the bomb or the fruit. Sign and representament are sometimes used as synonyms and at other times as a generic concept, as in the above quote. For example, elsewhere Peirce states: "My definition of a representamen is as follows: *A REPRESENTAMENT is a subject of a triadic relation TO a second, called its OBJECT, FOR a third, called its INTERPRETANT, this triadic relation being such that the REPRESENTAMENT determines its interpretant to stand in the same triadic relation to the same object for some interpretant*".[9] This definition of the sign, as I can see, is quite close to the definition Morris has put forth, in that it integrates the dynamic Peircian triadicity. The Peircian sign, if I use his definition, can also be represented more precisely with a triangle:

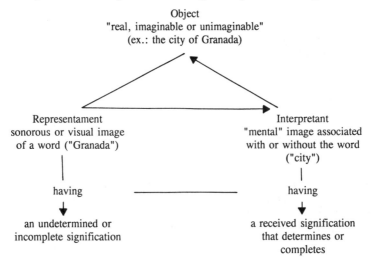

The representament, in itself, does not contain the meaning; it does not refer directly to the object. Before anything else, it has to pass through the interpretant, and it is this sign which refers to the object. That is, it completes the undetermined meaning of the representament. This provokes a mental image or interpretant in the interpreter, and this image is either associated with, or associates itself with, an object. An important point which arises from this understanding of the sign is that in order for an interpretant sign to say something about the object, it must be known beforehand. For example, if I do not know of the city of Granada (even if only by name), then the sign does not express anything for us, although it may have a linguistic meaning. Another example: if someone mentions the name of a person who is well-known in a given field to someone who knows nothing about that field, then the name does not say anything, it does not allow for knowledge to occur unless it is explained to or learned by this person. As I can see, this understanding of the sign is far from both the dualist Saussurian view (i.e. signifier/signified) and the Hjelmslevian view (which does not include the object, and in which meaning is found directly between signifier and signified).

This triadic view of the sign is triadic in another way as well. Not only is it triadic, one can also say it is has *trichotomies*, and these are explained in the table below. For Peirce: "Signs are divisible by three trichotomies; first, according as the sign in itself is a mere quality, is an acutal existent, or is a general law; secondly, according as the relation of the sign to its object consists in the sign's having some character in itself, or in some existential relation to that object, or in its relation to an interpretant; thirdly, according as its Interpretant represents it as a sign of possibility or as a sign of fact or a sign of reason".[10]

	First	Second	Third
Representant	Qualisign	Synsign	Legisign
Object	Icon	Index	Symbol
Interpretant	Reme	Decisign	Argument

In the first trichotomy (representant), the sign may be qualisign as first; as second, synsign; and as third, legisign. In the second trichotomy, the sign may be icon as first; as second, index; and as third, symbol. According to the third trichotomy, it may be reme as first; as second, it may be decisign; and as third, it may be argument. This trichotomous division relates each sign (first, second, third) to the other poles of the trichotomy; that is to say, each sign may be a *representament* as in 1, 2 or 3, i.e. in relation to its significant substance. Each sign may be an *object* in relation to the *form* of relation of the type of object to which it refers, and each sign may be an *interpretant* in relation to the *form* of interpreting each one of the signs. In this system, the second trichotomy is the most interesting one, for it is the most used in theatre. With respect to the other signs, a few words of explanation are needed.

The qualisign is a quality present as a sign, and for this reason it has to be present in some concrete form, or, using Peirce's expression, a materialization must occur. The synsign is also something real which can be said to exist through its qualities and it therefore involves a qualisign; that is, the qualisign exists only as a possibility of manifestation and it becomes manifest through a synsign. For example, if I wish to express a storm in theatre, it must materialize through the characters' gestures, the movement of their costumes, the blowing along of bits of paper, etc. The legisign is simply a conventional sign, such as a cross, the apple of the Judeo-Christian tradition, or the famous stairs in the *Oedipus Rex* produced by Josef Svoboda (National Theatre, Prague, 1963),[11] which symbolized the fall of man. Peirce, however, speaks of symbol as a *replica*, and it is important to clarify this point too, since we will speak of replica when discussing the icon. On this point, Peirce states: "Every legisign signifies through an instance of its application, which may be termed a *Replica* of it. Thus, the word 'the' will usually occur from fifteen to twenty-five times on a page. It is in all these occurrences one and the same word, the same legisign. Each single instance of it is a Replica".[12] In this case, replica means the exact reproduction of the fundamental properties of the sign 'the', but at the same time it is a symbol, for the article 'the' symbolizes the function of the article as defined in the grammar of a language. It is a symbol in the same way that all of language is a symbol. Peirce's distinction between legisign as a 'general type' established by society, or as a 'particular case' established through each application, which he calls replica, is the difference between *type* and *occurrence* (between *intension* and *extension*).[13]

According to the third dichotomy, the *reme* is an interpretant of qualitative possibility. That is, it may represent a possible object. A decisign is an interpretant as a signaller. An *argument* is a conventional interpretant. Peirce summarizes these interpretant relationships in the following way: "a Rheme is a sign which is understood to represent its object in its characters merely; ... a Dicisign is a sign which is understood to represent its object in respect to actual existence; and ... an Argument is a Sign which is understood to represent its Object in its character as Sign".[14] For example, if a weather vane indicates the direction of the wind, we have as a real representament the weather vane (an index) that produces a mental image - 'wind direction' - that is, its (decisign) interpretant, that refers to the real object before us (index) and that allows for the interpretation of the weather vane as indicating the direction of the wind. This same process can be applied to the first and third trichotomies.[15]

II. NATURE OF THE THEATRE SIGN

The first thing that I should say about the theatre sign is that it cannot be reduced to a single sign, and even less to minimal units of signification. Theatre is a place of privilege for the sign, because, in the stage space, *everything* is either an artificial or a natural sign. Everything is seen or perceived as a sign by the spectator; the plurality and polyphony of signs in theatre is immense.[16] From the moment the actor begins to move about the stage, or when the curtain goes up, the audience is in front of both a reality signified by means of the sign, and a system of signs, and thus it is difficult to speak of natural signs. The theatre sign, then, immediately shows itself to be an artifice.

A) *Signs of Signs*

If it is true that, in order to signify by means of the semiosis process, theatre must use signs that proceed from nature (lightning, rain, age, youth, etc.), from society (gestures, linguistic terms, dress) or from other artistic practices (architecture, painting, mime, music), then it is also true that these signs are never communicated directly but rather through other signs. This is the case even in realist or naturalist theatre, because the realist sign elaborated to achieve ‚mimesis ‚ is in fact an exterior sign and not truly real (I will return to this point in the section on the icon). Recalling Kowzan's thirteen sign systems,[17] these can be summarized, according to their nature, by quoting Petr Bogatyrev: "All theatrical manifestations are then signs of signs or signs of things".[18] It is this exact aspect or quality of the theatre sign - theatre sign as sign of another sign - that is theatre's most definitive characteristic. Kowzan's thirteen sign systems, which cover everything from the word to sound, *are signs of signs of the object*. Bogatyrev is correct when he differentiates between signs of signs and signs of the object, for these are distinct uses of the sign. The problem with Bogatyrev's terminology as well as that of Kowzan and Honzl, is that they did not conceive of these systems from a triadic perspective, and therefore, because they do not distinguish between *icon*, *index*, and *symbol*, their thoughts are not always clear.[19] If I take Umberto Eco's famous example of the drunkard put on a platform (on a 'stage') by the Salvation Army to show the importance of moderation and the evil caused by alcoholism, the situation is the following:[20]

Real drunkard ──▶ drunkard 'on stage' ──▶ sign of this ───
─── ▶ sign of a real drunkard ──▶ sign of moderation
    (index)   (symbol)

The real drunkard is a sign of real drunkenness because of the way he walks/talks/is dressed. Because he is on stage, he becomes the sign of drunkenness. The on-stage drunkard refers to the real drunkard and to his sign of drunkenness but, at the same time, he is an 'on-stage' sign of moderation. He does not refer to *a specific drunkard*, but rather to all drunkards. Thus, the 'on-stage' drunkard is a sign of a sign of an object. The drunkard, however, can just be a sign of an object, if he is taken only as a drunk and not as a drunk used to promote moderation. What is at play between the sign of a sign of a sign and the sign of a sign is the symbol and the index:

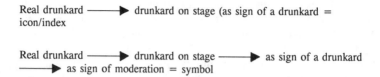

In fact, I could say that, in this case, there is a sign of a sign of a sign, if I first take the drunkard as an icon, then as an index, and finally as a symbol. This transformation of the sign will be examined in greater detail in the next section.

It is important to point out that besides the space change that renders the *sign staging* possible, *ostentation* plays a decisive role. Umberto Eco points this out when he argues that a body and a real state are being ostentated: "In the case of our elementary model of mise-en-scène, the drunk is a sign, but he is a sign that pretends not to be such. The drunkard is playing a double game: In order to be accepted as a sign, he has to be recognized as a 'real' spatio-temporal event, a real human body".[21] A sign of a sign of a sign of an object is what characterizes the theatre sign and constitutes one of its most dynamic and *mobile* features.

B) *The Mobility of the Theatre Sign*

This sign of a sign of a sign of an object that I have just described is characterized by what Jindrich Honzl calls the *mobility of the sign*. This consists of the constant mutation theatre signs experience. This mutation has a close relationship with the icon/index/symbol that I will discuss in the next section. At this point, the objective is simply to outline this second characteristic of the nature or specificity of the theatre sign. The mutation of the signs refers to the fact that the signs of a given substance assume the function of signs of a different substance, undergoing in this way a significant transformation. For example, the stage production of *King Lear* done by I. Bergman (Teatro Tivoli, Barcelona, 1985, Théâtre National de l'Odéon, Paris, 1984) makes use of the transformative potential of the sign to establish the set and props that create *the theatre object*.[22] In this play, the actors are transformed into objects in the strict sense of the term. They have various functions, for example: to divide the stage space in different ways indicating the divisions in the kingdom, or to act as walls or other interior/exterior divisions of space of the castle/asylum. As well, the actor's body serves as a prop: as a table or a chair, for instance. Whenever Lear and his companions sit down, they sit on the backs of kneeling characters who also serve as tables. In this stage production, the actors determined and created the stage space, and in fact all of the actors stayed on the stage throughout the play. When not acting, they were still, fulfilling the role of some object. In this way, there were no 'real' objects on the stage, for the 'props' and the 'set' were created by the actors' bodies. The simultaneous presence of all of the actors was justified by this transformability of actor/character into actor/object. In the production of *The Green Bird* by Beno Benson (Vienna, 1984), characters played the roles of animals, birds, statues, and trees. Thus, the body can acquire the iconographic properties of the object being played.

Inverse transformability (the process the material object experiences when it is stripped of its normal substance and acquires another) is a common practice in theatre. In Ariane Mnouchkine's productions (in which the body of the actor often plays an iconic/metonymic role), such as *Richard II*, for example, Richard II imitates a moving horse, and big pieces of linen in the background suggest Richard's feelings (Théâtre du Soleil, Cartoucherie de Vincennes, 1982). The transformability of the theatre sign is at the very essence of theatricality: in theatre, any sign has the potential of losing its own substance and acquiring another, without losing its effectiveness in the process. The effect this process creates can even be (and usually is) much more powerful than in pure iconic fiction. Thus, the creation of a stage space, or of various spaces and situations of enunciation, is surprisingly effective in *El romancero de Edipo* by Eugenio Barba (Nordisk Teater Laboratorium, Teatro Metrònom, Barcelona, 1985). All of the acting revolves around the body of the only character on stage. The same can be said for other recent stage productions, like *Ecrans noirs* by Pierre Friloux-Schilansky and Françoise Gedanken (Théâtre d'en Face, Centre Georges Pompidou, Paris, 1985), in which video, body, space, etc. are all used and intertwined, altering the way traditional theatre functions. This is so because video becomes part of the transmitting 'character', and not simply a supplementary means of expression for the performance, as it might be in a Brecht or Piscator production.

It is this particular function of the theatre sign that separates it from other performance signs (visual or auditive).[23] Transformability, claims Honzl, "is a rule, a matter of course, and therein lies its specific character".[24] Whether it be a sign of a sign, or a sign of an object, or a transformable or mutable sign, the theatre sign has a differentiating characteristic that is part of its function of production of meaning: redundancy.

C) *Redundancy of the Theatre Sign*

The redundancy of the theatre sign has to do directly with the communicative aspect of the theatre performance, with the transmission of the message, and with its reception by the audience. This function reinforces theatre communication by making the material signifying part of the stage signs much clearer. Thus, these signs (set, costumes, ideolects, gestures, etc.) acquire the function of signs producing meaning, and avoid significant neutrality. A third complimentary function of redundancy is the constant repetition of signifiers pointing to a single signified. If redundancy is to be understood in this way, that is, not only as an extra charge of meaning and information, but also as a function making signs *legible* and *translating* them effectively to the stage and public, then it is a fundamental and specific part of the performance and of the *work* of the theatre. Redundancy is not limited, as Michel Corvin claims, to pure communication of a message; it is also a producer of meaning.[25]

In all forms of theatre, there is redundancy in the discourse, characters, set, costumes, etc. For example, a stage, production intending to project a message of material and spiritual decadence and degradation of individuals or of a social class might use redundancy. This is the case in *Alamos en la azotea* by the Chilean playwright Egon Wolff (Teatro Municipal, Companía Teatro de Camara, 1981). This play expresses this degradation with stage spaces, costumes, sets and other things that reiterate this message: the room where Moncho lives, his own clothing, his occupation, not to mention the sister-in-law's discourse which literally *repeats* each of the aspects that the audience sees evolving from the play's opening. The material nature of the visual signifiers (room, clothing, work) is duplicated in the discourse.[26] In this way, any possible ambiguity about the message is completely avoided, and this redundancy sets the meaning right from the beginning of the performance.

Another interesting case is the production of *Le dernier marquis* staged by Armand Gatti (Atelier de Création Populaire, Centre Georges Pompidou, Paris, 1985): three groups of actors dressed as athletes compete to reconstruct the history of Maqui, the guerrilla of the Spanish Civil War. At the beginning, each of the actors narrates his or her own story using one of the many televisions hunging over the audience. In this way, the different versions of the Maqui stories intermingle. It is this redundance of the word and the visual component (from the televisions) that renders the intricate and difficult message/story comprehensible, for each object on stage has a role and nothing is neutral. The video narrates, as do the objects and characters, and these are the three levels participating in the construction of the figure of Maqui.

Reiterative production (i.e. the omnipresence of certain actions and objects) produces an accumulation of signifiers that often become a unified signified. For example, in the production of *Où sont les neiges d'antan?* by Tadeusz Kantor (Théâtre Cricot 2, Centre Georges Pompidou, 1982),[27] which is a mute performance, only the characters' reiterative gestures produce overall meaning and a complete picture. And Tadeusz Kantor is constantly present on stage, observing these movements, at times standing next to an omnipresent skeleton. The white clothing worn by all the characters also contributes to the creation of an image of death, suffering and total alienation. The specific signified of this image could either be understood as the alienation of the worker in capitalist or socialist society, or the annihilation of the Jews during the Second World War. Either way, these possibilities are determined by three main signifiers: repetitive movement, white costumes and the presence of a skeleton with the 'author-character'. Something similar occurs in the productions of *Waiting for Godot* by Samuel Beckett, done by Otmar Krejca (Théâtre Atelier, Paris, 1985), and of *La cantatrice chauve* by Ionesco (produced by Nicolas Bataille, Théâtre de la Huchette, Paris, 1985) in which the characters' discourse and the on-stage objects create an image of vacuity and circularity. In both these cases, the redundancy of the signifier creates a signified that could be said to be absurd: it points to a society that feels that its very existence has been transformed into the life of Sisyphus.

This is why Corvin is correct when he argues that redundancy is one of the central components "of the specificity of theatre if it permits the establishment of a typology of the possible correlations between the levels of expression and content".[28] The three aspects I consider specific to the theatre sign are: sign of a sign/sign of the object, transformability, and redundancy, and these function through a system or type of specific sign that I will now examine.

III. THE ICON, THE INDEX, AND THE SYMBOL ACCORDING TO PEIRCE

The sorts of signs that operate in the theatre performance can be reduced to three: icon, index and symbol. The various ways in which these signs operate, independent of their substance of expression, can be further categorized in three ways. It is in the way they function, and not in their substance, that they acquire their specificity. Before beginning a new definition of how these signs function, it is important to go back to the original one put forth by Peirce. Only then could we explain why the whole process of semiosis can be reduced to the triadic sign.

If I recall the table of the three trichotomies established previously I will observe that these three signs work according to the second trichotomy, where the icon is first, the index second, the symbol third, and all three are defined as they relate to an object. Peirce refers to this second trichotomy in several places in his writings, but I will concentrate only on a few definitions.

A) *The Icon*

According to Peirce: "An *Icon* is a Representamen whose Representative Quality is a Firstness of it as a First. That is, a quality that it has *qua* thing renders it fit to be a representamen. Thus, anything is fit to be a *Substitute* for anything that it is like".[29] That is, the icon in the *form of expression* (the most used) presents a few representative qualities that allow it to represent (to be the representamant of) the thing or object in question. The icon, then, should have a few of the traits or *properties* of the represented thing, and this is why one speaks of quality. On the other hand, the icon may substitute for, that is, represent, anything that its own traits include. This last point is important because the mobility of the sign (referred to in section II.B) is instrumental in theatre: everything can become an icon when the intention to represent (and not imitate) is there.[30]

In another place, Peirce claims:

> An *icon* is a sign which would possess the character which renders it significant, even though its object had no existence, such as a lead-pencil streak as representing a geometrical line.... An *Icon* is a sign which refers to the Object that it denotes merely

by virtue of characters of its own, and which it possesses, just the same, whether any such Object actually exists or not ... Anything whatever, be it quality, existent individual, or law, is an Icon of anything, in so far as it is like that thing and used as a sign of it.[31]

There are two important points to be made: first of all, the non-real (or immaterial) existence of an object does not impose its representation, for the icon always exists by means of a *synsign* that posits a *qualisign* (its qualities). For example, the unicorn does not exist as a real object, but it does as an imagined object, as shown in the Cluny tapestries in Paris. A line represents the ideal geometrical line that does not really exist in a material way, although it does as an object imagined geometrically. Secondly, every icon (quality) can be transformed into another sign, that is, into an index (*individual that exists*, or extended *individual*, in this case, understood as a philosophical category), or into a symbol (law, convention). Naturally, the icon is an *index* in a particular way, for, as I will see further on, the index does not *reproduce* qualities of the object. In any case, I can now say that the icon/index is intimately linked to theatre semiosis, and in fact it is rare to find them separated.

B) *The Index*

Whereas the icon signifies by means of resemblance, the index does this through an existential relationship: "An *Index* or *Seme* ... is a Representamen whose Representative character consists in its being an individual second"[32] and "An *Index* is a sign which refers to the Object that it denotes by virtue of being really affected by that Object".[33] As a second individual, and unlike the icon, the index always has a real, material existence and presence. On the other hand, there exists an existential relationship between the sign and its object, for the latter is affected by the former. For example, a weather vane represents (indicates) the direction of the wind. The weather vane is the signifier, a *synsign* whose interpretant it is to represent 'wind from the north, wind from the south', etc. However, it is actually the wind that has a direction and directs the vane, and therefore it is affected by the object that it signifies. This is why Peirce claims that "In so far as the Index is affected by the Object, it necessarily has some Quality in common with the Object, and it is in respect to these that it refers to the Object. It does, therefore, involve a sort of Icon, although an Icon of a peculiar kind; and it is not the mere resemblance of its Object, even in these respects which makes it a sign, but it is the actual modification of it by the Object".[34] Another difference between the index and the icon is the fact that, whereas the icon does not need the real existence of an object, the index does, for without it, the index would cease to exist. This view of index would have to be broadened if it were to be used to analyze the stage production, for if it is true that on stage Peircian indices do exist, it is also true that there exist indices that depart from the actual icon. In other words, the icon in theatre always presents an index. This is so because these are not pure or authentic indices as Peirce calls them, but rather, in a general way, they are iconicized indices. Thus, a character dressed in rags is the icon of a vagabond or homeless person; but at the same time, upon being ostentated on the stage, the character is recognised as such, precisely because of the costume the stage icon borrows from the real social object. This is how a vagabond or homeless person may refer to a state of events at a given time.

Finally, from a Peircian point of view, the index is distinct from the icon in that it is completely different from its object: for example, a weather vane (*representament*) and the north wind (*object*). These two objects do not resemble each other, as do, for example, a drawn line and the ideal geometric line.

C) *The Symbol*

The symbol may be made up of either an icon or an index, that is, of elements that come from these two signs. According to Peirce:

> A *Symbol* is a Representamen whose Representative character consists precisely in its being a rule that will determine its Interpretant.... A *Symbol* is a sign which refers to the Object that it denotes by virtue of a law, usually an association of general ideas, which operates to cause the Symbol to be interpreted as referring to that Object".[35]

When Peirce speaks of symbol, he is referring to the symbolic nature, for example, of language or logic. Words, sentences, etc., are symbols, and hence replicas.[36] Without rejecting this view of symbol, it is possible for the symbol in theatre to be understood in another way. Peirce's understanding of *structure* is useful here: he saw it as a symbol, or more precisely, as a rule or law of motivation between the sign and its signified as it relates to the expressed object. In the symbol there exists a will, and therefore an action that resides entirely in the interpretant. Whereas the index may exist without an interpretant, but not without an object, the symbol stops being a sign if it has no interpretant. In other words, if I recall the weather vane, even if it is not interpreted, its meaning is still indicated by the very presence of the object (another example is the smoke which comes from a fire). A symbol, however, cannot be a sign, unless it is decodified and understood in this way. Symbols operate by accumulation and by tradition, in accordance with social and artistic practice. According to Peirce, "Symbols grow. They come into being by development out of other signs, particularly from icons, or from mixed signs partaking of the nature of icons and symbols".[37] Whereas the icon is dynamically linked to the object it represents, and whereas the index is physically linked to its object, the interpreter has nothing to do with establishing these two relationships. In the case of the symbol, it is the interpreter who establishes this relationship and, of course, the social tradition.

The icon and the index are recognised and the symbol is interpreted. For example, in a dramatic/performance text, a king's crown (like the one in *Richard II* by Shakespeare/Mnouchkine, Cartoucherie de Vincennes, Théâtre du Soleil, Paris,

1982, which is a play that deals with power) could function in the following way (and in this case it does): as a crown/icon representing a crown/object that actually exists. But, at the same time, it is a crown/index because it *shows* who is the king or queen. Then it is transformed into a crown/symbol when it becomes the symbol of power at the centre of the kingdom, of the royal family and of all of the Bolingbroke action.

In relating the Peircian notions of icon, index and symbol to theatre, I have in fact adapted them to theatre, giving them a playful and functional dimension distinct from the logical understanding of these terms found in Peirce's writings.

IV. THE ICON, INDEX AND SYMBOL AT WORK IN THEATRE

In my opinion, these three signs constitute the sort of semiosis that characterizes theatre. In these three signs, all of the production of meaning is organized, independently of substance of expression of the signs in question. Furthermore, these three signs perform very specific functions in the theatre performance. To stage is first and foremost to *stage a sign*, to represent using signs: to mime and imitate the exterior world by means of icons, and to express them indexically and symbolically. Whereas the icon is essential for the projection and materialization of the image of a possible world, the index and symbol fulfil diegetic and interpretive functions.[38]

A) *Iconic Function*

1) The Icon as Code

The theatre iconization is mainly a semantic function. It never exists in a cultural vacuum, but, rather icons work according to a social code, a certain way of representing reality. Icons, and the manner in which iconization occurs is culturally coded. What Umberto Eco calls the "similar perspective structure",[39] refers precisely to the act of recognizing the code as such.[40] In this way, the resemblance between the iconic sign and the object it represents is guaranteed by the cultural space where the iconization occurs. This is why Western audiences with no exposure to Japanese Nô or to Kabuki do not grasp most of the iconization found in the masks and costumes. Thus, to represent an object iconically is "to transcribe according to graphic (or other) conventions the cultural properties which are attributed to it. A culture defines its objects by referring to certain codes of *recognition* which select the pertinent and characteristic traits of the content".[41]

It is important to stress that when I speak of iconic function I am not only referring to the fact that icons fills certain representative functions in theatre, but also to the way these functions are carried out. The similarities that the spectator notices between the sign and the object to which the sign refers (and that is intimately related to the mutability of the theatre sign) has to do with the following: the signifier, or as Eco calls it, the *imitant*,[42] may be distinct from the object. That is, its form can be distinct, but it must achieve the same function as the object by means of its iconic/kinesic signs. A good example of this use of the icon is Ariane Mnouchkine's production of *Richard II* (Cartoucherie de Vincennes, Théâtre du Soleil, Paris, 1982), where almost all of the 'props' were expressed in this way, especially the kinesic icons.

2) Visual Icon

The icon's main function in theatre is to represent or to materialize referents on-stage, and this materialization may be visual, linguistic or verbal. The term visual icon means any manifestation or actualization of physical referents on-stage and these can be of different substance of expression or materiality. One can distinguish between visual icons, icons related to the actor, and icons related to the object.

a) The Body

In the first case, the actor is an icon of the character being performed: the actor's body is, or pretends to be, the body of Hamlet or of Tartuffe or of Lear. The proof of this iconization is that, throughout history, a few characters have become supercodified, thereby creating a *vision* or presence every spectator expects. We all have an idea of how Hamlet, Lear or Tartuffe should appear. Indeed, when this codification established by iconic tradition is broken, malaise and alienation are experienced by the audience as a result. An excellent example of this is the production of *Oedipus Rex* done by Alain Milianti (Théâtre de la Salamandre, Théâtre National de L'Odéon, Paris, 1985) in which Oedipus is young, half bald, with long, thin hair that hangs around his bald spot; he is a barbarous Oedipus, a half-savage, and Jocasta is a man dressed as a woman, yet makes no attempt to hide his masculine voice.

b) Gestures

Another icon that forms part of the body of the actor is the kinesic icon. This comes into play when the actor imitates and creates a visual icon using gestures, or by making abstractions of certain properties of the imitated object. For example, in *El romancero de Edipo* by Eugenio Barba (Nordisk Teater Laboratorium, Teatro Metrònom 1982), the gestures of the actors' hands and arms function as signifiers, expressing the action whose object is absent. The kinesic icon is central to the production of iconic signs in theatre in general; but in the productions of Kantor,

Barba, Grotowski, Beckett, this icon is especially important. In these cases, the body becomes the *prime referent* for iconic inscription.[43]

c) Object/Mimetic Icon

The visual icon that reproduces objects can do it in two ways: either by representing a fairly close imitation of the object, and thereby producing a literal or mimetic icon (figurative decor), as is usually the case in realist theatre of the Meiningen or Antoine type or in the Free Theatre;[44] or by producing a contiguous or mimetic icon, that is to say, by reproducing only certain schematic traces of the object being suggested (a curtain in the background might be the only thing showing and its main function might be, for example, to create the atmosphere of a bourgeois salon). Perhaps one of the theatre forms that has used this most often is the theatre of Edward Gordon Craig. His stage productions would suggest, by means of curtains, light, and visual icons, that had very few or none of the properties of the imitated object. He was trying to create a referential illusion, and not the actual stage referent. Craig did this in *Acis and Galatea*, creating the illusion of a pastoral and springtime scene by using a transparent veil and light.[45] In this instance the sign or visual icon, in particular was allowed to produce signs of signs of the object in the way just discussed. In such cases, the mutability and redundancy of the sign are obvious, since they are accompanied by language and supported by visual icons.

3) Verbal Icon

a) Verbal Icon/Mimesis

The verbal icon consists of an ancient process used in the theatre to which I have already referred when discussing discourse in chapter I. This process consists of the representative function of language, that is, it consists of language's ability to express iconically. This type of icon can be subdivided into: a) verbal icons (which may or may not be redundant) which refer to the theatre object, whether this be a set or general scenography; b) verbal icons which refer to on-stage or off-stage actions. The first type (which Bogatyrev has called *stage scenography*)[46] occurs, for example, when the characters refer to that which the spectators can see and that which is supported by discourse, or when the object is imperceptible, thereby giving rise to the need for language. For example, in Tennessee Williams' play *Cat on a Hot Tin Roof* (National Arts Centre, Ottawa, 1984), this type of icon is used and is concretized in the imagination of the spectator. It is used especially often in European classical theatre and in Ancient Theatre, but it is also important in modern theatre, although its presence here is less frequent.

b) Verbal Icon/Action

The verbal icon also has the function of expressing actions that cannot be represented on stage. Depending upon the point in time in theatre history, this icon was used frequently in ancient and classical theatre because of the set restrictions; but it has also used in such modern productions as *Les Cenci* by Antonin Artaud.[47] It is also used when it is materially impossible to represent certain actions on the stage, as is often the case in the theatre of Lope de Vega or of Shakespeare, or in modern adaptions like *Lear* by Edward Bond, *Mutter Courage und ihre Kinder* by Brecht, and *Heroica de Buenos Aires* by Osvaldo Dragún. This type of verbal icon, called *oriented phantom deixis* by Honzl,[48] can also have a redundant function. That is, it can refer to actions that are actually occurring, or have happened, on stage. This is why Honzl considers the word to be one of the most important signs in the theatre performance - because of its capacity to iconize as well as to 'narrate' a story. A good example of this occurs in *Santa Juana de América*, by the Argentinean playwright, Andrés Lizárraga:

> JUANA: It wasn't easy finding the army coming from Buenos Aires. Nor climbing the hills with four small children, one of whom - the littlest one - was still eating at my breast. But hiding ourselves here and there, walking Indian and llama trails, we arrived at the town occupied by the Buenos Aires' forces. My husband still hadn't made up his mind to let me fight.[49]

B) *Indexical Function*

The theatre index has a very important function in the stage production because it contextualizes words in a variety of ways. The index, therefore, has a syntactic function. Like other icons, it obeys a cultural code that is often more rigorous than the codes of other icons, since these tend to vary greatly from culture to culture. In general, the theatre index tends to be systematized in accordance with the diegetic aspect.[50] One of the main functions, however, is the contextualization of both the discourse of the actors and the space and time in which this discourse is produced. It is often difficult to differentiate between an icon and an index, since, as we have already seen, every icon, in order to be a sign of a sign, is transformed into an index of something in the theatre. Unlike the icon, the index is always materially present on stage, precisely because of its indicative function. The index does not represent, it indicates, and therefore it has a single purpose, whereas the icon can be polysemic.

The indices can be divided into several types: gestural, spatial, temporal, social and environmental. However, the index also has a diegetic function in the theatre performance, and therefore I should consider this point before proceeding with on with the subdivisions.

1) Diegetic Function

This function is made up of three complementary sub-functions which provide a basis for the evolution of the characters' discourse. The theatre object has the central diegetic function, and it ensures fluidity, iconic linearity and continuity of discourse. The continuation or extension of the same set/space tells the spectator that he/she is still in the same space-time. On the other hand, by the same mechanism, the index may account for the rupture of a space-time, or it may maintain the space but change the time. The theatre objects, especially the set (and the props), have certain characteristics at the beginning of a scene; for example, those of a living room which at the beginning is well-furnished and elegant, but later is old and shabby: this is a case of the same space but different time. This is a characteristic of both naturalist and contemporary theatre. The index has a diegetic function because it contributes and is essential to the articulation and connection of concrete situations. That is, the index functions as a *situationeme* that links scenes and contextualizes them. Two pertinent examples come from *Waiting for Godot* by Samuel Beckett and *Les chaises* by Eugene Ionesco. In both cases, the tree and the chair, respectively, create spatial stability and mark time in a discourse that is ambiguous and apparently without direction. When the indices are props, they have a 'syntactic' function of the first order, and they guarantee the transmission of information.

Intimately linked to the diegetic function of the index, then, is the communicative function which ensures the transmission of the theatre message. This function provides a context for the senders of the signified, thereby creating an enunciative situation which agrees with the dramatic situation. The transmission of the message and the expression of utterances are also mediated by the theatre object (the set, music, lighting and other elements of the stage production that can be essential to the articulation and comprehension of the message). Some performance texts make use of spatial and temporal ambiguity - take for example the production of *Antonio, Nosé, Isidoro y Domingo* by the young Chilean author/director, Mauricio Pesutic (Teatro Ictus, Santiago de Chile, 1984). The stage space and the main prop, a sort of tri-pyramidal staircase a little more than a metre high, are the only indicators of stability orienting the discourse (other than certain reiterative sounds and lighting).

At the same time, as we saw in chapter I, discourse is fundamental in its function as diegetic *index*. Bits and pieces of discourse are always being connected and reconnected to other bits and pieces that emerge in the narrative syntagm. An exemplary case is that of *Hamlet*, a story made up of a series of parallel indexical discourses that all eventually develop to their ultimate consequences.

2) Gestural Index

The geste, as Ubersfeld has stated, has a dual nature: on the one hand, "it is the icon of a geste in the world since it is *recognized* as such and such a geste, but it can also be the icon of an element of the world which the geste 'describes' or evoques", and on the other hand, "the geste is the *index* of a behaviour, of a sentiment, of a relation with others, of an invisible reality".[51] In my opinion, *gesturality* functions dialectically: there is a coming and going between the word and gesture. A gesture can precede discourse that may then explain or corroborate this gesture, or conversely a word can be accompanied by a gesture that intensifies its meaning. In this way, the gesture functions as a 'saying-showing' mechanism in relation to the word of the *I/you*. In *Richard II* or *The Twelfth Night* (Shakespeare/Mnouchkine, Cartoucherie de Vincennes, Théâtre du Soleil, 1982), the gesture plays an essential role in the expression of a variety of emotions, whether it occurs either along with the word or previous to the word.

An important function of the gesture is its role as convergence/opposition for the utterances. In the previously cited cases, the gesture works in convergence with the discourse, but in Brecht's epic theatre, for example, the gesture can function in contradiction to discourse, thus provoking a division between the *being* and the *appearance* of a character. The utterance may express admiration, and the gesture disdain, or the utterance might express love, and the gesture, rejection, and so on. A good example of this type of gesture as counterpoint is provided by *Los siameses* by the Argentinean playwright Griselda Gámbaro; in this case, all of the activity of the siamese twins, Lorenzo and Ignacio, is articulated in utterances which are contradicted by their gestures. The same can be said of Molière's *Tartuffe,* where the main character has a pious discourse, but whose gestures reveal the falseness of this discourse. In all of these cases, the gesture has an indexical function which is essential to discourse, even in the case of the Brechtian *Gestus*, which is not a true gesture, but a social indexical attitude.[52]

No doubt, it is obvious that, when speaking of the indexical function of the gesture in general, I have in mind predominantly the performance text, for it is in the staging of discourse and language that the gesture is seen and functions in the double dimension mentioned above: that is, it is both iconical and indexical. For this reason, the gesture index has limited textual manifestation and is limited mostly to the stage. Furthermore, as was already stated in chapter II, the dramatic text is schematic and incomplete and is completed, only when staged, for "in its 'incompleteness', its need of physical contextualization, the dramatic discourse is invariably marked by a performability, and above all, by a potential gesturality".[53] The gesture may be instrumental in the comprehension of the message, in the silence left when discourse is absent. This is the case in *Waiting for Godot* and *Fin de partie* by Beckett, in *Antonio, Nosé, Isidro y Domingo* by Mauricio Pesutic (Teatro Ictus, Santiago de Chile, 1984), in *Yes, Peut-être* by Marguerite Duras (staged by Moni Greco, Théâtre des Déchargeurs, 1982), and in the theatre of Kantor, Grotowski and Barba.

I should also consider the role of the actor's body and gestures, for once these materialize, the actor becomes the character; icon and index become confused because, in this case, the sign is reflexive, carrying out an *indexical inscription* that becomes confused with the *iconical inscription*.[54] The spectator then *recognizes* the character through the character's gestures and costume, or by the didascalia included in the discourse, before the character's name has even been pronounced. One only has to think of various Russian, English, or French productions of Hamlet to agree with what I have just been saying.

3) Spatial Index and 4) Temporal Index

These types of index are very important for all sorts of theatre, not only for mimetic theatre. These indices are apparent in what we have called the *theatre object*. Every object on the stage is, at the same time, an icon and, automatically, an index. If we consider the fact that, in the stage production, everything becomes a sign and then a sign of a sign of an object, then the set, costumes, lighting, or music will function as either spatial or temporal indices, so as to indicate the historical period, which will be matched by the costumes. In fact, in more abstract theatre, like that of Tadeusz Kantor, the index-object plays a central role. This index reveals a whole variety of elements that contextualize the discourse, as is the case in *Grand et petit* by Botho Strauss (staged by Claude Régy, Théâtre National de l'Odéon, Paris, 1983); in this production, each scene depends very much on the index to spatialize and temporalize the discourse and dramatic situations.

The indexization of space and time thus defined permeates certain dramatic and performance texts in a special way. For example, in the opening scene of *Death of a Salesman* by Arthur Miller: "The kitchen at centre seems actual enough, for there is a kitchen table with three chairs, and a refrigerator".[55] Or in *The Straw* by Eugene O'Neill: "The kitchen of the Coarmody home on the outskirts of a manufacturing town in Connecticut.... Four cane-bottomed chairs are pushed under the table. The floor is partially covered by linoleum strips".[56] The spatialization-temporalization can be done in different ways in theatre: by the presence of objects or by allusion to these objects. For example, lighting can indicate a change of spatial or temporal state, as was done in the production of *King Lear* by I. Bergman (Tivoli, Barcelona, 1985; Odéon, Paris, 1984). The spatial-temporal index does not only fill a 'mimetic' (evocative) function; it also allows for contextual and spatial changes within fiction that would otherwise be very confusing for the spectator. In fact, one of the main tasks of every theatre director is to solve problems related to space and time, and these can only be dealt with indexically.

5) Social Index

The social index works by means of a mixture of gestural and discursive indices with the object. For example, an actor's gestures may consist of a coded gesturality from a different place, as is the case in *Ubú roi* by Anton Vitez (Chaillot, Paris, 1985), in which the gestures, furniture and costumes suggest that the characters are of the high bourgeoisie, while this is contrasted by scatological scenes that discredit their status as a wealthy, 'upper' class. This sort of index immediately sets the social surroundings in which a production/text is inscribed. In *Tres tristes tigres* by the Chilean playwright Alejandro Sieveking, the following can be read at the beginning of the first act: "An apartment in a building in the centre of Santiago, modern and elegant ... There are prints of good paintings on the walls. The furniture is of good quality, but there is a lack of unity in the style which betrays the ignorance of the owner who, evidently, has gone to some trouble to create an atmosphere of distinction".[57] The case of *Purple Dust* by Sean O'Casey is similar: "A wide, deep, gloomy room that was once part of the assembly or living room of a Tudor-Elizabethan mansion. The floor is paved with broad black and dull red flagstone. The walls are timbered with oak beams, and beams of the same wood criss-cross each other".[58] Even in plays where almost no overt information about the class status or social profile of the characters is given, this has to appear in some way in the production, and it often derives from the social dimension - the acting and dialogue of the characters. The appearance of this index depends a lot on the type of theatre. For example, in the theatre of the absurd, this dimension is secondary or non-existent as compared to the metaphysical or philosophical aspect of the text/representation.

6) Environmental Index

Finally, the environmental index is the index having to do with the affective and emotive part of theatre. For example, both music and lighting can indicate sad or happy states of being, or indicate the passage from reality to a dream world, without any linguistic mediation. In the production of *Hamlet* done by Anton Vitez (Chaillot, Paris, 1983), the play takes place in the dark, indicating the somber and tragic nature of its events. Special lighting was used each time the ghost of Hamlet's father appeared, so that it looked as if he was rising from the depths of the Earth and his gestures were in slow motion. The same can be said of the production of *La buena alma de Sechuan*, done by Giorgio Strehler (Teatro Piccolo de Milano, Théâtre Saint-Martin, 1982), in which the stage was a round, revolving surface, which was almost empty, gray, and covered with a layer of water. This created a sense of alienation which was accentuated by the robot-like gestural movements of the characters and by their computer-like discourse.

Environmental deixis is not limited to lighting, gesturality, costumes, music, etc. The theatre object can also have this deictic function. For example, in *Flores de papel* by the Chilean playwright Egon Wolff, the degradation of the physical space in Eva's apartment is a response to psychological degradation and this is deictically ostentated in the gradual deterioration of the furniture, walls and other objects. Costumes can also act as a sign-symbol of demoralization and breakdown, as is the case in this play, and in *Heroica de Buenos Aires* by the Argentinean playwright Osvaldo Dragún.

Throughout this detailed consideration of how the index works in theatre, I have observed how it is central to the function and to the intelligibility of theatre discourse. The theatre index is also specific to theatrical practice (textual and on stage). This unique use of index is perhaps one of the more specific features of theatre.

C) *Symbolic Function*

The symbolic function of the sign is mainly pragmatic because the symbol establishes direct contact with the spectator. This is because the relationship between the symbol and the symbolized object is arbitrary, and therefore the spectator must create a relationship not present beforehand, as is the case for the icon or the index. Of course, symbols are also culturally encoded (the flag signifies 'country' or 'nation'); but because of the very nature of the theatre performance (its ephemeral dimension and the constant creation and production of symbols), in each new production, the cultural code does not help us *to read* the symbols. The symbolic reading done by the spectator is always *in situ,* and works by the accumulation, development and reiteration of the same signifier (visual or verbal) or of a variety of signifiers that provide a common signified for the production. The symbol operates solely by means of connotation, unlike the icon and index which work through denotation. This arbitrariness is often extreme, as in the theatre of the 1920's and 1930's, and can only be reproduced and inter-connected as it relates to the totality of the signs produced on the stage: for example, the theatre of abstraction of Oskar Schlemmer, Bauhaus Theatre and Italian Futurist Theatre.[59] The main problem of theatre symbolization is the distance between the sign and its referent. Whereas this distance is insignificant in the case of the icon (because it is mimetic), and existential (contiguous, metonymic) in the case of the index, for the symbol, the distance is enormous, and its 'correct' interpretation or reading depends dialectically on the way the symbolic sign is produced and on the competence of the spectators.

At this point, it is time to formulate a distinction between visual and verbal symbols so as to analyze how symbolization occurs in the theatre performance.

1) Visual Symbols

In their pragmatic function, symbols are primarily visual and secondarily verbal. The actor's body and the body of the character he/she is playing can both become a symbol. The body of the actor can be symbolically inscribed, that is, it can connote a meaning that transcends its purely iconic dimension. For example, many characters from Greek theatre (Oedipus), European theatre (Segismundo, Tartuffe, Hamlet), and from modern theatre (Mother Courage, Ubu, Willy Loman) can be considered universal symbols. Because of the mode of presentation of the symbol (that accompanies the stage production), the symbol's connotation may be oriented in a certain way, for example, Oedipus may act as a symbol of incest in one production and in another, as a symbol of humanity's pride and final fall. Many of Molière's characters, like Tartuffe and the Avare, are highly coded types that symbolize hypocrisy and avarice.

The character's body can, in itself, symbolize various general aspects of humanity, stripped of all narrative elements. Wladimir Krysinski points out that in

Grotowski's work (as in that of Tadeusz Kantor and Eugenio Barba): "The body is symbolic to the extent that on the stage it becomes a machine producing signs which invoke the collective, cosmological and universal thematics of man".[60] In the productions done by Kantor, Barba, and Grotowski, the word has been almost eliminated: only body movement exists, repeating various rhythms and gestures that evolve on the stage. In these productions, it is the actor's body that produces the symbol in an accumulative and reiterative way.

As well as the actor's body, the theatre object also plays an important role in the production of symbolic signs. Even the empty space of *Waiting for Godot* is part of this, because it suits the message of the theatre of the absurd: this very emptiness is already a symbol of solitude and alienation. In some productions, certain objects become symbols: the drapes at the back of the stage in Ariane Mnouchkine's productions, the crown in *Richard II*, or the paper serviettes that Moncho makes in *Alanos en la azotea* by the Chilean playwright Egon Wolff, are symbols of solitude, decline, or poverty, respectively. In Tadeusz Kantor's theatre of death, for example, or in *Où sont les neiges d'antan,* the skeleton on stage becomes a symbol complementary to the constant reiterative movement of the actors, and it means that death is in vigil and awaits its victims.

2) Verbal Symbols

The verbal symbol comes from the use of language, which, through repetition of certain utterances, communicates or connotes meaning transcending the first, purely denotative level. For example, in *Antonio, Nosé, Isidro y Domingo* by the Chilean playwright Mauricio Pesutic, the slow, repetitive movements of the actors are accompanied by highly poetic and metaphoric language. The only way to understand the message is to let the utterances accumulate and to link them to the gestures and movements. Only at the end of the performance a concretization becomes clear, one that is some what different from what actually "seen" during the performance. The same can be said of the theatre of Genet or of García Lorca. In plays like *Bodas de sangre*, *La casa de Bernarda Alba* or *Les bonnes*, the language is highly metaphoric, which this forces the spectator to look for the hidden connotation.

Music, even sound, can play a symbolic role. However, this means of symbolizing is much more complex than visual means. In general, the way music and other sounds function is to support the action, but in other cases, it has its own function. One only has to think of the wails emitted by the actors in Kantor's *Où sont les neiges d'antan?* or in *Yes, peut-être* by Duras. Sound, along with gestures, is used in *El asesinato de X* by the Argentinean group Libre Teatro Libre. In this play, the language is veiled and the mechanical actions of the characters are, in some situations more symbolic than iconic or indexical. In fact, the characters' birth and their detachment from machinery is expressed through their breathing which slowly increases and grows in intensity, then decreases only to increase once again.[61] The use of music and sounds, however, is more often indexical or iconic than symbolic.

This rather detailed systematization of theatre semiosis as it relates to the three basic signs reveals the complexity involved in an analysis of stage production. Considering the exact role of the signs has not only helped to clarify the process of theatre semiosis, but has also, I hope, provided practical tools for the analysis of the theatre performance, which is particularly ephemeral, fortuitous and heterogeneous, due to its great diversity of substances of form.

V. THEATRE REFERENTIALITY

One element that is closely linked to theatre semiosis is referentiality, or, in other words, theatre's way of referring. I have touched on this problem throughout this chapter, especially when referring to the specific nature of the theatre sign and when discussing the icon. The problem of theatre referentiality is complex, for, on the one hand, there is the material presence of real objects and the actors' bodies, and, on the other hand, the fact that everything on the stage is fiction, a sign of something else that can have different referents (textual or socio-historical). The notions of referent and reference denote and connote many things, and thus it would be wise to consider these two notions, however briefly, so as to have a solid conceptual base before discussing theatre referentiality.

A) *Referent/Reference*

In general terms we can say that the referent is the real, extra-linguistic object (ex. the HOUSE) to which the reference or signified (meaning - house) refers by means of the signifying sign (*house*). In Saussurian terms, the acoustic or graphic image '*house*' expresses the concept 'house'. Nevertheless, the referent HOUSE is a generic abstraction which refers to a variety of objects called HOUSE.[62] This reference is the relationship that exists between words and objects, events or qualities that the words represent.

Gottlob Frege has pointed out an important distinction in his discussion of *meaning, denotation* and *representation*.[63] Every sign may have the same denotation (*Bedeutung*), but not the same meaning (*Sinn*); and a denotation may be expressed with different signs. For example:

(sign)		(meaning)
morning star		morning star
	(denotation)	
	Venus	
(sign)		(meaning)
evening star		evening star

The two expressions are two signs of the same denotation (Venus), but they have different meanings. On the other hand, the representation made of a sign is unique, even though it may be understood by two different people in the same way, for every representation is subjective and individual. Meaning, however, is social, and is part of language. At the same time, the same representation is not always associated with the same meaning, because this, too, is subjective. This difference that Frege establishes follows from the "mode of denotation of the object",[64] for: "The difference persists, nevertheless, between meaning and representation; albeit only in the form in which they are linked to the word. There is nothing to prevent several individuals from grasping the same meaning; but they cannot have the same representation".[65] Thus, according to Frege, meaning is established as follows:

    denotation = object   meaning (social)

    Sign = name   representation (individual)

This model is important for my purposes, for theatre semiosis operates more by representation than by any other method. The sign refers to an object (its denotation), and the denotation has a meaning (social); but at the same time, there is an individual interpretation or meaning. In theatre the theatre object refers to itself simply because it is on-stage, but it also refers to a real object; these are 'equal' in denotation although they are not equal in their material nature and properties. Other components of the performance, the scenography and the discourse all pass through this process of *representation*, including music, lighting, sounds, descriptions, characters' comments, and so on.[66]

From these comments, I can see that the referent is the object to which signs refer. This object may or may not exist: it might have a real existence in the exterior world or it might simply be an object of discourse, having an existence in the universe of the discourse with *zero denotation*.[67] For example, the term *chair* has a real denotation in the exterior world, whereas *unicorn* has only a fictive one; but nevertheless both terms denote. One denotes a material object and the other, an imaginary object, as one can see from the Gobelin tapestries of Cluny in Paris.

B) *Theatre Referentiality*

The entire problem of theatre referentiality resides in the dual nature of the theatre performance to which Roland Barthes has accurately referred as "*the effect of the real*".[68] This effect of the real or reality consists of the fact that the performance *stages a referent* or that it fabricates and constructs a real context on the stage because the objects, words and actors have a true, material existence. On the other hand, however, these referents are not real because they are signs of signs of what is being represented: the objects represent a time and a space, connective words the word comes from the dramatic text and is fiction, and the actor is a character.

Therefore, everything on-stage is not considered real (despite its material qualities), but is considered, rather, as a sign that refers to reality. Curiously, in theatre, a 'de-realization' of what is seen and heard occurs. On the one hand, this process presents itself as real, and, on the other, it negates this reality. This is what Anne Ubersfeld has called *denegation*; as indicated in chapter I, it consists of the process by which theatre presents itself as something real, but at the same time *says* that it is a sign, a simulacrum, an illusion.[69] In theatre, everything appears to be saying 'what is on the stage is a lie, but is fooling us into believing it is true'.

1) Denegation

Denegation is the very essence of theatre. It can work in two ways: a) by means of mimetic illusion (the iconic sign refers directly to the reality - this is 'realist' theatre) or; b) by means of rupture with mimesis (the sign refers to itself - non-realist theatre). These two forms of denegation constitute two different theatre practices. The first tries to reproduce a mould of reality; but, paradoxically and indirectly, it is clearly theatre, fiction. The process of denegation here does not function from what is iconized, but from everything involved in the performance: the stage-theatre hall division (darkness-light), the changes in the scenography, the presence of actors whose names are known (Hamlet: Fontana, Richard II: Bigot, Willy Loman: Hoffman), etc. In a word, all the elements put together in view of creating similitude are also the signs that reveal their artifice and fabrication. For example, in the staging of an archeological museum in *La pregunta perdida* by Joan Brossa (produced by Hermann Bobbín, Barcelona, 1985), the factual ostentatious reproduction of the museum produces the effect of denegation. The characters actually drink and eat and this creates a feeling of distance in the audience which in turn provokes an effect opposite to the one the production was ostensibly seeking. This is because the spectator 'de-realizes' the object, translating it into a sign of something that he/she does not have to accept as a real sign, because whatever is on the stage is a sign of a sign of an object.

The other form of denegation is the sort of reproduction that declares itself as artificial, fictive and theatrical. Every form of stage practice, from the beginning of the twentieth century until today, has been defined by a recuperation of the properly theatrical, of the playful ostentation. One only has to think of Artaud or Brecht. Brechtian theatre is based on theatricality and the reflexive nature of the sign that actually creates itself. The distance effect caused by the characters (imitating but not incarnating, speaking in quotes), by other components of the production (lighting, film projections, etc.), and even by the story structure (fragmented, autonomous scenes) all inform us that 'we are in the theatre'. In non-illusionist theatre, what is most real and fundamental is the message and playfulness, and not the referential illusion.[70] An exemplary case is that of *Commedia dell'Arte*, where the playfulness and imitation of certain social types is what has defined this stage practice as one of the most *theatrical* theatre forms in the history of theatre.

In the end, denegation can be explained and defined by what has sometimes been called the "referential real, a real that is transformed into a sign" (Ubersfeld)[71] or the "referential illusion, sign that is transformed into reality" (Pavis).[72] The position Ubersfeld adopts on this point is two-fold: on the one hand, the stage production is something real, something which is physically present and which refers to reality, and on the other, this reality is transformed into a sign.[73] Patrice Pavis' view, however, seems more precise. He argues that the process is the opposite: the performance sign presents itself as real in the stage production, when in fact it is not. It creates a referential illusion, or rather, a simulacrum of a referent, and this is exactly what is being staged. A sort of *simulation* occurs which can never be confused with exterior reality, as realist as the production may be.

2) The Theatre Referent

The complexity of the theatre referent is determined by the referential multiplicity that exists in the theatre performance. There are at least three types of referent that occur in the stage production: a) the text the stage production is staging; b) the stage as its own referent; c) the exterior world.

a) Stage Production/Text

In the first case, the performance has as its referent *the dramatic text* being staged, and it shows itself mainly through words in the form of dialogue set in a given situation, that is, in a fictive world whose referent is the text (the textual referent). In this way, a first referent would be the fictive word. For example, every reader familiar with *Hamlet* or *Waiting for Godot* has this text in mind and contrasts or compares it to the performance text. The reader, therefore, does refer to the dramatic text as a first referent.

b) Stage Production/Stage Production

In the second case, the textual referent is generally accompanied by a stage referent consisting of the set, the characters/actors, the costumes, etc. The world inscribed in the textual referent is iconized as a visual or stage referent that contextualizes the discourse and creates a referential context, thus creating a referential simulacrum. This stage referent functions automatically because there is no transcription of the text; rather, it is created each time the same text is produced stage. Whereas the textual referent is invariable because it is set by the dramatic text, the stage referent is always new, never the same. Thus, the spectator in the audience has as referent the actual stage, for there are objects to which he/she may refer - concrete, visible, comprehensible signs.

c) **Stage Production/Exterior World**

In the third case, the stage referent refers to the exterior world, for this referent *represents*, or has staged, sign referents that have a real existence in the world and that could be called a *real referent*. This is why I disagree with André Guimbretière when he claims that "The referent is *that about which something is said* in the discourse, *that with regard to which* the speech act is carried out; and not what is said in the discourse, which is properly speaking the signified".[74] Signs in discourse never exist isolated from communication, and signs are the very means by which people relate to the world. The stage referent functions as an icon (visual and verbal) of the exterior world.

As for the first and third points, there are various things I should highlight and explain. A problem arises as a result of the world signified by the textual referent (and also by the stage referent). This is because the referent's status as fiction can vary depending on whether the referent of the world is based on a reality that has truly existed or whether this world is strictly fictive. We do not wish to discuss fiction here but rather to identify the differences that exist in the way of denoting what is fiction. If a dramatic or performance text has as referent a past reality (a historical referent) or a contemporary reality (a current referent), or if, in fact, it is an imaginary reality, then there are two ways of denoting fiction. In the first case, the fact is that there is a historical/contemporary reality that is transformed into fiction and is altered in such a way as not to impede the reality from being considered as real. In the second case, if it is pure fiction, that is, a DT or PT that is not based on an existing reality, then it is a fictive referent.

The following example illustrates what I have been saying. Andrés Lizáragga's play *Santa Juana de América*[75] takes a historic fact from Latin American history ("From 1809 until 1925 great liberation movements made their presence felt in High Peru. They were, perhaps, those who had the most popular roots in the bloody Indoamerican struggle which gave us our independence from Spain ... and this is the story of some of their actors". Epigraph to the play). This history is projected into the present. Hence, the referentiality of these texts is highly complex: the performance has as referent the dramatic text, and at the same time it creates its own referent in the stage production, which makes reference to the outside world (through iconization). It also has a dual referentiality - historical and current - by means of the discourse. On the one hand, the performance refers to the situation of the fight for the land during Latin American Independence, and on the other hand, it refers to the present-day situation of the peasant, showing that the oppressive situation of the past and present is one and the same (the character Indalecio says: "The war is not over!... The war is not over, my lieutenant colonel...! No!).[76]

After this long discussion, perhaps I have only pointed out the obvious. At the same time, however, the highly complex signification systems of the theatre semiotization process has been made more explicit. Every semiotics researcher trying to puzzle out and explain the production of meaning in theatre needs a metalanguage to describe the complexity inherent to this particular form of semiotics I call theatre.

1 word 2 tone	pronounced text	actor	auditive signs	time	auditive signs (actor)
3 mime 4 geste 5 movement	corporal expression			space and time	visual signs (actor)
6 make-up 7 hairdo 8 costumes	actor's corporal appearance		visual signs	space	
9 props 10 set 11 lighting	aspect of the stage	outside the actor		space and time	visual signs (outside the actor)
12 music 13 noise	non-articulated sound effects		auditive signs	time	auditive signs (outside the actor)

ENDNOTES
CHAPTER III

1. "Le signe au théâtre", *Diogène*, 61 (1968), 59-90.

2. *Collected Papers of Charles Sanders Peirce*. Volume V. *Pragmatism and Pragmaticism*. Edited by Charles Hartshorne and Paul Weiss. (Cambridge: Harvard University Press, 1934), p. 332.

3. "Foundations of the Theory of Signs", in *Foundations of the Unity of Science*, Vol. I, Nos. 1-10. Third printing (Chicago and London: The University of Chicago Press, 1971), pp. 79-84.

4. *Problèmes de sémiologie théâtrale* (Montréal: Presses de l'Université de Québec, 1976), p. 5 (our translation).

5. "Semiotics of Theatrical Performance", *The Drama Review*, XXI, 1 (March 1977), 112 and "Elementos preteatrales de una semiótica del teatro", in *Semiología del teatro*. José Maria Díez Borque and Luciano García Lorenzo, editors (Barcelona: Editorial Planeta, 1975), pp. 93-102; also J. Honzl's "Dynamics of the Sign in the Theatre", in *Semiotics of Art*, Prague School Contributions, edited by Ladislav Matejka and Irwin R. Titunik (Cambridge, Mass.: and London, England: The MIT Press, 1976), pp. 74-93 and "La mobilité du signe théâtral", *Travail théâtral*, 4 (1971), 5-20.

6. *Logical Investigations*, Vol. II, Investigation I, "Expression and Meaning". Translated by J.N.Finlay (New York: The Humanities Press, 1970), p. 269.

7. *The Meaning of Meaning* (New York: Harcourt, Brace and World, 1923), p. 2.

8. *Collected Papers of Charles Sanders Peirce*, vol. II. *Elements of Logic*. Edited by Charles Hartshorne and Paul Weiss. (Cambridge: Harvard University Press, 1932), p. 169.

9. *Collected Papers of Charles Sanders Peirce*, vol. I. *Principles of Philosophy*. Edited by Charles Hartshorne and Paul Weiss. (Cambridge: Harvard University Press, 1931), p. 285.

10. *Collected Papers of Charles Sanders Peirce*, vol. II, p. 142.

11. For more on the theatre of Josef Svoboda, see the book by Denis Bablet, *Svoboda* (Lausanne: Editions L'Age d'Homme, 1970).

12. *Collected Papers of Charles Sanders Peirce*, vol. II, p. 143.

13. "The *intension* of a concept consists of the qualities or properties which go to make up the concept. The *extension* of a concept consists of the things which fall under the concept; or acccording to another definition, the *extension* of the concept consists of the concepts which are subsumed under it". Dagobert Runes, editor, *Dicionary of Philosophy* (New Jersey: Littlefield, Adams, 1962), p. 147-148. See also Rudolf Carnap, *Meaning and Necessity*, second edition (Chicago and London: The University of Chicago Press, 1956), pp. 23-31.

14. *Collected Papers of Charles Sanders Peirce*, vol. II, p. 144.

15. See also: Timothy J. Reiss, "Peirce, Frege, la verité, le tiers inclus et le champs pratiqué", *Langages*, 58 (1980), 103-127.

16. See the previously quoted articles by Kowzan, "Le signe au théâtre", 63, and the article by Jindrich Honzl, "La mobilité du signe théâtral", 5-20.

17. See the table at the end of this chapter for what Kowzan calls "systems of signs in the theatre". It comes from "Le signe au théâtre", 83.

18. "Les signes du théâtre", *Poétique*, 8 (1971), 529 (our translation).

19. See for example, Kowzan's "Le signe au théâtre", 64.

20. "Semiotics of Theatrical Performance", 110-113.

21. *Ibid.*, p. 111.

22. According to Ubersfeld: "Everything on the stage thereby acquires *ipso facto* the character of an object: the theatre object is a thing, taken up and recomposed by the theatrical activity: everything that is on the stage, whether it be deposited there by chance, becomes a signifier simply by its presence in the universe of the stage, a universe recomposed by the artistic work of the stage", *L'école du spectateur. Lire le théâtre 2* (Paris: Editions Sociales, 1981), p. 126 (our translation). See also Maryvonne Saison, "Les objets dans la création théâtrale", *Revue de métaphysique et de morale, LXXIX*, 1 (janvier-mars 1974), 253-268, and Anne Ubersfeld, *Lire le théâtre* (Paris: Editions Sociales, 1982), pp. 194-202.

23. For more on the 'contamination' of theatre by the media of communication and their inter-relationships, see the excellent article by Patrice Pavis, "El teatro y los medios de comunicación: especificidad e interferencia", *Gestos*, 1 (avril 1986), 11-24.

24. "La mobilité du signe théâtral", *Travail théâtral*, 4 (1971), 16 (our translation). See also Gianfranco Bettetini, *Produzione del senso e messa in scena* (Milano: Studi Bompiani, 1975).

25. Michel Corvin states that "Redundance is then much more a condition *sine qua non* of the transmission of the message than a principle of the production of meaning". "La redondance du signe dans le fonctionnement théâtral", *Degrés*, sixième année, 13 (printemps 1980), c20 (our translation).

26. In *Teatro chileno contemporáneo* (Santiago, Chile: Editorial Andrés Bello, 1982), pp. 127-184. [It includes *El tony chico* by Luis Alberto Heiremans, pp. 11-84 and *El árbol Pepe* by Fernando Debesa, pp. 83-126].

27. For more on the theatre of Tadeusz Kantor, see *Le théâtre de la mort*, texts compiled and presented by Denis Bablet (Lausanne: Editions L'Age d'Homme, 1977).

28. "La redondance du signe dans le fonctionnement théâtral", c22 (our translation).

29. *Collected Papers of Charles Sanders Peirce*, vol. II, p. 157.

30. For a general view of the icon, see the study by Umberto Eco, "Pour une reformulation de concept de signe iconique: Les modes de production sémiotique", *Communications*, 9 (1978), 141-191, and "Sémiologie des messages visuels", *Communications*, 15 (1970), 11-51.

31. *Collected Papers of Charles Sanders Peirce*. Volume II. *Elements of Logic*, p. 170 and 143.

32. *Ibid.*, p. 160.

33. *Ibid.*, p. 143.

34. *Ibid.*, p. 143.

35. *Ibid.*, pp. 165 and 143, respectively.

36. On replica, see Umberto Eco, "Pour une reformulation du concept de signe iconique", *Communications*, 9 (1978), 145-146.

37. *Collected Papers of Charles Sanders Peirce*, vol. II, p. 169.

38. On the icon, the index and the symbol in theatre, see Patrice Pavis, *Problèmes de sémiologie théâtrale*, pp. 55-64; "Théorie du théâtre et sémiologie: sphère de l'objet et sphère de l'homme", *Semiotica*, XVI, 1 (1976), 45-86; "Représentation, mise en scène, mise en signe", *The Canadian Journal of Research in Semiotics*, IV, 1 (Fall 1976), 63-86.

39. "Pour une reformulation du concept de signe inconique", 153 (our translation).

40. For Umberto Eco: "A process of *recognition* takes place when a given object or event, produced by nature or through human action (intentionally or unintentionally), a fact among facts, is interpreted by a receiver as the expression of a given content, be it a function of a correlation already predicted by a code, or a function of a correlation established directly by the receiver. This act of recognition permits the identification of the object in terms of *imprint, symptom or index*". *Ibid.*, p. 167 (our translation).

41. *Ibid.*, p. 160 (our translation). According to Eco: "We can define the *iconic code* as a system of graphic means of perceptive units and codified cultural units, or the pertinent units of a semantic system which results from a codification of previous perceptive experience". *Ibid.*, p. 161 (our translation).

42. *Ibid.*, p. 161.

43. According to W. Krysinski, "With semiosis thus installed in narrative and representational theatre, it follows that the inscription, or if one prefers, the textualization of the body in this theatre is of a triple nature: iconic, indexical and symbolic". "Semiotics Modalities of the Body in Modern Theatre", *Poetics Today*, II, 3 (Spring 1981), 147. See also Anne Marie Gourdon, editor, *Formation du comédien: Les voies de la création théâtrale*, vol. IX, (Paris: Editions du Centre National de la Recherche Scientifique, 1981); Wladimir Krysinski, "El cuerpo en cuanto signo y su significado en el teatro moderno: De Evreïnoff y Craig a Artaud y Grotowski", *Revista Canadiense de Estudios Hispánicos*, VII, 1 (Fall 1982), 19-38; Anne Ubersfeld, *L'école du spectateur*, pp. 165-238; and Jacky Martin, "Ostention et communication théâtrale", *Littérature*, 53 (1984), 119-126.

44. On these two types of theatre, see *The Director and the Stage* (London: Methuen, 1982), by Edward Braun.

45. For information on Craig's productions see Edward Braun's book, *The Director and the Stage*, pp. 77-94; and on Craig's views on theatre, see his book *The Theatre Advancing* (New York: Arno Press, 1979) and *On the Art of the Theatre* (New York and London: Heinemann Educational Books, 1980).

46. "Semiotics of Folk Theatre", in *Semiotics of Art*, Prague School Contributions, edited by Ladislav Matejka and Irwin R. Titunik (Cambridge, Mass. and London: The MIT Press, 1976), p. 35.

47. See Artaud's view on *Los Cenci* in "Artaud's Theatre of Cruelty", in *The Director and the Stage* by E. Braun, pp. 191-200.

48. "The Hierarchy of Dramatic Devices", in *Semiotics of Art*, p. 124.

49. (La Habana, Cuba: Casa de las Américas, 1975), p. 85 (our translation).

50. This is the function that Patrice Pavis attributes to the index in *Problèmes de sémiologie théâtrale*, pp. 55-64; and "Théorie du théâtre et sémiologie: sphère de l'objet et sphère de l'homme", 45-86 and "Représentation, mise en scène, mise en signe", 63-86.

51. *L'école du spectateur*, p. 197 (our translation). See also the excellent articles on geste by Patrice Pavis, in *Voix et images de la scène* (Lille: Presses Universitaires de Lille, 1982), pp. 83-92.

52. See "Mise au point sur le *Gestus*", by Patrice Pavis in *Voix et images de la scène*, pp. 83-92.

53. Keir Elam, *The Semiotics of Theatre and Drama* (London and New York: Methuen, 1980), p. 142.

54. See Wladimir Krysinski, "Semiotics Modalities of the Body in Modern Theatre", p. 147.

55. (New York: The Viking Press, 1972), p. 11.

56. (New York: Vintage Books, 1951), p. 57.

57. (Santiago, Chile: Editorial Universitaria, 1974), p. 76 (our translation).

58. (London: MacMillan London, 1980), p. 119.

59. See Oskar Schlemmer, *Théâtre et abstraction*. Translation, preface and comments by Eric Michaud (Lausanne: Editions L'Age d'Homme, 1978); Eric Michaud, *Théâtre au Bauhaus* (Lausanne: Editions L'Age d'Homme, 1978); Giovanni Lista, editor, *Théâtre futuriste italien*, vol. I and II (Lausanne: Editions L'Age d'Homme, 1976).

60. "Semiotics Modalities of the Body in Modern Theatre", 158. See also *Towards a Poor Theatre* (New York: Simon and Schuster), by Jerzy Grotowski.

61. For further information on this play, see Fernando de Toro, *Brecht en el teatro hispanoamericano contemporáneo* (Buenos Aires: Editorial Galerna, 1987), pp. 157-159.

62. See Rudolf Carnap, *Meaning and Necessity*.

63. *Ecrits logiques et philosophiques*. Translation and introduction by Claude Imbert (Paris: Editions de Seuil, 1971), pp. 103-106.

64. *Ibid.*, p. 106.

65. *Ibid.*, p. 106 (our translation).

66. Frege's distinction is similar to the one made by other language theoreticians. For example, Benveniste claims: "language carries reference to the world of objects, both globally, in its complete utterances, in the form of sentences, which relate to concrete and specific situations, and in the form of inferior units which relate to general or particular 'objects', taken from experience or forged by linguistic convention. Thus, each utterance, and each term of the utterance, has a referent of which knowledge is implied by the native use of the language". "Les niveaux d'analyse linguistique", in *Problèmes de linguistique générale, I* (Paris: Editions Gallimard, 1966), p. 128 (our translation). Wittgenstein uses the concepts of *use* and *meaning*, establishing a dual notion of use: on the one hand, it is employment (*Verwendung*) - effective and observable practice, and on the other, it is use (*Sprachgebrauch*) -normative and socially coded practice. See *Philosophical Investigations*, second edition, translation by G.E.M. Anscombe (Oxford: Blackwell, 1958).

67. C.I. Lewis notes that the *denotation* of a term is the class of all real or existing things to which this term correctly applies and a term that does not name anything has a *zero denotation*. "The Modes of Meaning" in *Semantics and the Philosophy of Language*. Leonard Linsky, ed. (Champaign: University of Illinois Press, 1969), p. 53.

68. "L'effet du réel", *Communications*, 11 (1968), 84-89 (our translation).

69. *Lire le théâtre*, pp. 46-50, *L'école du spectateur*, pp. 43-51 and 311-318, and "Notes sur la dénégation théâtrale", in *La relation théâtrale*, texts compiled by Régis Durand (Lille: Presses Universitaires de Lille, 1980), pp. 11-26.

70. Artaud claims that: "The theare will never find itself again-i.e., constitute a means of true illusion-except by furnishing the spectator with the truthful precipitates of dreams, in which his taste for crime, his erotic obssesions, his savagery, his chimeras, his utopian sense of life and matter, even his cannibalism, pour out, on a level not counterfeit and illusory, but interior". *The Theatre and Its Double*. Translated from the French by Mary Caroline Richards (New York: Grove Press, 1958), p. 92.

71. *L'école du spectateur*, pp. 38-39.

72. *Voix et images de la scène*, pp. 15-17.

73. *Lire le théâtre*, pp. 27-37 and "Sur le signe théâtral et son référent", *Travail théâtral*, 31 (avril-juin 1978), 120-123.

74. "Approche du référent", *Degrés*, première année, 3 (juillet 1973), f7 (our translation).

75. See Fernando de Toro, "Ideología y teatro épico en *Santa Juana de América*", *Latin American Theatre Review*, XIV, 1 (Fall 1980), 55-64; and "El teatro épico hispanoamericano: estructuras de convergencia", *Ibero-Americana*, XIX-XX, 2-3 (1983), 69-85.

76. *Santa Juana de América*, p. 150 (our translation).

CHAPTER IV

THEATRE RECEPTION

> Not only does the stage action influence the audience, but the audience also influences the stage action ... The audience is therefore omnipresent in the structure for stage production.
> Jan Mukařovský, *Structure, Sign and Function.*

I. RECEPTION THEORY

Theatre semiotics has been concerned with various aspects of the phenomenon of theatre for about two decades now, especially such problems as the text-performance, theatre discourse and the production of meaning, just to name a few. However, one area that remains still unexplored is that of theatre reception - with the exception of a few studies by Patrice Pavis,[1] Marco De Marinis,[2] and André Helbo,[3] who have been the most productive researchers in this area. It should be noted that the researchers of the Prague School had already done some research on theatre reception, but without formulating any complete theory or systematization.[4] The situation with respect to literature reception is quite different, given the reception theory that has been developing from Roman Ingarden[5] to the work done by the so-called School of Constance (made up of Hans-Robert Jauss, Wolfgang Iser, Wolf-Dieter Stempel)[6] to the work of Umberto Eco.[7] Perhaps one of the reasons why theatre semiotics has not dealt with this area is because of the hermeneutic nature of reception theory. This characteristic of reception has meant that reception theory has lacked rigor and thus appears to be far from semiotics. Despite this fact, it is time that semiotics integrated, or rather, incorporated reception into the very centre of semiotics, especially as it relates to theatre where the audience-stage relationship is fundamental since without an audience or spectator, the performance is obviously not possible. Hence, in this chapter, I would like to establish a theoretical and operational point of reference for theatre reception that is inspired by a few of the studies mentioned above.

Reception theory, or theatre aesthetics as it is sometimes called, takes as its main object of study the relationship between text and reader. This aesthetic did not begin with the School of Constance, as is often thought, but with Roman Ingarden and the Czechoslovakian theorists, such as Felix Vodička and Jan Mukařovský.[8] These authors are of interest for this study insofar as they provide a conceptual and theoretical base for the elaboration of a theory of theatre reception. At this point in this study, my intention is simply to discuss certain key notions as they relate to the objective of this book and to delineate some new theoretical perspectives.

A) *Places of Indetermination*

In two of his major works, *The Cognition of the Literary Work of Art* and *The Literary Work of Art*, Roman Ingarden[9] employs a series of concepts that will be central to this book: *objectivization, actualization, concretization* and the places of indetermination (*Unbestimmtheitsstellen*). The places of indetermination in the literary work are those places that are not determined by the objective strata of the narrative: they are that part of the work that the reader must complete. It is that which is not said, but is suggested, by the text. On this notion, Ingarden maintains that: "I call the aspect or part of the portrayed object which is not specifically determined by the text a 'place of indeterminacy'. Each object, person, event, etc., portrayed in the literary work of art contains a great number of places of inderterminacy, especially the descriptions of what happens to people and things".[10] These places of indetermination exist simply because it is impossible to determine all that is narrated, and thus, the reader is required either to *fill in* these places or to leave them as they are. According to Ingarden, this implies two different attitudes: either a) to leave them intact, that is, not to fill them in, or b) to fill them in, which requires going beyond what the text itself suggests.[11] The first process is difficult to carry out, for in general our reading habits encourage us to fill in these places of indetermination. In theatre, the director can, with precision, play on not *reading* the text, and leave it with the places of indetermination intact so that the audience will have to perform its own *reading* of the text. This was the case, for example, in the staging of *Hamlet* done by Anton Vitez (Chaillot, Paris, 1983). Vitez refused to make *his own* reading of the text, leaving total freedom to the spectator.[12] Ingarden attributes indetermination to the schematic nature that is characteristic of every work of art.[13] The process of filling in the places of indetermination is done by *objectivization,* then *actualization* and finally *concretization*.

B) *Objectivization*

The first step or level of the filling-in of these places of indetermination occurs through *objectivization* which consists of "the transition from the intentional states of affairs to the objects portrayed in the literary work".[14] The notion of 'states of intentional things' refers to the objectivity presented and determined by the text, while the notion of 'described objects' refers to the expansion of these objective realities as a result of imagination filling in the places. The actual objective realities are those things which make up the narrated world - persons, things, processes, events, etc. Objectivization is the extension or expansion of the objective strata of a work.

The objectivization process consists of imaginative processes that mould and complement the objective situation. Upon reading a piece of theatre, or, for that matter, a novel, a whole imaginative dimension of places comes into being: for example, the atmosphere or profiles of characters. These exist not in the text, but in the reader's imagination. This process is also present in theatre: even though, on the stage, there exists a first step in the filling-in process of objectivization, there always remains something that the spectator has to fill in, to complete.

C) *Actualization*

The various examples of objective reality, or more precisely, the process of objectivization, is mediated by the process of actualization before becoming a concretization. In my opinion, however, Ingarden's work contains a central difference. According to Ingarden: "The objectification and concretization of the objects portrayed in the literary work of art go hand in hand with the actualization and concretization of at least a goodly number of schematized aspects".[15] Here, we have both concepts clearly set apart, for while objectivization is the expansion and the *imaginative figuration*, *actualization* is the experience of these objective realities, the tested representation of a concrete form through objectivization. *Actualization* is the very *perception* of the suggested objective realities.[16] It is through the actualized aspects that "the things portrayed appear with a greater plasticity and distinctness, they become more vivid and concrete, and the reader seems to enter into direct intercourse with them".[17]

D) *Concretization*

Both objectivization and actualization are transformed into concretization. This concept appears to be used in different ways, and so, before defining my own position and use of the term, it is important to consider Ingarden's various uses. In *The Literary Work of Art*, the above concept has the following meanings:

1) concretization: interpretation ("But the very possibility that one and the same literary work can allow any number of concretizations, which frequently differ significantly from the work itself and also, in their content, differ significantly among themselves ...", p. 252).
2) concretization: perception of the work ("These concretizations are precisely what is constituted during the reading and what, in a manner of speaking, forms the mode of appearance of a work, the concrete form in which the work itself is apprehended", p. 332)
3) concretization: concretion of the schematic ("The most radical difference between a literary work and its concretizations appears in the aspect stratum. From mere preparedness [*Parathaltung*] and schematization in the work itself, aspects attain concreteness in the concretization and are raised to the level of perceptual expe-

rience [in the case of a stage play] or imaginational experience [in a reading]", p. 339). In this case, concretization would appear to be confused with objectivization and actualization.

4) concretization: manifestation of the objectivization ("The concretization of a literary work is furthermore distinguished by the fact that a truly explicit *appearance* of represented objectivities occurs only here ...", p. 341).

5) concretization: knowledge and aesthetics ("Concretizations constitute, as it were, the connecting link between the reader and the work and emerge when the reader approaches it cognitively and aesthetically", p. 352).

6) concretization: manifestation of the actualization ("the potentialities contained in the work itself ... are transformed into actualities in the concretizations", p. 337).

In *The Cognition of the Literary Work*, there are other applications:

7) concretization: filling in ("I call this complementing determination the 'concretization' of the portrayed objects. In concretization the peculiar cocreative activity of the reader comes into play. On his own initiative and with his own imagination he 'fills out' various places of indeterminacy with elements chosen from among many possible or permissible elements", p. 53).

The concept of concretization implies and includes the concepts of objectivization and actualization, and this is why there are so many uses of the term, for every interpretation-understanding-experience-apprehension of a work involves the whole process, that is, the circuit that exists because of the places of indetermination:

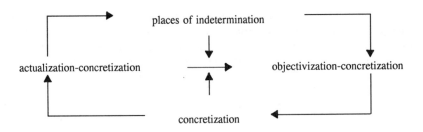

The following quote by Ingarden presents this circuit in its full complexity: "As I have already mentioned, if one wants to achieve an aesthetic apprehension of the work, one must often go far beyond what is actually contained in the objective stratum of the work in the process of objectifying the portrayed objectivities. One must 'concretize' these objects at least to a certain degree, and within boundaries set by the work itself".[18] In this way, the concept of concretization is to be understood as being broad and complex and the result of experience in all its totality.

For Ingarden, a series of concretizations constitutes the meaning of a work, the meaning of which is forever changing because every concretization is determined by the moment and the culture of an era. This point is important, for it introduces the role of the reader (spectator) as central to the production of meaning, and as a sort of co-producer of the work. This is why, when speaking of the reader, Ingarden refers to the activity of reading as a co-creative activity. Once expressed, the literary work 'lives' in a series of concretizations. Furthermore, it lives because it changes or is changed at the intervention and emergence of new concretizations.[19] Thus, the structure as well as the meaning of every work is not static, but, rather, dynamic. Ingarden contextualises concretization, and the role of the reader becomes an instrument: texts change because their respective readings-concretizations change, and this occurs because of the fact that the *social context* and its framework is altered. Every era has its own form of understanding, its own reading, its own ethical and aesthetic norms.[20] At the same time, concretizations differ radically from the work itself (its immanent meaning), mainly due to the fact that the concretization (objectivization-actualization which is subject to the social context) endows a work with a dimension that it lacks, overcoming its schematic nature. In my opinion, however, the reading of a work *is* its concretization. Ingarden seems to suggest that the work is one thing and its concretizations another, without in fact recognizing that a work without the concretizations it receives in a given moment of time, or those it has received throughout history, does not exist.

Because the concretization is dynamic, and undergoes a series of metamorphosis, it is very important for history, since our *understanding of how a work functions according to a reading process* is determined by the norms and codes of a given historico-cultural situation which conditions the concretization. Nevertheless, a word of warning is necessary: where does the concretization occur? Where is it recorded? To date, the most extensive and efficient means of accounting for concretizations lies with the critics - critics being understood in both the broad and restricted senses of the word - that is to say, in journalistic comments (magazines, newspapers, documents, radio, television) and in literary science. Only through these sources might generalizations be arrived at, for the 'critics' never postulate an implicit reader.

From a semiological point of view, Ingarden's notions and conceptualization of the *work of art* can be systematized using the terminology of Jan Mukařovský. On the one hand, there is the *work-thing* or signifier, and on the other hand there is the *aesthetic object* which possesses a signified within a given *social context*. Thus, Mukařovský states that, "the objective study of the phenomenon 'art' must regard the work of art as a sign composed of a sensitive symbol created by the artist, a 'signification' (= aesthetic object) deposited in the collective consciousness, and a relation to the thing signified, a relation which aims at the total context of social phenomena".[21] Mukařovský's conceptualization of the receptive circuit is important, for it introduces the notion of *social context as an intermediate between the notions of signifier and signified* from which signification necessarily emerges.

E) *Horizon of Expectation*

I have considered some aspects of Ingarden's work because, in my opinion, most of what has been proposed thus far in theatre aesthetics has come from him, although certain of his notions have been refined in the process. Perhaps his most important contributions are the concepts of *horizon*, *effect* (*Wirkung*), and *reception*. Whereas Jauss considers effect to be in the text, claiming it is the text that determines it and hence links it to the past of the text, he believes reception is in the present, in the reader who reads the text according to the rules of his or her present. Fundamental to this distinction is the role of the reader. For Jauss, the reader is everything and it is the dialogue between reader and text that makes literature what it is and makes it exist as it does.[22] In fact, according to Jauss, the work is nothing more than the result of the convergence of the text and its reception, and thus the work can be fully understood only in its successive historical 'concretizations'.[23] This understanding of the literary work, in which the role of the reader is favoured, is rooted and articulated (effect-reception) in questions-answers: the text gives an answer to questions put forth by the reader. The problem with this view of the role of the reader lies in the fact that ancient texts provoke questions in the reader (much less provide answers) only with great difficulty. It is more probable that the literary text is able to respond at any moment in time, but in different ways, to the questions posed throughout history.[24]

Implicit in the notions of effect and reception is the notion of horizon of expectation. This is a complex system made up of diverse elements such as aesthetic conventions, reading codes, messages the reader expects, the types of structures of given genres. Thus the horizon of expectation either responds to the aesthetic and ideological expectations of the audience at a given moment, or it does not respond to these expectations (if a rupture or change of horizon occurs). There is a sort of circular relationship between the *internal horizon* and the audience's horizon of the work, for in Jauss' view, the receiver and the reception of a work are already inscribed in this work because of its relation with previous works, that is, in the way it contains many of their norms. The notion that the reader's horizon is already in the work is the same one that Y. Lotman proposes when he claims that: "This phenomenon is bound up with the fact that any text (and especially a literary one) contains in itself what we should like to term the *image of the audience* and that this image actively affects the real audience by becoming for it a kind of normalizing code".[25] In a word, the horizon of expectation has to do with the means of reception to which the audience is accustomed.[26] The problem that arises here is that, when reading texts from the past (including those thirty years and older), the reading is done from the present, in which a contemporary horizon exists and, as Jauss seems to suggest, it is only through the fusion of present and past (or historical) horizons that meaning is produced.[27]

The concept of horizon appears to be useful insofar as each text contains a literary horizon of expectation. This is especially the case when one is dealing with a new piece that has a social or trans-subjective (or current) horizon of expectation, and this involves a certain kind of reception. In fact, in the two types of horizon mentioned above, there is a fusion of a synchronic type with a diachronic type. In this way, meaning will be created by the intersection of the reader's synchrony with the diachrony of the work. The aesthetic distance that the reader perceives is due to the mutation of the horizon (*Horizontwandel*) because of the fact that the reader possesses another horizon. One can say the same with respect to change when new pieces appear. What the reader perceives is a change of *horizon* of expectation, between the literary and the social.[28]

Perhaps, the most important factor that could be taken from the theory of reception aesthetics is the new status assigned to the reader. The unilateral relationship of text-meaning-reader, that is, the idea that the reader is located in a passive receptive role (where the text ensures its own meaning, which the reader simply *reads* in the text), is replaced by the idea that there is a dialectic articulated between text, receiver and meaning, in which the reader and the text both have a *productive* nature. It is this joint creative activity that creates the ultimate meaning of the text. This co-creative view of the production of meaning is very useful for the theatre performance, for in the theatre performance, as we will see, there exists a series of co-creators, and the process is quite a bit more complicated than in a simple reading of a text.

In summary, the reader plays an essential role in the construction of meaning of a literary (or performance) text, and this construction is made up of both the literary and the social horizon of expectation. This is where the text and the reader are inscribed in a social context which may or may not be shared (the present/history). The process of comprehension of a text is achieved through concretization, and this implies objectivization and actualization of the objective strata. The *meaning*, that is, the reception, depends in the end on the effort of the reader or readers. To be precise, one should say that to speak of readers in the abstract sense is not very useful because every text has an effect (*Wirkung*) and a reception, but these will vary depending on the audience as well as on the writer's ideological position.

One should begin with the premise that writers are historical actants of a specific practice: the practice of writing. For this reason, it is important to discuss what Jauss and other aesthetic theorists seem to have forgotten: the socio-economic class of the writer and his or her position whithin that class.[29] Let us distinguish between these two things, for belonging to a given class does not necessarily mean adopting a position whithin that class. Generally, for many Latin American writers, to belong to a class is not the same as accepting a place therein. Here I subscribe to Jacques Dubois's definition of 'class position' as

> the manner in which an individual perceives, conceives and lives his/her situation in the social field or again the way in which he/she gives values to his/her personal adventure in terms of class relations and social antagonisms. Thus, this position presupposes a dawning of awareness which is expressed as both affirmation and denial.[30]

II. THEATRE RECEPTION

In addition to the concepts presented thus far, I must include several concepts that are appropriate for theatre reception. This area, as I have already pointed out at the beginning of this chapter, is the one that needs the most elaboration, since the studies done on the subject have only just begun.

Attempting a systematization of theatre reception is a difficult task since the actual performance leaves only a few traces once it is completed - the production text, the critic's comments, interviews with the director or some other related group, comments and description of the production, photos, videos, films, and a variety of other materials.[31] None, or almost none, of these post-performance 'traces' tell us anything about the relationship that is established between the spectators and the performance, or about the interpretation or reading that the spectators make of a given perform-ance. On the other hand, almost all of the research has been done from a theoretical point of view; little research has been done on the public from an empirical perspec-tive.[32] Despite the difficulties, we can establish certain criteria for a model of theatre reception from the data provided in the actual theatrical situation.

From the moment the public begins to watch a performance, a distance, or a specific type of relationship or convention, is established. Part of the theatre space, whatever this may be, is the actual stage; the other space is the actual space occupied by the audience. This distance always exists, even in extreme cases like that of Grotowski, who brought this relationship to its limits (the extreme case is the *Happening*). Here, this relationship is paradoxical, since on the one hand it is stating, 'I am theatre', 'I am an illusion', and on the other hand, it seeks to be perceived as reality, supported by the actual voice and bodies of the actors. The theatre relationship can function by accentuating the distance, as in the case of Brecht's epic theatre (*Verfremdungseffekt*), or by decreasing the distance, as in naturalist theatre (*Einfühlung*). The form of this relationship does not matter; what is important is to show how this distance functions, and the mechanisms through which the *artefact (play-thing)* (signifier) and its aesthetic object (signified) must pass before being fully comprehended.

A) *Mode of Production and Reception*

The mode of theatrical production is very different from that of literature, for a novel is produced and consumed by individuals, which implies that there is no mediation between the producer and his or her product:

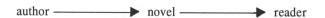

author ⟶ novel ⟶ reader

Although this process may share many extra- and intra-literary elements with theatre, I can also say that it is radically different from a strictly theatrical process:

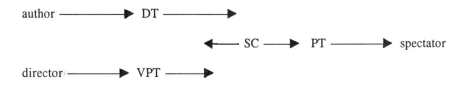

The author and the director are producers of text: the former produces the dramatic text (DT) and the latter produces both the virtual performance text (VPT) and the performance text (PT). The reception of this PT by the spectator is mediated by the social context (SC), which determines and influences the concretization. The general social context (SC) or cultural setting can be shared by both poles of the circuit, but the theatrical mode of production is mediated by everything involved in the staging, and this implies a production system. I point this out, because theatre, more than any other art, must always pay attention to reception, to the spectator to whom the work is directed, and thus the production process is fundamental and central to the creative act in theatre. The fundamental feature in the mode of theatrical production is the fact that in this mode, there exists a *double concretization* and because of this, a double *production* of meaning: one is done by the director and the other is done by the spectator.

Before providing details on this double concretization, I should briefly discuss the status of the concretized object, for it is not a question of a monocoded object. I know that the theatrical performance has a contradictory dual status: everything on stage is real yet nothing is real; that is, the material dimension of the performance is real - actors, objects, costumes, etc. - but at the same time none of these are real, because they are signs of signs and because it is fiction. Let us recall that the costumes are never the actual costumes of the specific era, but rather a sign of those costumes. This is why I could say that theatre is a semblance or a referential illusion. Therefore, from the very moment he or she assumes his/her role, the spectator is confronted with a sign that functions as a reality without actually being one. At this point, a special form of perception intervenes: on the one hand, there is the *possible world* of the dramatic universe created by the fiction, and on the other hand there is the real world to which the spectator belongs (we will return to this point). In this way, this material world to which the spectator belongs and the fiction that unfolds tend to relate to each other, and thus the fiction becomes intermingled with the world of the spectator. The referent of the work of art, or of the play as a play-thing-artefact (signifier), and the aesthetic object (signified) is created by the fiction, and this referent, once it has passed through the *social context*, can be understood due to the referential illusion it creates, for the *possible world* and the real world have links whose nature permit the actualization of both worlds through iconization, indexation and symbolization. These links are reinforced by two other components besides fiction: language and ideology. These components are *displayed* or iconized in the same way as fiction, and the form used to iconize them has a lot to do with the directorial practice; indeed, it is the next topic.

B) *Directorial Concretization*

Once it is transformed into a performance text, a dramatic text implies a directorial mediation, a first *reading*, prior to the spectator's reading. First of all, the theatre director performs a dramaturgical reading, through which the plot of the text in question, as well as its structural articulation and the ideological components that compose the structure are analyzed. Then, this reading is moulded according to the aims of the performance text structure, thereby organizing the forms of enunciation, the system of gestures, the proxemics and kinesics, the construction of characters, and, finally, the inscription of all of this into a structured space that includes various systems of expression such as the set, the music, the lighting, etc. The convergence of the dramaturgical work and the performance work results in the director's concretization, that is, in the interpretation or reading the director delivers to his or her public.

This concretization is determined by various elements that can be summarized in Patrice Pavis's notion of *metatext*.[33] The metatext should not be confused with the intertext, which has to do with the relationship of texts among themselves, for indeed the metatext is a much more elaborate concept. Metatext includes the cultural setting, or that which Marco De Marinis has called *General Cultural Context* (GCT);[34] that is to say, the metatext is composed of non-dramatic texts, the director's ideological position, his/her idea of the performance, of history and its place in the social context, and the general knowledge of both the director and of the spectator. Because of the GCT, the DT, transformed into performance text, passes through the filter of the director, who imposes in a certain way a concretization onto the public. But the relationship of the director with the text cannot lose sight of the public, to whom the performance is directed, or of the relationship of that DT with history. For example, if one has a classic text or simply a non-contemporary text, the director can either adapt this text, as was often the case in Brechtian or Artaudian works, or attempt a reconstruction of the original work. Whatever the position of the director, a guide or conductive system must be set up to allow the public to perceive and trace a direction in the performance text. This may be achieved by a number of different means: a) the conductor system could be based on the narrative path if the plot were organized in such a way that the spectator would be able to follow it without a major lapse; b) the plot could be organized around a generic path, where the very genre would itself establish a horizon of expectations, as is the case in tragedy, comedy, satire, etc.; c) the ideological route, in which the spectator could recognize certain utterances and gesticular attitudes pertaining to one ideology or another; d) the generic path could be used for the opposite effect, that is, when the genre is taken apart in order to say the opposite of that which is normally inferred by the genre, keeping only the label of the genre. For instance, the plot could be altered as well, especially in an adaptation, changing at the same time the public's horizon of expectations. I only have to think of Edward Bond's *Lear* or Jean Anouilh's *Antigone*. The same is feasible with respect to ideology, where ideologically marked dramatic texts undergo an ideological inversion in the performance text. This whole process of changing or conserving the text passes through the filter of the director and establishes itself in its concretization.

One aspect that is at times fundamental in various productions is the ambiguity that permeates the performance text. This ambiguity can proceed from the actual text or from the director, who could choose to resolve, conserve or create this ambiguity. There may exist an ambiguity that is programmed into the text, but ambiguity may also emerge from the aesthetic and ideological distance between the dramatic-performance text and the public. Examples of the above are found in the production of *Oedipus Rex* by Alain Milianti (Théâtre National de l'Odéon, Paris, 1985) and in *Hamlet* by Vitez (Chaillot, Paris, 1983). In the latter, Vitez decides not to resolve the ambiguities, and leaves it up to the public to resolve them. However, the simple fact of accentuating textual ambiguity already constitutes a decision to adopt a position, a concretization. I should point out that the *way* of structuring the signifier of a PT in relation to its signified is always mediated by the social context in which it is inscribed, and the fact that it is an ancient text has little or no bearing. Thus, from a Marxist point of view, Lope de Vega's *Fuenteovejuna* was staged in Moscow as an example of class struggle, when in fact there is simply no class struggle is not at all, nor does it have much to do with reality as it was presented.[35] Dramatic texts like *Die Heilige Johanna der Schlachthöfe, Galileo Galilei* and *Die Tage der Commune* by Brecht would be difficult to stage in a country like Chile, since any of the progressive theatre groups of that country would do a reading related to their current social context. Thus, it is important to realize that the director must always consider this social context and the ever-changing horizon of expectations. In fact, the director must often articulate historicities of either the literary and social context of the dramatic text, or of the literary and social context of the public, and its system of ideological and aesthetic expectations. It is obvious that the work of the director, particularly as it relates to the message transmitted by the fiction, will be reduced to the construction of a referent. The dramatic text creates a referent by means of the fiction, a referent that is a pure referential illusion since it has no existential value. Nevertheless, the DT maintains a mimetic relationship with the referent of the real social context; hence, the possibility of transmitting this fictitious referent to the public's reality.

The mediation of the director is not the only form of mediation between the PT and the public; there is also the mediation of the scenographer and that of the actor. One should not forget that the public attending the theatre performance is exposed to a constant bombardment of the most diverse systems of signification (music, costumes, objects, actors, voice, gestuality, lighting, etc.), whereas, when confronted with the DT, the public confronts one single system of signification: the language articulated in dialogue, and, in the best of cases, a few stage indications of the DT.

Every actor performs his or her own concretization of the DT, and particularly of the character represented by the actor: in the actor's performance, there is always something of the character and something of the actor him or herself. In fact, when we speak of Hamlet, we often have in mind one concretization or another of, for example, Lawrence Olivier or Derek Jacobi, and when we claim that this character is not Hamlet or Oedipus, it is because, according to our interpretation, the character is not legible or recognizable. When exposed to Alain Milianti's production of *Oedipus Rex* (Théâtre de la Salamandre, Théâtre National de l'Odéon, Paris, 1985), the critics as well as the public react against Milanti/Blanc's concretization of Oedipus, who is traditionally portrayed presented as an austere character possessing great dignity (similar to Lear) and elevation. In this staging, however, Oedipus is relatively young, dressed almost like a caveman and acting in a semi-wild manner. The actor, Christian Blanc, displays the character through his voice and his body gestures as well as his costume: in this case, this is a signifying body. This tangible dimension of the character, absent from the DT, is in itself a concretization that the public has to confront from its own metatext.

Something similar could be said about Peter Brook's *Mahabharata*, K. Michael's *Bérénice*, Maurizio Scaparro's, Josef Svoboda's, Pierre Albert's and Josep Maria Flotas' *Cyrano de Bergerac* (Companía Josep Maria Flotas, Poliorama, Barcelona, 1985). The scenography plays a central role in this case, for it makes functional use of the theatrical space and object and this constitutes a concretization different from the traditionally arranged stage. The convergence of the concretizations of Scaparro, Svoboda, Albert and Flotas yields a synthetic whole that fits into the global concretization of this performance text.

C) *Spectatorial Concretization*

The receptive practice, that is, the concretization process and the manner of carrying out this work in relation to a performance, is of great complexity, for the theatrical performance is ephemeral; and thus any attempt to systematize the reception process encounters obstacles that at first seem insurmountable. Thus, the best means of delivering the most precise and concrete results on the above topic would be to establish a model of theatre reception capable of dealing with the difficulties of this semiological task.

Patrice Pavis proposes a model that can account for the process of reception and the various stages that are implied in reception. The model consists of a reception circuit that is articulated in the following manner:

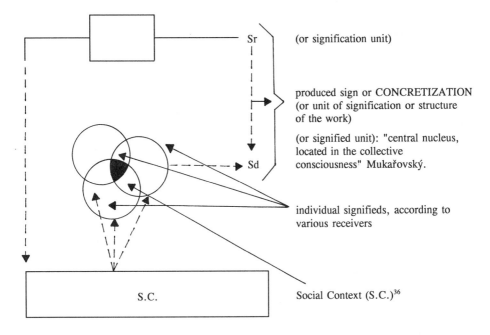

On the one hand, the model proposes a signifying structure (Sr) that is a structured referent. In the unfolding of the performance this is what the spectator gradually perceives, and at the end of the process of perception the spectator receives an *artefact* or structure of the performance. At this level, we observe that the receptive process through which the spectator goes is a *productive* one, in the sense that it is the spectator who organizes the structure. Undoubtedly, the performance text proposes a structure; but this can be perceived and broken down into various segments by the spectator. In this way, the structure of a given performance text is not something immutable; on the contrary, it is dynamic, given to the structuring activity of the spectator. On the other hand, the signified (Sd) of the performance text is central or nuclear, being shared by all the spectators and foreseen by the performance text - it is a product of the labor of the theatrical director who carries out its concretization. At the same time, there are the individual or multiple concretizations done by each of the spectators. This process of signification is carried out in stages: first the *fictionalization* of the aesthetic object or referent, then the *textualization of the ideology*, and finally the *ideolization of the text*. These three stages are mediated by the *Social Context* that both the director and the spectator share. At this level, the spectatorial metatext comes into play, for, ultimately, it is the confrontation of both metatexts that produces the concretization. The metatexts can diverge, that is, express different concretizations, one belonging to the director and the other to the spectator.

The importance of the model proposed by Pavis lies in the fact that it incorporates the social context into the semiotic process as a mediating category. The concretization is not given beforehand *in toto* by the performance text; it is the result of a directorial concretization that proceeds from the directorial metatext, and then is confronted by the spectatorial metatext. Both metatexts have something in common: the social context. In other words, meaning is not formed directly from the signifier to the signified. Rather, it goes through the circuit Sr → SC → Sd. The social context, according to Pavis, "is both produced by the work, in its reference to a possible world, and formed by the conditions of reception of the work. It is at times the context in which the producers of the text are inscribed, at other times the reception situation in which it is perceived in the present".[37] It must be pointed out that the process of concretization carried out by the spectator is not as subjective as one might think. The variety of concretizations results from the *variability* of the three components of the circuit: a) the social context that implicates the artistic tradition; b) the ideological and literary norms, which change with time (as well as from culture to culture); c) the signifier which changes insofar as the divisions made of the text are not always the same (on the contrary, they change from period to period, and even from one production to the next). If it is true that at the structural level the performance text imposes a signifier on the spectator, it can also be said that the manner of perception of this structure may vary. The variation of the signified is simply the product of the changes undergone by the signifier and the social context. In this way, the variety of concretizations of a performance text might be explained by the changes that take place in the three elements of the receptive circuit.

In this receptive activity, a triple reading may occur, as proposed in the following model:

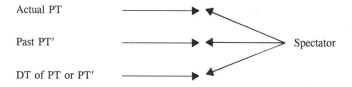

First of all, there is the reading of the PT occurring on the stage before the spectator; then, the spectator acquires another concretization from the same DT realized in another PT' by a different director. Finally, the spectator can also have read the DT that he or she is perceiving or has perceived as PT or PT'. Thus, both the PT' and the PT as well as the DT influence the spectator's reading/concretization of the new PT.

D) *Process of Concretization*

Concretization takes place through two distinct processes related to the social context. On the one hand, there is a movement from the performance signifier to the social context; that is, the way the performance text is seen by the social context of the spectator. On the other hand, is a movement from the social context to the performance signifier, which provides certain messages and the imaginary referent (the fiction) for the PT. The convergence of these two processes constitutes the spectator's concretization.

1) From the Social Context to the Signified

a) Fictionalization

The fictionalization phase consists of the confrontation between the possible world proposed by the DT/PT and the real world of the spectator. What is important in this process is that the fiction of the performance creates a referent, one that is imaginary and without any real existence. This referent has first to pass through the SC in order to be understood. First, the artefact (the signifier) is structured by the spectator - that is, the fiction and its components are articulated in a coherent structure, from which meaning emerges and the concretization is realized. Thus, fictionalization is the first and most important of the stages, since it determines the subsequent stages (textualization of the ideology and ideologization of the text). In the process of fictionalization, therefore, there is a double spectatorial task: structuration and concretization:

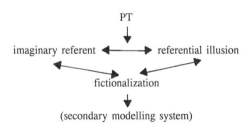

The PT, or rather the fiction itself, creates an imaginary referent: characters, plot, scenography, decor, dialogical discourse, etc. This imaginary referent, composed primarily of an oral component (dialogue) and a visual component (space and the theatrical object), produces a referential illusion that allows for the fictionalization process to proceed. This entire operation may be called a *secondary*

modeling system (SMS). This concept, introduced by Yuri Lotman,[38] is to be understood in the following manner: the SMS is a product of the horizon of expectations and the reading code of the reader/spectator, which is based on the signifying artefact (the DT/PT). I are dealing with what Rien T. Sehers refers to as the *superstructure*, which is constructed on the first model.[39] However, the notion goes beyond the meaning normally attributed to this word. The first meaning of this word comes from the fact that a *secondary modeling system* is actually a second language - for example, the cinema, the theatre, etc., which are communicative structures built on and from natural language (= first system). Thus, art, in general terms, is a second system, a second language. But the system that is referred to here is another one that, in actual fact, is found in the semantic components (ideological, ethical, aesthetic). In this sense, then, this second system is complete in that it incorporates the three stages of concretization and is a significant structure (signifier, signified, social context) confronted by the imaginary referent or illusion of the dramatic/performance text.[40]

The establishment of the fictionalization, the structure/meaning, is obtained from the Social Context. That is, the performance text is *filtered* through the Social Context and then constitutes the structure/meaning. What allows the spectator to relate the possible world to the real world are those referents of the former which can be related to the latter, and this process is also achieved by means of components of an ideological, aesthetic and ethical nature.

b) The Ideologization of the Text

This stage of the concretization consists of the formalization of an ideology for a given text. One is not concerned with form here, but with ideological components transmitted through the possible world; the imaginary referent expresses a world view, a proposal of the real world. For example, Brechtian texts institute a textualization of ideology which is later taken up by the various playwrights (particularly Latin American). These texts contain ideological contents recognizable not only in their manner of enunciation, but also in the semantic charge they carry. The ideologization of the text goes through the same process as the textualization of the ideology through the autotextual and intertextual. No doubt, there is a dialectic relation between ideology and the ideologization of the text, since the text normally contains some ideology, or in other words, every text which is articulated in a given syntax transmits content of some kind. This, however, is not always the case, for there may exist a clear distinction between the textualization of ideology and the ideologization of the text, as is the case in the works of the Chilean playwright J. Radrigán, where these two aspects are not dialectically opposed, but rather diametrically opposed.

The ideologization of the text is not only a productive act of the producer who disseminates the ideological components of his or her text, but also by the receiver of the message, who ideologizes the text from *places of indeterminacy* as textual blanks. That is, the receiver projects *his* or *her* ideology, which originates from the social context. The producer of the text (author or director) performs a semanticization of the fiction (which is not yet structuration of fiction, for this would mean that the signifying part of the sign was being obeyed) which is in turn convergently or divergently re-semanticized by the receiver. If the director is working with an old or distant text, he or she may semanticize it by bringing that fiction closer to our reality, or by making the text allude to present reality without being too explicit. For instance, current Chilean theatre often operates through veiled discourse, ideologizing the text in an oblique way; but this obliqueness is not beyond the horizon of expectation (the reading code) of the spectator.

2) From the Signifier to the Social Context

The DT, like the PT, proposes and imposes a structure independently of what the spectator/reader does. The textualization of the ideology consists of imposing ideology in the very form of the text, in its signifier. That is, the discourse as well as its expression will be ideologically labelled. According to Pavis, the textualization of the ideology consists of the inscription of ideology as a textual operation upon the real. It passes from a discursive referent and from an undifferentiated and particular ideology to a precise or final text concretized in a type of signifying structure.[41] What is occurring here is the inscription of the social dimension into the form, or of an ideological form inscribed *as* form, with the chosen form being the mark of the social. In other words, this is a structuration of ideology *as text*.

This process, or rather, textualization, occurs through the autotextual and/or the intertextual. As I have already shown in chapter II, the autotext is self-revealing with respect to its processes of construction and autonomous structure, insofar as it has its own form of expression. But at the same time, the autotextual text is transmitted and supported by the intertextual or the diversity of texts that are inscribed in or are automatically associated with the intertext. For example, texts by the Chilean playwright Egon Wolff, such as *Flores de papel* or *Los Invasores*, are texts where the ideology of the dominant social formation is inscribed into the texts' structures, into characters' discursive positions, etc. This text has an organization that is entirely its own, a sort of 'this is how I say it'. But, at the same time, this text is supported by the intertextual space composed of other linguistic texts, for example, theatrical (as in the dramatic texts of Sergio Vodanovich, Alejandro Sieviking, etc.) with which it shares common structures from participating in an ideology that is textualized in the text. This is how the text's proposed/imposed signifier can pass through the text to the social context where the spectator is situated. What has been previously said must not be forgotten: the social context is produced by both the producer of the text trying to create a possible world and by the reception conditions of the text. According to Pavis, "It is at times the context in which the producers of the text are inscribed, at other times the reception situation in which it is perceived in the present".[42] The intertextuality of the text is what allows the text to transmit or refer the text to other texts that might or might not themselves be artistic, for example, political texts, domestic texts, etc. The whole process of dual theatre reception can be summed up in the following model of theatre reception (see next page).

The process of reception/communication is a complex one, since it involves not only the relationship between stage and the audience, but also the production of the DT/PT, where a concretization takes place. The source of the receptive chain lies in the producer, whether this be the author, the *dramaturg*, or a collective group. This transmitter produces its text and is conditioned by the performance context (PC) (which determines the form of production of the text and the dramatic writing codes to be used) and at the same time by the social context (SC), which determines the ideological position, the cultural setting, intertexts, etc. Consequently the DT proposes a signifier (Sr) and a signified (Sd). Then the director and his team (actors, scenographers, etc.) carry out a concretization which transforms the dramatic text into a virtual performance text, and which materializes in a performance text proposing its own Sr and Sd. The directorial concretization is also determined by the PC and by the SC with which it shares the cultural environment. At this point, the signification of discourse takes place through the dialogue of the actors. This PT is concretized by the spectators from the discourse of the actors and from the various components of the performance text. The spectatorial concretization, like that of both the director and the writer, is determined by the PC, that is, by the DT and by the SC, in the intersection of both texts resulting in the final and ultimate concretization of spectatorial activity.

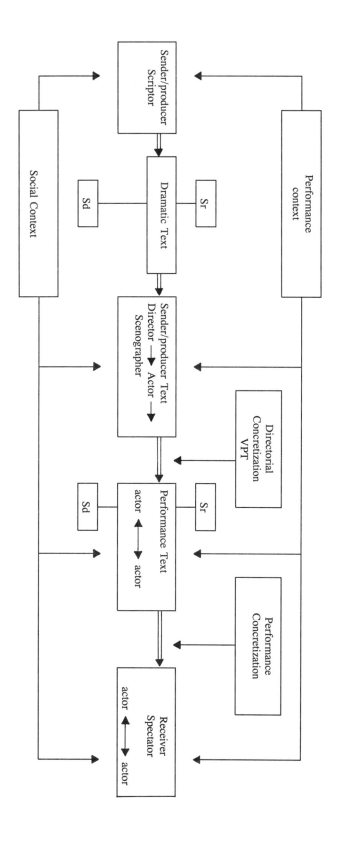

III. NEW PERSPECTIVES

The model proposed in the above section discusses concretization at a general and theoretical level and considers the abstract spectator. The empirical dimension of the process, however, has not yet been examined. It is absolutely necessary to complement these receptive theories with an empirical approach in order to verify them. In what follows, some theoretical hypotheses regarding the spectators' receptive activity will be introduced, using some of the most recent research done in this field.

In this newly-developing field which could be called socio-semiotics, two main areas must be defined: a general theoretical level which will establish the general hypotheses, and a second level which will determine the methodology that will account for the object of study. In the following, the principle characteristics of this form of socio-semiotics will be outlined.

A) *Object of Study*

The central object of study is the spectator, a fundamental point in reception studies; this spectator, however, is the concrete, real spectator who goes to the theatre. Up until now, most studies on the process of reception have been concerned with an abstract approach, hypothesizing the ideal spectator and what or how this hypothetical ideal spectator should read the stage. Nevertheless, as De Marinis, a pioneer in this new field of research, points out, "in general, we have carefully avoided posing the problem of a true pragmatic and operational reformulation of the semiotic and all of its equipment/accoutrements/apparatus/machinery, such a reformulation being, in my view, necessarily subordinate to the choice of the real receiver as the central theoretical object".[43] What I am dealing with, then, is a new theoretical/empirical approach that will analyze what the spectator does based on real data which is beginning to be compiled from empirical studies verifying theoretical proposals related to the data. Some of the most important studies in this field are:

a) The work of Frank Coppieters, who has done excellent research by studying an audience's reactions to performances that have taken place in Amsterdam and New York; he reveals his methodology (ethnogenic approach) and he has also completed a survey of the spectator's *memorial experience*. In order to do this, he used various methods including interviewing the spectators, filming the audience's reactions, and assissting the relationship between the position of the spectators in the audience and their reactions. Perhaps the central point in his study is the fact that it is one of the rare empirical studies of the theatre spectator who tries to verify the spectatorial memory and its way of operating.[44]

b) Another important study is the one by Henry Schoenmakers and Ed Tan that researches the reception process from an experimental point of view: that is, interpretation, emotion, and appreciation. Very much like Coppieters, they make use of various types of tests, interviews and questionnaires. In one way, this study suggests that the cognitive dimension predominates over the emotive one.[45]

c) Similar research has been done by Cosimo Minervi, who also uses interviews and questionnaires to study the spectator's interpretive processes on micro- and macro-structural levels. This study furthers the levels proposed by De Marinis.[46]

d) Marco De Marinis and Leonardo Altieri have completed a very interesting study which furnishes valid results on spectatorial reception. In their study they analyze the relationship between *competence* and *comprehension*. Their most significant result is an acknowledgment of the motivation, stimulation, and emotive and axiological components in the spectatorial concretization. De Marinis and Altieri clearly show that the cognitive component plays a role that is never completely determinant in the comprehension of the performance.[47]

e) Michel Jaumain's excellent study, carried out in seven theatres, consists of a survey of the type of audience, the sort of theatre people want in Brussels, and the rate of theatre attendance. This study is useful inasmuch as it offers a model for methodological and empirical research; but it lacks the theoretical framework necessary as a guide to empirical work.[48]

f) Finally, the study by Anne-Marie Gourdon is perhaps the best of all; it is very comprehensive, including methods and techniques of analysis, audience composition in the theatres studied, spectators' motives for attending certain performances, etc. Every empirical study should consult the results obtained by Gourdon.[49]

I can deduce from these studies that the object of study has been extended in the following ways: a) the attempt to establish a new model of theatre reception, which specifies distinct processes (levels) of the spectator's receptive activity; b) the study of the continual dialectic relationship between audience and stage, spectator and director, manipulation and interpretation, passive and active subject; c) the incorporation of cognitive and emotive activities that until now have been ignored in studies on reception in general. Neither the cognitive dimension, nor the emotive dimension should be favored, for this would result in a subjective and romantic view of the receptive activity.

B) *Levels of Receptive Activity*

Based on some of the above studies, as well as on the work of Stanley Schachter[50] and M.W. Eysenck,[51] Marco De Marinis proposes five basic levels: 1) perception, 2) interpretation, 3) emotive and cognitive reactions, 4) evaluation, and 5) memorization and recollection. These five levels constitute the model of theatre comprehension and reception.[52]

1) Perception

The first level consists simply of the recognition and identification of expressive elements (verbal and non-verbal) of the performance. This has to do with the perception of *signifiers* which in fact determine to a large extent the spectator's attention to the focalization and re-focalization process. What is important at this level is to establish how spectatorial attention is captured. Without a doubt, the spectator's receptive activity is the result of a dialectical interaction between the text's strategies and the spectator's own activities. According to De Marinis, the focalization may be realized by means of either a *"process governed by data"* or *"a process governed by concepts"*.[53] In the first case, focalization, de-focalization, re-focalization, and, therefore, attention, are determined by the performance text itself, by the productive activity (director), by the reception context, and by the approximation strategies of the spectator. In my opinion, at this level, one must determine *in situ* strategies, because in every theorization it is difficult to arrive at precise general postulates. Each PC has its own strategy, its own way of appealing to the spectator or getting the spectator's attention. The semiotic dimension of the process controlled by the information is of prime importance, since the production of signs is transmitted intimately with the spectator's perceptive activity. Any theoretical generalization will have to refer to a *model spectator*, which is what I did when I established my model in the previous section. It is not so much an imaginary spectator, as De Marinis has pointed out,[54] but rather the general spectator.

The second level deals with the spectator's receptive activity: with his/her horizon of expectations, theatrical competence, culture - in short, with the ensemble of his/her knowledge. Thus, the dialectical relation of these two focalization modalities determines the attention, since this is a determinant factor in the spectator's receptive activity.

2) Interpretation

Interpretation has to do with cognitive comprehension operations which according to De Marinis may be subdivided into three categories: a) *pragmatic interpretation*; b) *semantic interpretation*; c) *semiotic interpretation*. These three sub-levels seem to constitute the central point of the spectator's receptive activity, and in my opinion they are far more important than De Marinis's macro levels 3, 4, and 5. It is at this level that the interpretation of the PT takes place.[55]

a) Pragmatic Interpretation

Pragmatic interpretation concerns itself with the double recognition achieved by the spectator *before* the performance takes place - that is, with the recognition that the event announced (by programs, posters, etc.) is a theatre performance, and placing that theatrical event within an aesthetic category, a given genre, that is a type or class of PT. This level is significant in that it predisposes the spectator to a series of receptive, attentive, and focalization processes, and in this sense motivates the spectator's horizon of expectations. This *para-textual* pragmatic interpretation predisposes the spectator's entire receptive activity.

b) Semantic Interpretation

Semantic interpretation is the result of level (1), for the spectator assigns a meaning, or to be more precise, a concretization, to a given performance, based on the elements provided by the PT and the spectator's theatrical competence. According to De Marinis, this concretization occurs in two contexts: a) at the *micro-structural level;* and b) at the *macro-structural level*. The first deals with the immanent, inductive interpretation which derives from the elements provided by the PT, at its *surface* level, as a material entity (discourse/staging). It is a punctual interpretation, relevant to a given PT. In the second context, one is dealing with a global, comprehensive interpretation; it operates at a deep level assigning a meaning to the PT which transcends the local or punctual meaning.

c) Semiotic Interpretation

Semiotic interpretation is concerned with the spectator's perception of *signifiers*, that is, with the identification and recognition of conventions and theatre codes. It has to do with the grasping of the *expressive level* that governs and determines the PT. This level, then, is of great importance, perhaps of the greatest importance, for it is in the comprehension of the signs that the spectator decides about the sub-levels (a) and (b). On this point, De Marinis comments:

> While semantic interpretation focuses on the *meaning* of the performance ... which is to say on *what* it is, semiotic interpretation ... mainly focuses on *how* it is, which is to say on the theatrical *signifiers* and on the stylistic deviations ... that constitute them. Semiotic interpretation focuses on the form and rhetoric which organize the production, and how they are a means of conveying given contents.[56]

3) Emotive and Cognitive Reaction

Up until this point, theatre reception studies have largely ignored the emotive dimension of reception, that is to say, of the role emotions, stimuli, impulses, etc., play in reception. Generally speaking, the approach used has been primarily cognitive in nature and has disregarded the fact that comprehension originates at an emotive level as well. Nevertheless, it is my opinion that one has to proceed with extreme caution in this field, if one is to avoid rampantly subjective views. In this respect, the studies already carried out by Eysenck, Schachter, Schoenmakers and Tan are very important, for they reveal the dialectical relationship between cognitive and emotive components.

The emotive component is extremely difficult to measure, since I do not have a methodology that allows us to verify the hypothesis just put forward, namely that cognition and emotion are central components in receptive activity. Questionnaires, interviews, and the like, are not sufficient to verify this dimension, which is in fact psycho-physiological and needs very precise tools of verification, such as measuring the spectator's pulse or filming the reactions of a group of spectators chosen before a given performance. This type of research requires follow-up of the same group of spectators with various stages of verification and tests and this requires an ideal working situation. For now, this is an area which has yet to be developed.

4) Evaluation

This area has so far been completely disregarded by theatre semiotics. The main reason for the neglect of evaluation lies in its 'subjective' and thus non-scientific nature. Nevertheless, as soon as theatre semiotics introduces the problem of theatre reception, whether this be from the aesthetic/social point of view or from the empirical perspective, then the question of evaluation becomes central and must be incorporated into reception. The importance of evaluation is evident in the studies of, for example, Schoenmakers, and Gourdon.[57]

By evaluation I understand the act performed by the spectator in relation to a given PT. The evaluation has to be analyzed as it relates to perception, interpretation, and cognitive/emotive reactions, for evaluation is the *result* and integral product of the receptive activity of the spectator. Evaluating a PT means relating the intra-textual and the para-textual, the spectator's theatrical and cultural competence. In this way, I believe that evaluation is not arbitrary, for it is determined by the preliminary processes and is not purely a question of taste, devoid of any receptive context.

5) Memory and Recollection

Bernard Beckerman has introduced the distinction between *theatrical experience* and *memorial experience*. According to Beckerman:

> The memorial experience is not distinct from the theatrical but merely a continuation beyond direct contact with the presentation. The form of action induces the theatrical experience directly but has an indirect effect upon the memorial experience.... Once removed from his fellow spectators, he gains a new perspective of the work. Responses elicited in performance may seem alien in retrospect. The process of rumination alters the work.... Memory plays tricks. We think we saw actions which were merely described or remembered by the characters, and we fill in the details of the sketch of life shown to us.[58]

The real difference between both types of experience resides in the fact that *theatrical experience* is the experience lived in the performance, whereas *memorial experience* is what is recollected from that experience. What is important here, as Coppieters has correctly pointed out, is that mnemonic experience gives us a fairly accurate idea of the spectator's experience, in spite of the fact that this may be fragmented and distorted.[59] It is equally important to point out that this mnemonic experience includes not only the immediate theatrical experience, but also preceding theatrical experiences that are part of the mnemonic experience and thus play a role in the spectator's present experience.

The only way to reconstruct the theatrical experience is through the mnemonic experience. This reconstruction may also be accomplished by an evaluator/analyst who attempts to record a spectator's or group of spectators' reactions, generating in this way his or her own perception of the spectator's theatrical experience.

C) *Methodology*

1) The Selection of the Corpus

A methodology which will produce the results and verification of my hypothesis is still being elaborated, and I am beginning to work in this direction.[60] However, I am able to suggest some preliminary methodological procedures.

One of the most important points, as noted by Coppieters,[61] is the selection not only of an audience, but also of the performance that will allow for certain generalizations. Thus, it is fundamental to select people who represent typical members of a given collectivity and, at the same time, performances which may be considered *types*. This first stage is fundamental, for the audience cannot be chosen at random. For this reason, initial selection criteria have to be established, possibly with a questionnaire that would provide data on the spectators to be studied. This questionnaire would give a clear and precise idea of the public being subjected to analysis.

With respect to the selection of the performance type, this may be decided in relation to the chosen audience. One must choose here between a performance that *suits that particular* audience's aesthetic parameters and theatrical competence, and a contemporary (for example, avant-garde) performance which would be typical of contemporary theatre. What I am trying to say here is that, if we hope to arrive at conclusions regarding the reactions of concrete spectators to a given performance, it does not make sense to analyze an audience's reaction to a performance if that audience has not been selected for a number of reasons - ideological, cultural, fondness of a certain type of theatre, etc.

Another problem is encountered as one tries to define what is *typical*, for here too there are many variables. If we think of a country like Canada, composed mainly of a very large technical/professional middle class, which contains a sector which attends a variety of artistic activities (doctors, professors, government employees, etc.) and which has a general cultural competence, it is possible to speak of a *typical, uniform* audience. From Vancouver to Newfoundland I find these same sectors participating in the same cultural events. Furthermore, in this respect, this Canadian audience is not very different from a European one. Perhaps the only difference is that, generally speaking, a European audience is larger and more theatrically and culturally competent than a Canadian audience. Also, in some countries like Canada, France and Italy, some promotion of theatre occurs within the school system, and one would have to analyze this milieu separately. Whatever the case, the establishment of a *typical* audience must be done in relatively large sectors to avoid fragmentary conclusions about the process and activity of reception.

2) Evaluation and Survey Methods

The methods of analyzing spectatorial reception at my disposal may be numerous, but I have to devise methods that will allow for the integration of results and avoid overly detailed and fragmented methods. Some of the methods used by Coppieters, and De Marinis and Altieri provide a starting point, and we can suggest others.

a) Questionnaires

One of the more effective methods of analyzing spectatorial reception is with questionnaires that address the spectator's theatrical and mnemonic experience. These questionnaires may take two forms. On the one hand, there are direct interviews with a given number of spectators. These interviews, as carried out by Coppieters, can be complemented by audiovisual materials of a given PT.[62] On the other hand, questionnaires may be answered in written form by the spectators. In fact, it might be methodologically pertinent that certain spectators of a given group be given interviews and others be given questionnaires.

The form these interviews/questionnaires may take should be flexible and, as Kahn and Cannell have shown, the sequence of ideas in the questionnaire should follow "the logic of the respondent".[63]

b) Recording Reactions

Another method that might prove useful to theatre reception analysis would be to register spectators' reactions. These can be recorded in two ways: internally and externally. For instance, the internal method would consist of measuring the heartbeat or any of the various neuro-physiological reactions of the spectators. This would indicate the type of stimuli and instinctive emotions felt during the course of the performance. The external method might consist of filming the individuals in the audience so as to observe their external reactions and general behaviour, not only in relation to the performance, but also in relation to other members of the group.

These various forms of analysis of the receptive process would mean working systematically with a group of spectators, as if it were a laboratory situation. This would require a very developed level of systematization and resources. In my case, I have followed up on two of Frank Coppieters' recommendations. First of all, I will evaluate the spectatorial reception of two or more 'typical' but spatially and temporally separated groups in Bologna and Ottawa to a 'typical' performance. The second recommendation is that this type of research must be multi-disciplinary - that is, it must include semioticians, sociologists and psychologists, all providing different methods that will make possible a comprehensive approach to theatre reception.

Without a doubt, this empirical dimension must be integrated into the reception model proposed above (section I), for I should not limit myself to empirical data given that the social context and its relationship to artistic production also contribute in determining theatre reception. In this chapter, I hope to have shown how theatre concretization is as much the result of the social dimension (social context) as it is the individual (emotions, theatrical competence). This is why this research has to integrate other disciplines into semiotics. If this is not done, theatre semiotics will not achieve its goals.

ENDNOTES
CHAPTER IV

1. For example: "Production et réception au théâtre: la concrétisation du texte dramatique et spectaculaire", *Revue des sciences humaines*, LX, 189 (janvier-mars 1983), 51-88; "La réception du texte dramatique et spectaculaire: les processus de fictionnalisation et idéologisation", *Versus*, 41 (May-August 1985), 68-94; "Pour une esthétique de la réception théâtrale", in *La relation théâtrale*, exts compiled by Régis Durand (Lille: Presses Universitaires de Lille, 1980), pp. 27-54; "Per un'estetica della ricezione teatrale. Variazioni su alcune relazioni", in *La semiotica e il doppio teatrale*, edited by Giulio Ferroni (Napoli: Liguori Editore, 1981), 187-218; "Vers une socio-critique du théâtre?", in *Voix et images de la scène. Pour une sémiologie de la réception*, new edition revised and expanded (Lille: Presses Universitaires de Lille, 1985), 309-316; "Du texte à la mise en scène: l'histoire traversée", *Kodikas/Code*, VII, 1-2 (1984), 24-41.

2. "Toward a Cognitive Semiotic of Theatrical Emotions", *Versus*, 41 (May-August 1985), 5-20; "L'esperienza dello spettatore. Fondamenti per una semiotica della ricezione teatrale", *Documenti di Lavoro*, Università di Urbino, 138-139, Serie F, (noviembre-deciembre 1984), 1-36; "La recherche empirique sur la réception théâtrale: de la sociologie à la sémiotique", (1985), mimeograph, 6 pages; "Il lavoro dello spettatore. Un' indagine sul pubblico di teatro", in *Sociologia del lavoro* (1985), mimeograph, 31 pages; *Semiotica del teatro* (Milano: Studi Bompiani, 1982), pp. 156-212; "Problemas de semiótica teatral: la relación espectáculo-espectador", *Gestos*, 1 (avril 1986), 11-24; "Theatrical Comprehension: A Socio-Semiotic Approach", *Theatre*, XV, 1 (Winter 1985), 12-17.

3. "Construir la coherencia. El espectáculo teatral", *Gestos*, 2 (September 1986), 29-38; "Approches de la réception. Quelques problèmes", *Versus*, 41 (May-August 1985), 41-48; "Le discours téâtral: une sémantique de la relation," in *La relation téâtrale*, texts compiled by Régis Durand (Lille: Presses Universitaires de lille, 1980), pp. 97-106; "The Semiology of Theatre or: Communication Swamped", *Poetics Today*, II, 3 (Spring 1981), 105-111.

4. For example, see Jan Mukařovský, *Structure, Sign, and Function*, translated and edited by John Burbank and Peter Steiner (New Haven and London: Yale University Press, 1978), pp. 201-219; Felix Vodička and O. Obelic, *El mundo de las letras*, 2nd edition (Santiago, Chile: Editorial Universitaria, 1971); Felix Vodička, *Die Struktur der literarischen Entwicklung*, translated by Christian Tuschinsky, Peter Richter and Frank Boldt (München: Wilhelm Fink Verlag, 1976). Other studies can be found in the journal *Versus*, 41, and in *La relation théâtrale*, quoted above. See also the excellent study by Hans-George Ruprecht, *Theaterpublikum und Textauffassung* (Frankfurt am Main und München: Herbert Lang Bern, 1976) and the article by Frank Coppieters, "Performance and Perception", *Poetics Today*, II, 3 (Spring 1981), 35-48.

5. *The Literary Work of Art*, translated with an introduction by George G. Grabowicz (Evanston: Northwestern University Press, 1973) and *The Cognition of the Literary Work of Art*, translated by Ruth Ann Crowley and Kenneth R. Olson (Evanston: Northwestern University Press, 1973).

6. For example, *Ästhetische Erfahrung und literarische Hermeneutik I* (München: Wilhelm Fink Verlag, 1977) and *Pour une esthétique de la réception* by Hans-Robert Jauss, translated from the German by Claude Maillard, preface by Jean Starobinski (Paris: Editions Gallimard, 1978); *Der Implizite Leser: Kommunikationsformen des Romans von Bunyan bis Beckett* (München: Wilhelm Fink Verlag, 1972) by Wolfgang Iser; "Aspects génériques de la réception", *Poétique*, 39 (1979), 352-362, by Wolf-Dieter Stempel.

7. *The Role of the Reader* (Bloomington, Indiana: Indiana University Press, 1984). For a global view of reception theory, see the excellent book by Robert C. Holub, *Reception Theory*. (London and New York: Methuen, 1984) and by Terry Eagleton, *Literary Theory: An Introduction*. (Minneapolis: University of Minnesota Press, 1983), chapter II.

8. For example, the already quoted book by Felix Vodička, *Die Struktur der literarischen Entwicklung*, and by Jan Mukařovský, *Aesthetic Function, Norm and Value as Social Facts*, translated by Mark E. Suino (Ann Arbor: University of Michigan Press, 1970).

9. See note 5.

10. *The Cognition of the Literary Work of Art*, p. 50. Referring to the literary work, Ingarden says: "At least some of its strata, especially the objective stratum, contain a series of 'places of indeterminacy.' We find such a place of indeterminacy wherever it is impossible, on the basis of the sentences in the work, to say whether a certain

object or objective situation has a certain attribute". *Ibid.*, p. 50.

11. *Ibid.*, p. 52.

12. From the point of view of reception esthetics, *reading* must be understood as a type of concretization or interpretation that the director or spectator carries out. That is, it is any process that implies staging a play, or a scene. For example, Patrice Pavis speaks of a reading of a reading: "Reading the staging ... is, therefore, at the same time and/or separately 1. reading the dramatic *text* performed ... 2. reading the performance *text* in which the dramatic text is inserted, 3. reading the reading of the dramatic text carried out by the practitioners of theatre". "Production et réception au théâtre: la concrétisation du texte dramatique et spectaculaire", 72 (our translation).

13. See *The Literary Work of Art*, pp. 251-252.

14. *The Cognition of the Literary Work of Art*, p. 41.

15. *Ibid.*, p. 55.

16. *Ibid.*, pp. 55-61.

17. *Ibid.*, p. 62.

18. *The Cognition of the Literary Work of Art*, p. 50.

19. See Hans-Robert Jauss, *Pour une esthétique de la réception*, 45. (I am not using Jauss' English translation of 1982 (University of Minnesota) since is a radically different text and many of the chapters contained in the French edition do not appear in the English one.

20. See Roman Ingarden, *The Literary Work of Art*, p. 348.

21. "Littérature et sémiologie", *Poétique*, 3 (1970), 389 (our translation).

22. On this point, refer also to Wolfgang Iser: "The Reading Process: A Phenomenological Approach", *New Literary History*, III, 2 (Winter 1972), 279-299.

23. *Pour une esthétique de la réception*, p. 246.

24. This would seem to be Jauss' response when he says: "It is because of its *form*, its specific artistic quality, transcends the practical function of language which makes of a given work the testimony of given epoch, maintaining open and therefore present, in spite of the time that passes and changes, its *sigfinication* conceived as the implcit answer which speaks to us in the work". *Ibid.*, p. 247.

25. "The Text and the Structure of Its Audience", *New Literary History*, XIV, 1 (Autumn 1982), 81.

26. On the other hand, the concept of horizon of expectations implies that the reader must know the previous norms or codes if he or she hopes to evaluate a given text. Also, this concept implies that the text in question has a horizon that is determined by the appearance of the work at a given moment. That is, the horizon of a work is the initial horizon, when the work first appears, since this horizon is inscribed into the work itself.

27. *Pour une esthétique de la réception*, p. 259.

28. See my article, "El teatro en Chile: ruptura y renovación. Perspectiva semiológica de los fenómenos de producción y recepción en los últimos doce años", in *Le théâtre sous la contrainte* (Aix-en-Provence: Université de Provence, 1986) and in *Conjunto*, 68 (avril-junio 1986). Rita Schober proposes the term *Rezeptionsvorgabe* which she defines in the following way: "a neologism comprised of two factors of correlation and thus it contains an entire program. The work and the reader conserve relative autonomy. The work provides, from the author, potential meaning (*Sinnpotential*), structured virtual signification, by means of an overall strategy of the effect to be created (*Wirkungsstrategie*)". "Réception et historicité de la littérature", *Revue des sciences humaines*, LX, 189 (janvier-mars 1983), 14.

29. In this respect, the paper by Mannfred Naumann is interesting: "Literary Production and Reception", *New Literary History*, VIII, 1 (Autumn 1976), 107-126. In this case, the emphasis is on the material aspect of the production of cultural objects as well as their relationship to ideology and infrastructure in society.

30. "Sociologie des textes littéraires", *La pensée*, 215 (octobre 1980), 90 (our translation).

31. Examples of this material can be found in the series *Les voies de la création théâtrale* (Paris: Centre National de Recherche Scientifique), 13 volumes still in the process of being written; or the review under the direction of Giorgio Strehler, in the ninth volume, *Théâtre en Europe*; or the book by Edward Braun that was quoted previously, *The Director and the Stage* (London: Methuen, 1982); not to mention the many programs and newspaper reviews kept since 1900 in the Biblioteca Argentores in Buenos Aires.

32. This work has just begun, especially by Dutch researchers such as Frank Coppieters, Henry Schoenmakers and Ed Tan (see note 43 and 44, respectively) and by researchers such as M. De Marinis (note 43). See also Patrice Pavis, "Vers une sociocritique du théâtre?" pp. 309-316.

33. See "Production et réception au théâtre: la concrétisation du texte dramatique et spectaculaire", 87-88.

34. See *Semiotica del teatro* and "Le spectacle comme texte" in *Sémiologie théâtrale* Lyon: Université de Lyon II, CERTEC, 1980), pp. 195-258.

35. See my article "Estructuras de convergencia en el teatro del Siglo de Oro", in *Texte-Kontexte-Strukturen*, Beiträge zur französischen, spanischen und hispanoamerikanischen Literatur. Festschrift zum 60. Geburtstag von Karl Alfred Blüher. Edited by Alfonso de Toro (Tübingen: Gunter Narr Verlag, 1987), pp. 265-282.

36. Patrice Pavis, "Production et réception au théâtre: la concrétisation du texte dramatique et spectaculaire", 65.

37. *Ibid.*, p. 66 (our translation).

38. "The Text and the Structure of Its Audience", 81-88.

39. "A propos de la nécessité de la collaboration entre la sémiologie et l'esthétique de la réception", *Degrés*, huitième année, 24-25 (hiver 1980-81), h7.

40. Sehers establishes the following model:

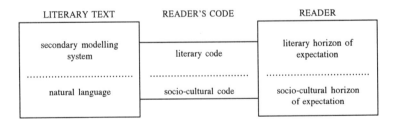

41. *Marivaux à l'épreuve de la scène*. Paris: Publications de la Sorbonne, 1985.

42. "Production et réception au théâtre: la concrétisation du texte dramatique et spectaculaire", 66 (our translation).

43. "La recherche empirique sur le réception théâtrale: De la sociologie à la sémiotique", mimeographed in 1985 (our translation).

44. "Performance and Perception", 35-48.

45. Henry Schoenmakers and Ed Tan, "'Good guy bad guy' effects in Political Theatre", in *Semiotics of Drama and Theatre*, edited by Herta Schmidt and Aloysius Van Kesteren (The Hague: John Benjamins, 1984), pp. 467-508.

46. Cosimo Minervini, *Sémiotique de la réception théâtrale*, tesis de licenciatura, Universidad de Boloña, 1983.

47. Marco De Marinis and Leandro Altieri, "Il lavoro della spettatore: Un'indagine sul pubblico di teatro".

48. "Approches méthodologiques de l'audience théâtrale", *Cahiers théâtre Louvin*, 49 (1983). This issue is entirely devoted to this topic.

49. *Théâtre, Public, Perception* (Paris: Editions du Centre National de la Recherche Scientifique, 1982).

50. "The Interaction of Cognitive and Physiological Determinants of Emotional States", in *Anxiety and Behavior*, edited by C. Spielberger (New York: Academic Press, 1966). See also, S. Schachter and J.E.Singer, "Cognitive, Social and Physiological Determinants of Emotional State", *Physiological Review*, LXIX, 5 (Septembre 1962).

51. *Attention and Arousal. Cognition and Performance* (Berlin, Heidelberg, New York: Springer Verlag, 1982).

52. "L'esperienza dello spettatore. Fondamenti per una semiotica della recezione teatrale", 3.

53. "Problemas de semiótica teatral: la relación espectáculo-espectador", 11-24. See also: "L'esperienza dello spettatore. Fondamenti per una semiotica della recezione teatrale", 138-139, Serie F, (November-december 1984), 5.

54. "Problemas de semiótica teatral: la relación espectáculo-espectador", 11-24. See also, "La recherche empirique sur la réception théâtrale: De la sociologie à la sémiotique".

55. For more detail on these levels and processes, refer to "Theatrical Comprehension: A Socio-Semiotic Approach", and "L'esperienza dello spettatore. Fondamenti per una semiotica della recezione teatrale".

56. *Ibid.*, 14.

57. *Théâtre, Public, Perception*. In this excellent book, Gourdon deals with the main problems, as for example: the methodology and techniques of enquiry (pp. 11-18); the composition of the theatre audience (pp. 19-24); performance perception (pp. 117-196), etc. This study provided a working model that initiated current theatre semiotics.

58. *Dynamics of Drama* (New York: Knopf, 1970), p. 157.

59. "Performance and Perception", 45.

60. Marco De Marinis and I presented a paper on this subject at the First World Congress on Theatre Sociology in Rome, June, 1986, now published: Marco De Marinis, "Sociologie du théâtre: un réexamen et une proposition", and Fernando de Toro, "Towards a Socio-Semiotics of the Theatre", in *1er Congrès Mondial de Sociologie du Théâtre*, edited by Roger Deldime (Roma: Bulzoni Editore, 1988), pp. 67-82 and 83-122 respectively.

61. "Performance and Perception", 36.

62. *Ibid.*, pp. 38-39.

63. *The Dynamics of Interviewing* (New York: Wiley, 1957), p. 161.

CHAPTER V

TOWARDS AN ACTANTIAL MODEL FOR THEATRE

> The question of *what* a tale's dramatis personae do is an important one for the study of the tale, but the questions of *who* does it and *how* it is done already fall within the province of accessory study.
> Vladimir Propp, *Morphology of the Folktale*.

One of the fundamental tasks proponents of theatre semiotics have proposed is the formulation of a 'grammar' of the actions of the DT/PT in order to distance semiotics from substantialist practices in which the character is often considered as almost a real being. At the same time, theatre semiotics must establish some model or deep structure explaining actions in theatre. This area of research has been developed considerably, especially in the narrative and more recently in theatre.

The aim of this chapter is both to examine the various attempts at an actantial specification in theatre and, thus, to contribute to the development of this specification. First of all, however, it is important to explain, however briefly, why one would want to systematize characters' actions.

I. BACKGROUND

We owe the first actantial systematization to Vladimir Propp with his famous book *Morphology of the Folktale*,[1] published in Russian in 1928. Propp's main objective was to find a deep structure common to all the Russian folk tales that made up his corpus. In order to do this, he based his work on the notion of *function* (which would later be taken up by the French Structuralists in the 1960s).[2] This notion was central to his success, for it is based on the character's action and not on what he or she thinks or says. Propp's work was the basis of what eventually became the actantial formulations of Greimas and Souriau,[3] when he concludes that "a tale often attributes identical actions to various personages. This makes possible the study of the tale *according to the functions of its dramatis personae*".[4] The ultimate result of Propp's research brought him to the conclusion that all the Russian fairy tales share the same type of deep structure composed of a limited number of functions. He organized these functions into sequences or areas of action that structure the tale.

Etienne Souriau, using methodologies very similar to those of Propp, elaborated an actantial model based on his definition of *dramatic situation*. Souriau's main goal was "to discern by analysis the great 'dramatic functions' upon which the dynamic of theatre rests" and "to study morphologically their principal combinations".[5] The similarity of the above with Propp's proposal is significant, especially when one considers that Souriau was not aware of Propp's work.

The definition of the dramatic situation was central to the formulation of the dramatic situation's functions. According to Souriau, "A dramatic situation is the *structural figure* depicted, in a given moment of the action, by a *system of forces*; - by the system of forces present in the microcosm, the stellar centre of the theatrical universe; and incarnated or animated by the principal characters of that moment of the action".[6] This system of forces is composed of the dramatic functions. Right from the beginning, Souriau limits the dramatic function to concrete characters; the function belongs to the system and the character belongs to a given dramatic text. That is, the function constitutes the deep structure of a dramatic text, whereas the diverse situations in which the character can be found constitute the superficial structure. The system of actantial structures is stable and the same in every dramatic text and what changes is its 'combination', which, according to Souriau, can generate two hundred thousand different dramatic situations.

The actantial model that Souriau created includes six functions that are organized in the following manner:

* the incarnated thematic force
* the representative of the desired Good, the desired Value
* the actual holder of this Good
* the opponent
* the arbitrator who attributes the Good
* the helper, who has come from one of the previous forces

This model presents several significant problems. First of all, Souriau does not distinguish between the receiver and the sender of the action. Consequently, it is difficult to distinguish between the motivation of the subject (that which moves the subject to act) and the action of the subject. In Anne Ubersfeld's proposed model, to be considered later on, this problem is clarified,[7] for (as she points out) one is dealing with two actantial functions rather than one. The second problem is that the arbitrator is a redundant function because of the fact that it cannot be adopted or assimilated by the helper, a function that Souriau leaves unclear. Despite these problems, however, this model is a first attempt at systematization, and unfortunately it was not developed further by critics until Anne Ubersfeld's proposal some thirty years later.

II. THE ACTANTIAL MODEL

The actantial model was introduced into theatre by Anne Ubersfeld who, with some modifications, took it from Greimas. In this explanation, I shall make a few more.

The term actant, first coined by Greimas, is a function (actantial) not to be confused with the notion of character which is always individualized by distinctive features which render the character different.[8] The actant has a universal quality: an actant can be a character, a group of characters, a collective character, an inanimate object or simply an abstraction like justice, liberty or God, etc. Within a dramatic work, a character can simultaneously or successively adopt different actantial functions. For example, a character can adopt the actantial function of subject and sender of the action. The actant can be absent from the stage and in that case, its presence is solely textual; that is, it is present in the discourse of other subjects of the utterance.

Building on Greimas and Ubersfeld, the following basic actantial model can be formulated:[9]

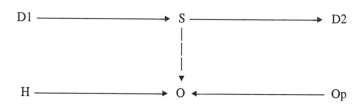

According to Greimas, the actantial model is the extrapolation of syntactic structure.[10] Thus, within the model,

> An actant identifies with an element (lexicalized or not) which assumes a syntactic function in the base sentence/phrase of the story: there are the *subject* and the *object*, the *receiver*, the *opponent* and the *helper*, whose syntactic functions are obvious; the sender, whose grammatical role is less visible and who belongs, if one may say it, to a previous sentence/phrase ..., or according to the vocabulary of traditional grammar, it is a causal object.[11]

The model is derived from these six actantial functions distributed into binary groups of opposition: subject vs. object, sender vs. receiver, helper vs. opponent.

Some of the actantial functions may be empty in a given DT; that is, one of the lexicalized elements may or may not be absent in one of the functions. For example, the function of receiver may be empty and this would indicate the absence of a motivating force (or cause) of an action, this being the distinctive feature of that play.

The function of helper may be absent, emphasizing in this way the solitude of the subject. Various elements may be present simultaneously in relation to the object. The same can occur with the functions of opponent, sender, receiver and subject.[12]

A) *Subject/Object*

The basic syntactic axis is composed of the subject/object pair. This axis that unites the subject to its object of desire is indicated by an arrow which shows the direction of its search (↓). Hence, when one wants to identify the main subject of action, this can be done only in relation with the object. In this way, there is no such thing as an autonomous subject in the DT/PT, but rather a subject-object. Ubersfeld points out that "the subject in a literary text is the one around whose desire the action, that is, the actantial model, is organized, the one we may take as the subject of the actantial phrase, the one whose positivity of desire, along with the obstacles it encounters, brings about the movement of the whole text".[13] Thus, the subject contains a series of precise characteristics: above all, it has to be a force directed towards an object; it can be a collective, but never an entirely abstract entity. In other words, it has to be anthropomorphic. The object of the subject's search can be individual, abstract or collective. Its dependence is determined not only by its relationship to a subject but also by its relationship to the sender, especially if the subject and the sender are made up of two different actors. (See below for further explanation of the actorial function).

B) *Sender/Receiver*

The sender/receiver pair has the following function: the sender has the function of motivator or promotor of the directed action of the subject; the receiver has the function of receiver or detainer of the action of the former. The sender (D1), which is usually not lexicalized, constitutes a motivation which determines the subject's action, which is why it is so important. From the D1 one can determine whether the subject's action is solely individual or whether it is ideological as well. If the arrow from the D1 to the S goes to O as well, then this is what Ubersfeld has called the psychological triangle:[14]

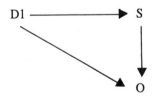

The triangle shows the dual character of the subject's action: it is both psychological and ideological. For example, in many dramatic texts one will often observe the formation of this triangle, for the subject's desire is not determined by solely individualistic factors; instead, ideological factors also play a role. Both the personal desire and social conscience of the subject cause the subject to act. The sender can be dual, with lexicalized and non-lexicalized actants. For example, in one of the first scenes of *Santa Juana de América* by Andres Lizárraga, what motivates Juana to marry Manuel is as much the mother as it is Eros.[15]

The sender is very important because it, too, indicates whether the subject's action is individual or collective. If it is individual, the arrow should go from the subject and object to the receiver but if the action is carried out with the intention of procuring collective gain or for a third party, then the arrow will go from the subject and object to the receiver. Ubersfeld calls the formation of this second triangle the 'ideological triangle':[16]

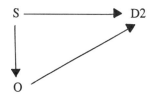

In many dramatic texts, the subject obeys this triangle, for its action has a collective purpose and not just an individual one.

At the levels of both reception and the actantial model, there exists a dual receiver-spectator: one within the world of the stage and the other outside that world. The first consists of the actantial receiver who receives the message from an enunciating character. The second is the spectator-receiver to whom the message of the dramatic text is addressed. This actantial function is of importance, for in the very unfolding of the performance, the spectator-receiver tends to identify him or herself with the actantial receiver.

C) *Helper/Opponent*

Finally, the helper/opponent pair can have quite a mobile function. At a given moment in the action, the helper can become the opponent and vice versa. This pair continually maintains a tight relationship with the subject/object axis. The opponent can oppose either the subject or the object or both simultaneously. These different relationships are expressed in what Ubersfeld calls the active triangle.[17] The arrow of desire (↓) directing the action of the subject and determining the function of the opponent can be present in different ways, depending on its relationship to the subject or the object. If the opponent opposes the subject and not the object, the following triangle will be seen:

If the opponent opposes the object of the subject, the following triangle will be seen:

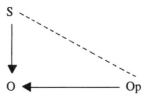

However, at this point it is important to indicate the possibility of a third triangle besides the two Ubersfeld discusses. In this triangle, the opponent opposes both subject and object:

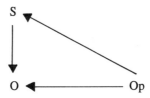

In the case of the actantial function of helper, one also has to decide whether this function is the helper of the subject or of the object. As in the previous case, I propose a third triangle that accounts for help for both the subject and the object. If the help is for the subject, the following triangle will be observed:

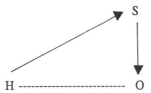

If the help is towards the object of the subject:

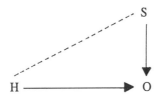

And if the help is directed to both the subject and the object then two solid line arrows will go from the helper to the subject and the object:

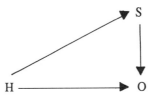

D) *Actants, Actors, Roles*

The actants, as already mentioned, are abstract units found in every DT/PT, independent of the superficial structure. The actants are manifest in the DT/PT through the actors. According to Ubersfeld, "The actor is a lexicalized unit of the literary or mythic narrative",[18] or in other words, the actor is the realization or individualization of an actant. This lexicalisation consists of a generic name, for example, father-actor, people-actor, king-actor, etc. According to Greimas, the actants belong to the narrative syntax, whereas the actors belong to the specific discourses in which they show themselves.[19] This same phenomenon occurs in theatre; hence, concepts elaborated for the narrative can be applied in theatre.

Quoting Greimas once again, "if an actant (A1) can be manifest in the discourse by several actors (a1, a2, a3), the inverse is equally possible, a single actor (a1) being the syncretism of several actants (A1, A2, A3)".[20] Greimas presents these models with the following diagrams, where A = actant and a = actor:

In this way, the actor is never confused with the actant, although the actor is a more specific abstraction because it is the actual realization of one or several of the actants. The actant is an element of the deep structure whereas the actor is an element of the superficial structure, belonging to a specific text. According to Ubersfeld, "There are a certain number of semes which correspond to and characterize the actor as lexeme".[21] The actor is characterized by: a) his or her own process in which he or she plays a role of nominal syntagm related to a fixed verbal syntagm (Y deceives X); b) a number of differentiating features with a binary function: man/woman, old person/young person, etc. In this way, two characters can have the same characteristics and carry out the same action, making up a single actor. The actor, therefore, as a unity of dramatic discourse, forms part of an intersection of a number of paradigms and syntagms, which is the actor's process. Three characters constituting a single actor may reveal various differences when analyzed paradigmatically. Thus, a character, for example Hamlet, has the actantial function of subject and the actorial function of prince.

What allows actor and actant to combine in characters is *role*. This function runs the risk of being confused with that of actor. They are, however, two distinct functions. I prefer to use Greimas' definition of role from *Du sens*. Here he claims that *role*

> at the level of discourse is manifested, on the one hand as a qualification, an attribute of the actor, and on the other hand, this qualification, from the semantic point of view, is nothing but the denomination subsuming a field of functions (that is, of behaviours actually noted in the narrative, or simply implied). Consequently, the minimal semantic content of the *role* is identical to that of the actor, *with the exception of the semes of individuation* which the latter does not possess: the role is a figurative, animated entity, but anonymous and *social*; the actor, on the other hand, is an individual who integrates and assumes one or more roles.[22]

As with the function of actor, role is a mediator between the abstract actantial code and the concrete manifestations of the text (characters). Depending on the theatre code (comedy, tragedy, etc.), it is possible for the actors to have roles determined by a single function imposed by the code itself. One only has to think of characters like those found in the *Commedia dell'Arte* (Arlequin, Pantalone, Scapini) or of the 'gracioso' of the Spanish theatre of the Siglo de Oro to find examples where roles are determined by the code. Thus, the 'gracioso' or Arlequin are not actors but roles. A good example of this actor/role codification comes from the *Gruppo teatro laboratorio de Verona* (Théâtre Lucenaire, Paris, 1985) where, despite the fact that the performance was in seventeenth-century Italian, the audience could easily follow the plot because of their performance competence.

It is important to point out that every character can have its original role taken away to be recodified with a new function. Galileo of Bertolt Brecht is one example of this. The main distinction between actor and role is that role is determined by a number of distinctive features (a function) and an actor is a specific process (Y loves X, having the role of seducer). The dramatic play, according to Greimas, occurs on three distinct levels: "the *roles*, elementary actantial units corresponding to the coherent functional fields, enter into the composition of two sorts of larger units: the *actors*, units of the discourse, and the *actants*, units of the narrative".[23] Thus, the basic, superficial unit of drama, which may be atomized into actant, actor and role, is the character.

Starting with character as subject of an act of enunciation (*énonciation*) and of the discourse and, thus, of the utterance (*énoncé*), it is possible to determine with precision the object of the character's desire as well as the main action. It is also possible to write the basic phrase or equation that will formulate the actantial model. In this way, the semic input "Y wants revolution" (as in *Santa Juana de América*) generates a dramatic situation and at the same time an actantial model that accounts for all of the actants, present or absent, lexicalized or non-lexicalized.

The analysis of the concept of character has to be done by studying the different paradigms to which this concept belongs. An inventory of these paradigms can be organized into three different diagrams or tables:[24] a) the first accounts for all of the actants of the DT at the micro-sequential level and this helps to establish the characters' relationships within each actantial model; b) a second table accounts for the lexicalized actants (present or absent) for each DT at a macro-sequential (MS) and a super-sequential (SS) level; c) a final table considers each character individually so as to observe the character's evolution throughout the work. For example, with respect to *Oedipus Rex*, the following tables can be made:

I. **Actantial Function: Micro-Sequences**

	Sender	Subject	Object	Receiver	Helper	Opponent
S1	Plague Hunger	Citizens of Thebes	Save the city	City of Thebes	Oedipus	———
S2	Oedipus	Creon	Meeting Laius' assassin	Oedipus	Apollo's oracle	———

II. Actantial Functions: Macro-Sequence and Super Sequence

	Sender	Subject	Object	Receiver	Helper	Opponent
MS1	The city	Oedipus	The guilty	The city	The city Creon	
MS2	Knowing/ discovery	Oedipus	Place of origin	Oedipus	Jocasta Tiresias Pastor Messenger	Jocasta Tiresias Pastor
SS	The city	Oedipus	The guilty Place of origin	The city	Jocasta Creon Jocasta Tiresias Messenger	Tiresias Pastor

III. Derivation of Roles and Actantial and Actorial Functions

	Characters	Actant	Actor	Role
S1	Citizens of Thebes	Subject	Citizen	Protector
	Oedipus	Helper	King	Agent
S2	Creon	Subject	Prince	Messenger
	Oedipus	Helper Receiver	King	Protector

These three tables show three forms of systematizing theatre action and of accounting for the actantial totality of the DT/PT; thus, they provide a fairly detailed and exact description of the actions of the text. This systematization is based on my definition of sequence (S) which presumes that everyone has a previous understanding of the definition of dramatic situation.

E) *Sequences*

Establishing actantial models of the DT/PT is primarily an activity of segmentation of the dramatic syntax of the DT/PT and this can only be done through the formulation of sequences integrating the different actantial models. The term *sequence* refers to a piece of action with linear development that is complete in itself (coherent). Global sequence (super-sequence) is composed of: 1) an initial situation,

situation, 2) the text-action, and 3) a situation of arrival. The super-sequence, however, can be divided into smaller ones, if internal structural ruptures in the DT/PT are desired. In this case, two further distinctions have to be made: a) micro-sequences and b) macro-sequences.

1) Micro-sequence

The micro-sequence is the sequence that corresponds to the scene from traditional theatre or simply to the entry and exit of characters onto and from the stage. Every time a sequence is isolated, an actantial model must be formed, one that expresses the central event of the sequence. In this way, one can segment the DT into a series of micro-sequences expressed in micro-sequential actantial models (as in table I).

2) Macro-sequence

The macro-sequence normally corresponds to the act in traditional theatre, or to a division that occurs within the structure of the DT/PT, as in *Oedipus Rex*. The macro-sequence is made up of a number of micro-sequences that compose the act or some other interior division of the DT/PT. The macro-sequence must also be expressed in an actantial model that reveals the focus or nucleus of the dramatic situation. Thus, the text has to be divided into a series of micro-sequences (see table II).

3) Super-sequence

The super-sequence, as mentioned above, is the global or total sequence of the DT/PT. This sequence is formed by all the macro-sequences together. The super-sequence should reveal the basic dramatic situation of the DT/PT, that is, what Souriau calls the directed force (see table II).

The actantial model is not only useful for describing and revealing the structure of the action of a DT/PT; it can also reveal the ideology inherent in each actantial position, determined as it is by the actantial inter-relationship of the various characters or abstract entities. The virtue of this way of analyzing action is that it avoids other more subjective and substantialist forms of characterization, for it is based on function and not on what some critic thinks or feels. Without doubt, like all models, this particular model is somewhat mechanical, but at least it provides a needed instrument for the analysis of action in theatre.

ENDNOTES
CHAPTER V

1. *Morphology of the Folktale.* 2nd edition revised and edited with a preface by Louis A. Wagner, new introduction by Alan Dundes (Austin: University of Texas Press, 1988).

2. See for example the article by Roland Barthes, "Introduction à l'analyse structurale des récits", *Communications*, 8 (1966), 1-27.

3. For example, in *Du sens* (Paris: Editions du Seuil, 1970) or *Sémantique structurale* (Paris: Librairie Larousse, 1966); and *Les deux cent mille situations dramatiques* (Paris: Flammarion Editeur, 1950), respectively.

4. *Morphology of the Folktale*, p. 20. He adds: "*Function is understood as an act of a character, defined from the point of view of its significance for the course of the action. Ibid.*, p. 21.

5. *Les deux cent mille situations dramatiques*, p. 6 (our translation).

6. *Ibid.*, p. 55 (our translation).

7. *Lire le théâtre* (Paris: Editions Sociales, 1982), pp. 58-118.

8. See Greimas, "Les actants, les acteurs et les figures", in *Sémiotique narrative et textuelle* (Paris: Librairie Larousse, 1973), pp. 161-176, and *Sémantique structurale*, pp. 175-178; and Darko Suvin, "Per una teoria dell'analisi agenziale" *Versus*, 30 (September-December 1981), 87-109. Finally, there is also the paper by Mihai Dinu, "The Algebra of Scenic Situations", in *Semiotics of Drama and Theatre*, edited by Herter Schmidt and Aloysius van Kesteren (The Hague: John Benjamins, 1984), pp. 67-92. This study approaches the problem mathematically, and comes up with an actantial configuration that is in fact of little practical use.

9. In *Lire le théâtre*, Ubersfeld introduces changes to Greimas' actantial model as proposed in *Sémantique structurale*, pp. 180-181. This is Greimas' model:

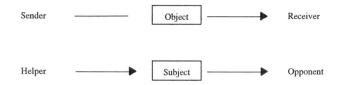

What Ubersfeld has done is to change the position of subject and object, for in principle, "I prefer that they (the arrows) converge in the object, insofar as the conflict develops *around the object*". *Lire le théâtre*, p. 70.

10. *Sémantique structurale*, p. 185.

11. *Lire le théâtre*, p. 68 (our translation).

12. For more on the relationship between subject and object, sender and receiver, helper and opponent, see *Sémantique structurale*, pp. 176-178 and my book, *Brecht en el teatro hispanoamericano contemporáneo* (Buenos Aires: Editorial Galerna, 1987).

13. *Lire le théâtre*, p. 79 (our translation).

14. *Ibid.*, pp. 86-88.

15. See my article, "Ideología y teatro épico in *Santa Juana de América*", *Latin American Theatre Review*, XIV, 1 (Fall 1980), 55-65, and *Brecht en el teatro hispanoamericano contemporáneo*.

16. *Lire le théâtre*, pp. 88-89.

17. *Ibid.*, p. 85.

18. *Ibid.*, p. 107 (our translation).

19. *Sémiotique narrative et textuelle*, p. 161.

20. *Ibid.*, p. 161 (our translation).

21. *Lire le théâtre*, p. 108 (our translation).

22. *Du sens*, p. 256. See also, *Sémiotique narrative et textuelle*, pp. 169-175 (our translation).

23. *Ibid.*, p. 256 (our translation).

24. Regarding this topic, refer to the appendices in my book *Brecht en el teatro hispanoamericano contemporáneo*.

CHAPTER VI

THEATRE HISTORY AND SEMIOTICS

> Voici une histoire de la littérature (n'importe laquelle; on n'établit pas un palmarès, on réfléchit sur un statut); elle n'a d'histoire que le nom: c'est une suite de monographies, dont chacune à peu de choses près, enclôt un auteur et l'étudie lui-même; l'histoire n'est ici que succession d'hommes seuls; bref ce n'est pas une histoire, c'est une chronique.
> Roland Barthes, *Sur Racine*.

I. GENERAL BACKGROUND

The notions of description and history have until very recently been mutually exclusive. The contradiction between these two notions, which are in fact two distinct *ways* of looking at the literary phenomenon, lies in the opposition between the synchronic and the diachronic perspective. Until the advent of the Russian Formalists, and the subsequent development of Structuralism and Semiotics in the late nineteenth and early twentieth centuries, the study of literature was primarily historical.[1]
The main characteristic of this approach can be resumed in one word: the *reconstitution* of the literary work, that is, of the genesis of a work, its period and the current to which it belongs, the life and ideas of the author, the cultural atmosphere, etc. The main problem with this historiographical approach is that the analysis revolved *around* the literary object and ignored the object itself, since the actual object was not yet defined.[2] Another fundamental problem is that the historiographical approach avoids the question of *how* form and content evolve in the historical process that constitutes the diachronic axis. Nor does it try to explain why these changes occur. History only served as a background to render the texts comprehensible, especially from a philological and at best, philosophical perspective. In examples where historical change was considered, this was usually understood as a 'natural' logico-causal evolution - it was simply a mechanical process. A period or movement evolved in a natural way into another period or movement, and no rupture was recorded. Thus, Romanticism evolved 'naturally' from Classicism and then it became Naturalism and so on.

This historiographical approach was criticized and abandoned by the Russian Formalists who emphasized the *literarity* of the literary work - that is, the specific nature of its structure. Thus, the focus of literary inquiry became synchronic and descriptive in nature. Starting with the famous formalist studies, the synchronic descriptive approach evolved, continued with the Prague School and eventually led to Structuralism and Semiotics. What characterised this new way of looking at and confronting the literary text is the description of how the text functions and the abandonment of the diachronic approach. The Formalists, however, did not completely ignore the problem of history, and many of their contributions in this area are still valid.

One of the problems that attracted attention was that of *literary variability* - that is, the evolution or change of a literary series.[3] This evolution was not thought to be autonomous and separate from the rest of the culture that produces literary texts. On the contrary, Tynianov claimed that "The study of literary *evolution* does not reject the dominant signification of the principal social factors, on the contrary, it is only within this framework that the signification may be elucidated in its totality".[4] Despite the early efforts by the Russian Formalists, and due to the new orientation that had been created in the area of criticism, literary history was neglected for many years because it was considered a futile and unnecessary effort.[5] As a result of the adoption of new analytical methods emphasizing the literary text rather than its surroundings, and due to the over-reaction against old methods, some even concluded that history lacks a well-defined *object* of study.[6]

II. THE CURRENT STATE OF AFFAIRS IN HISTORIC RESEARCH

The divorce between literary history and literary criticism or science originated in a historic reality: literary science abandoned any historical pretensions it had when it came to be believed that literary history brought little or nothing to the study and knowledge of literature. Thus, modern Structuralism has been invaluable and has contributed enormously to the study of the literary object, eliminating all forms of impressionism that were so characteristic of anecdotal historical 'methods'. The basis of modern literary science consisted of more and more elaborate and refined theoretical models for the analysis of literary texts, from Vladimir Propp's excellent work to the studies of Tzvetan Todorov, Gérard Genette, Claude Bremond, Patrice Pavis, Marco De Marinis, just to mention a few.[7] However, if a synchronic study of the literary text wishes to be complete and if it hopes to explain the literary *change* and not simply reconstitute historico-literary fact, then it must include a diachronic approach.

This position of considering synchrony and diachrony, description and history, as mutually exclusive, non-complementary approaches requires that we reconsider the role literary history has played in the study of literature.[8] Such a reformulation might be a cause for worry for many critics who, for such a long time, bothered only with description and synchrony. This new historical approach is being done from various perspectives which have in common the integration of description into the sociocultural context and an attempt at explaining literary change.[9] Such studies have proposed 'a new literary historiography' and have presented provoking and suggestive ideas on the renovation of literary historiography, but they rarely propose norms or theoretical models that would allow theorists to confront the many problems facing literary history. In general, these attempts have concentrated more on highlighting or indicating the problems in the old and new methods suggested by contemporary critics than on presenting new proposals on *how* the literary phenomenon should be studied.[10] What has been lacking is a theoretical and methodological proposal for this 'new' history. In the trajectory new research has followed, few researchers have dealt with this complex problem. The only convincing examples are Juan Villegas, Michel Riffaterre and Hans-Robert Jauss, at least with reference to what we have just been discussing. The point here is not to say that they have not resolved all the problems; they have, however, established operational theoretical models for the diachronic analysis of literary texts. The three studies mentioned deserve our attention and we will consider them briefly so as to point out where we agree and disagree.

In his excellent article "Pour une approche formelle de l'histoire littéraire", Michel Riffaterre proposes a literary history beginning with a triple analysis: a) the relationships between texts, genres and literary movements; b) the observation of how a reading of a text can change; c) the re-establishment of the true significance of the text.[11] These three proposed levels are based on an idea of what constitutes or should constitute literary history, as seen from the viewpoint of stylistic analysis. For Riffaterre, "literature is not made of intentions, but of texts; ... texts are composed of words, not of things or ideas; ... the literary phenomenon is not situated in the relationship between the author and the text, but rather in the relationship between the text and the reader".[12] With respect to the first level Riffaterre proposes, the following needs to be questioned. No doubt, the study of the relationships between texts, their relationship with the genre and with the various literary currents is useful, for the text-text relationship can show formal or other types of similarities or differences with texts of the same period. The relationship of these texts with the genre and different aspects of genre may help to explain these components of rupture. The problem, however, is to explain how this textual relationship occurs, and what norms should be followed when establishing the tri-partite relationship (text-text, text-genre, text-movements). Riffaterre appears to propose a functional analysis,[13] but in that case one would have to specify what the *components* of this analysis are.[14]

The 'history of successive readings', which is in fact Jauss's proposal and, in a certain way, Riffaterre's proposal as well, appears to contain the key to literary history: "The response of the reader to the text is the only relation or causality which can invoke an explanation of literary facts".[15] A distinction is made between two types of perception or reading; the first consists of the first readings by the first readers and the second consists of readings by later readers. The relationship these readers establish with the text, which Riffaterre considers to be immutable,[16] is the following: the first readers carry out a reading *in* the current linguistic code (code of the linguistic context) which is the same as that of the text, and later readers perform a reading in codes of their own context, which is different due to the distance between the reading and the text. Riffaterre, however, makes an interesting point with respect to the text. If it is true that it is immutable because its code is secure and given, it is also true that the text is in a constant state of flux. This statement is important, for on the one hand, it recognises the permanence of the textual code while on the other, it introduces a dynamism in the reading process and the ever-changing *social context*. In this way, a history could begin with a systematization of the *various readings* readers have done in distinct moments of time. There are problems that arise, however. In my opinion, the changes of forms of literary evolution are not subordinate to or determined by the process of reading. I do not share the view that history is made up of textual interpretations, that is, of purely hermeneutic work. I believe it involves situating and systematizing the *change of the signifying system* as a system and relating it to other outside systems that also play a role in the change of the signifier/signified. The reading process can not, in itself, alter or explain structural changes; rather it can only work on the level of meaning, which is undoubtedly always changing. But we still have not explained how or why ruptures and mutations in a given signifying practice occur.

Finally, the concept of the *reconstituted* 'original' meaning of the text is debatable, at least in the way Riffaterre has presented it. For him "the true, the only, original signification of a text is the one its first readers gave it.... It is their reactions which permit [the original meaning] to be discovered".[17] The concept of original meaning is erroneous, for a text is always interpreted to some extent in each moment of its history. When the social context changes, the ways of perceiving or reading a text change too. Therefore, its interpretation and decodification changes along with the code of the moment when the reading occurs. Each reader reads from his/her own code and it is difficult, if not impossible, to establish an original meaning. It is correct, however, to say that the distance between a medieval or renaissance text and a modern reader is immense, and this means that the immediate referents to which the text refers are not present, and thus an effort of *reconstitution* of the original meaning of the text occurs. But, how is this done? This is not a useless question since when this occurs, it is based on this very process of reconstitution, one that is usually impossible to do because of the lack of data relating to the reader's *horizon of expectations* (*Erwartungshorizont*) and the *reception* of these texts within this horizon. Furthermore, it is impossible to read an ancient or past text without the text being processed through the receptive context of a reader at a given moment. This is inevitable. It does not appear feasible to read a text using a social context that is not one's own. Even in those cases where a reconstitution of the horizon of expectations and of the receptive impact is possible, this does not mean that the reading or interpretation of this text - that is, its *concretization* - has a significant influence on our interpretation. At best, it could show us how a text might have been interpreted at a given moment or it could clarify lexical and semantic contexts and other parts of the linguistic code whose referents escape us today. No doubt the reconstitution of the context is necessary for establishing the components of a text's contextual production, but it is not required for the actual analytical process concerned with the organization of signs in the signifying system.

The work of Hans-Robert Jauss appears to be one of the more serious efforts of contemporary historiography. His excellent work on reception inevitably forced him to confront the problem of history and then to propose a history based on aesthetics of reception. According to Jauss, this reception depends on the "degree to which it can take an active part in the continual integration of past art by aesthetic experience".[18] Jauss proposes seven theses for the elaboration of a literary history using the reception of texts. They can be summed up in the following manner:

1) aesthetics of reception and impact;
2) horizon of expectation;
3) aesthetic distance and change of horizon of expectation;
4) past and present understanding of the work: reconstitution of the horizon of expectations;
5) diachronic study of reception;
6) synchronic study of the literary referents of a period;
7) study of the relationship between the immanent development of literature and the general process of history.

In general terms, Jauss's article proposes a concrete means (theoretical/methodological) for elaborating history; this is its main value, more than any actual results, which are in fact debatable. His theses are coherent, yet conflicting. For Jauss, "History of literature is a process of aesthetic reception and production which take place in the realization of literary texts on the part of the receptive reader, the reflective critic and the author in his continued creativity".[19]

The main problem with this view of history is that it puts the accent on *reception* (for the critic and the reader are both receivers) and also on the actual production of texts within a given context. But one wonders if a history of literature based on reception is truly possible. No doubt the reception of texts can have its own history, but this history does not explain literary change, for it is difficult to accept that the role of the reader is central in literary change. The point here is not to deny the (dialectical) role of the reader. This role, however, is no more important than the historical reality of the moment or than the text-text and text-context relationships. Moreover, to claim, as Jauss does in his third thesis, that: "It is only in view of such a horizon change that the analysis of literary effect achieves the dimension of a literary history of readers and provides the statistical curves of the historical recognition of the bestseller",[20] appears to be an overestimation of the role of the reader. No doubt, what is sought (*statistical curves*) is achieved, but this explains neither what change occurs nor how the change in the horizon of expectations occurs. It is the text itself that changes and the reader perceives this change, and if this is what Jauss is saying, then it is accomplished in the statistics. It is important to state that what is actually being proposed is a history of reception and not of literature.

The literary text does not change simply because the receiver acknowledges this change. On the contrary, the change is first noticed and then the reader confirms it. Change may or may not be noticed by contemporary readers comparing current texts with past texts because the social context, the reader and the producer of texts are all constantly changing. Also, the change may be noticed in the present moment or noticed years later, but the concrete change occurs in the first text. This is not to deny in any way whatsoever the *productive* activity of the reader, but idealist notions of the reader deciding everything must be avoided.

The method Jauss proposes could be very useful in trying to understand remote past texts, but even in those cases one must be careful, for, as Gadamer comments: "Understanding is always the process of fusion of such horizons which seem to exist independently".[21]

With respect to the problem of synchrony, while he adopts important elements from the Russian Formalists, Jauss questions the most valuable part of their work - that is, the change or formal variability of texts. Although one might agree with the importance of "the ordering of the individual work in its 'literary series' so that its historical position and significance in the context of literary experience can be recognized",[22] it is hard to agree with Jauss when he says that: "Literary history as 'literary evolution' presupposes the historical process of aesthetic reception and production up to the observer's time as a condition for the communicating of all formal contrasts or 'qualities of difference'".[23] This argument merits an objection: it is highly subjective to base literary evolution on the receiver of the text or in the historical changes in reception. The main problem here is the lack of scientific rigor, for *the search for meaning*, the objective of hermeneutics, has always lacked a systematic approach when faced with the literary phenomenon and, thus, has special difficulty with *continuity of meaning* or reception at a given moment in time. Furthermore, there is difficulty in determining the only actual material object of study: the literary text. The following statement by Jauss is especially significant and useful, although his perspective on the impact (*Wirkung*) of a work is debatable:

> The new becomes a historical category when the diachronic analysis of literature is forced to face the questions of which historical forces really make the literary work new, to what degree this newness is recognizable in the historical moment of its appearance, what distance, route, or circumlocution of understanding were required for its full realization, and whether the moment of this realization was so effective that it could change the perspective of the old and thereby the canonization of the literary past.[24]

In contrast to the problems we find in Jauss' understanding of synchrony, his understanding of diachrony is undeniably valuable and essential (paradoxically) to the formulation of a diachronic axis. He proposes taking synchronic slices at different moments in their process, then establishing relationships between contemporary texts and hence, categories, so as to attain a general system. The establishment of the historical character of the literary fact is extremely important, for it

149

> appears exactly at the intersection of the diachronic and synchronic approaches. It must be possible to analyze the literary horizon of a certain historical moment as that synchronic system in which simultaneously appearing works can be received diachronically in relation, and in which the work can appear as of current interest or not, as fashionable, out-dated or of lasting value, or before its time or after it.[25]

The third study that is worthy of consideration is that of Juan Villegas. Even though it was on lyric poetry, this study deals with aspects common to literary history in general, and more notably, Latin American literary history, where solid studies simply do not exist. From a theoretical point of view, this present study is closest to Villegas'.[26] One of the central points in Villegas' theory is the importance he attributes to the structure of the literary work and the change a system undergoes. He claims that "on the basis of the individual analysis of a series of works one may postulate structures which recur in a historical moment, suggesting certain general traits which explain the community. There must be a literary change or a stage of a possible periodization when the structural changes are such that they form a different system".[27] I will not discuss this quote immediately since it will be referred to in my theoretical proposal. I should only remark that the connection between structure and change is fundamental when doing history, for such a link unites the axes of synchrony (structure) and diachrony (change). Based on this fundamental hypothesis, I can now develop a theory that goes beyond the periodization and historization to which we are accustomed.

A second important point in Villegas' theory (and in this area he is closer to Riffaterre and Jauss) is the connection of the literary work and its formal components to ideological and historical components. That is, he believes that it is the social context that produces literary texts. For Villegas, the literary work "is not an entity which is explained only in relation to itself, rather it is in relation with or conditioned by factors which are apparently external and whose influence is diverse in sense and proportions, in the distinct instances of the creative process".[28] Social context was discussed in relation to reception (chapter IV). No attempt at doing history can be successful solely from a formal perspective, for although such an approach does reveal how forms function, it fails to explain why certain forms emerge at a given historical moment.

The structure-context relationship implies the need for developing a periodization method since current ones contain more problems than solutions.[29] On this very point, Villegas claims that "literature as history conforms to a series of instances - the periods - in which diverse systems co-exist - based upon visions of the world - one of which supplies the defining character of the period. In each period, moreover, the world visions are found in diverse stages of development".[30] Although I agree with the main part of this statement, I object somewhat to the idea of accounting for the process of change or rupture with an appeal to a 'world vision' because it puts emphasis on the semantic component of the text rather than on the system that makes up the period, which seems much more important (I will return to this point later).[31]

Much of what Riffaterre, Jauss and Villegas argue could be integrated into a model for the literary text, with connections being made to other texts in the historical context. I have considered these three theoreticians because of their theoretical and methodological proposals. Additionally, they have also created new interest in the areas of literary history, literary theory and the descriptive methodologies of literary theory. Unfortunately, this type of research has been largely ignored by literary historians in Latin America. For this reason, I will now present an example of how Latin American historiography has evolved thus far.

III. THEORY OF LITERARY HISTORY IN LATIN AMERICA: ONE EXAMPLE

A) *The Generational Method and Literary Currents*

In Latin America, the theory of literary history has focused mainly on what are called the 'generational method' and the 'literary current method' beginning with the work of Pedro Henríquez Ureña and continuing with Max Henríquez Ureña, José Arrom, Enrique Anderson Imbert, Fernando Alegría, Cedomil Goic, Luis Alberto Sánchez and Jean Franco.[32] These two 'methods', especially the generational approach, represent the way literary history has been confronted. Despite its many advantages, however, the generational method is not able to provide a theoretical framework, let alone a methodological one, that can explain literary change or the development of literary systems in the diachronic axis. Its very nature invalidates it for strictly historical work. In response to these and other criticisms of and objections to the generational method, Arrom states:

> It appears, in the first place, as an instrument of critique and it is not. It is a procedure for ordering, not for analyzing and evaluating. A literary creation is not explained *by* the generation. Situating a work within a historical ordering neither highlights its merits nor points out its faults. One avoids, certainly, falling into inapproriate conclusions. One relates the work with others within a causal current and it acquires a meaning which isolated it does not have. Consequently, this method does not judge. It situates, relates, illuminates and enriches.[33]

Arrom's statement invalidates this method as an instrument for literary history, simply because to historicize means *to explain and to systematize* literary creation into various synchronic systems projected into the diachronic axis that constitutes the *historical process*. Furthermore, again according to Arrom, this method is not an instrument of criticism and even less of analysis: its main purpose is to arrange. But it is obvious that to arrange authors and texts is far from doing literary history.[34] In any case, Arrom's point is useful in that it identifies the limits of the generational method. It is essentially a means of periodization, but even then it is questionable.[35]

B) *Periodization*

Periodization is certainly necessary in order to locate and explain literary systems at given points in history and to relate them to preceding and later systems. The problem arises when we ask the question: how do we periodize? By centuries? (The fifteenth or seventeenth, for example?) By eras? (The Renaissance, Baroque or Classical?) According to historical eras? (Victorian?) By generations? (The '27' in Spain?) As Oldrich Belic has argued, these different ways of forming periods work according to practical criteria of classification, description, etc.[36] However, such periodization should be more scientific, and its goal should be to define objectively these periods in the diachronic axis. A change in period should imply a change in the *system of expression*. Belic argues that periodization "should be literary, that is, one should study the evolution of literature as literature; or, more concretely, one should fix the periods and discover the changes between periods with the help of criteria which are uniquely and exclusively literary".[37] According to Belic, these uniquely literary criteria should be obtained from the empirical study of systems making up the period, the alteration of which would create a new period. These criteria should be clearly identified, for they, too, can be diverse: the criteria could include changes in content, form, genres or style. A change in a *system* creates changes in all of the components of the system, and this is what brings about the new system or subsystem.

Although these and other comments by Villegas are helpful, the problem of periodization is not yet resolved. Belic and Villegas are correct in stating that periodization should begin with the actual literary facts, in the texts at our disposal, that are seen as part of historical reality. The analysis of these texts is what allows us to periodize. Also, the *description* and *explanation* of the evolution and change should lead to the formation of systems and subsystems determining a period. But in order to do this, a methodology has first to be elaborated.[38]

Various Latin American critics doing literary history of Latin America have criticized the generational method of periodization. However, they have not (with the exception of Villegas) proposed a new appoach to the problem. In fact, there is some limited discussion on the topic of what European and North American critics are doing in this area: that is, the integration of literary theory, criticism and methodologies into the study of history. At the same time, in Latin America opposition has grown to theories and methods elaborated in a non-Latin American environment. Concerning the first point, Roberto Fernández Retamar has argued that: "Literary history and criticism are the obverse and the reverse of the same task: a literary history which seeks to avoid critical valuation is unachievable; and a criticism that pretends to be unconnected to history is useless and insufficient (thus both maintain essential relations with the corresponding literary theory)".[39] As for the second point, there is a strong preference for proposing one's own methods, that is, methods born of Latin American criticism. This is so because it is commonly thought that methods developed elsewhere have evolved from objects and realities which are alien to the Latin American continent.[40]

Mario Benedetti claims that in the same way that Latin American writers have created their own forms of expression (which, I should point out, is only partially true), Latin American critics "must also create our own critical focus, our own methods of investigation, our valuation with particular signs, which arise out of our conditions, our needs, our interests".[41] This statement contains a huge error, in that the advances and results of literary science cannot simply be ignored as Retamar and others[42] appear to do in a somewhat hurried and superficial way. Ignoring valuable contemporary literary theory amounts to putting oneself at the margin of history, or, at best, attempting to discover what is already known. What is valid in the arguments of Benedetti, Retamar, Rincón, Labastida and others is that theory and its methods should be applied in relation to the object being studied. That is, theory should serve as a research guide, as a means of discovering and explaining objects.

In Europe, theoretical development was always concurrent with a body of critical work - from Aristotle's *Poetics* to the new criticism of the "Tel Quel" group - and such critics as Artaud, Craig, Piscator, Brecht, Grotowski, Butor, Robbe-Grillet, to name a few, have been critics as well as producers. Their contribution has been to systematize European cultural and artistic objects. In Latin America, on the other hand, this is exactly what has been and continues to be lacking. Furthermore, much of Latin American artistic creation is heterogeneous, and in many cases consists of adaptations of other models that are absorbed into the culture. One can say that there is a sort of formal "impurity" in Latin American art when compared to the original model. The intersection of cultures and forms from *here* and *there* means that Latin American literature is a difficult phenomenon to systematize. But this does not mean that arbitrariness should reign. The lack of systematic studies is becoming obvious and hence the need to systematize grows, especially in the area of theatre criticism where almost nothing is being done.[43] One suggestive and revealing study, though perhaps limited in its scope, is by Marta Lena Paz who correctly points out that "perhaps the first thing that emerges with priority over all other questions is the methodological aspect".[44] The development of methodologies and corresponding systematizations is necessary in Latin America due to the qualitative heterogeneity, disproportionate quantity and relative lack of theory. Foremost in importance is a systematization of the qualitative heterogeneity, for theatre is in constant transition and it is non-uniform when compared to the other cultural objects of Latin America. Roberto Fernández Retamar is certainly correct when he comments: "Metropolitan literatures have behind them a process of decantation which, although it does not exclude the need for restating the question, allows for a certain amount of play in the study of these letters, a security which we usually lack ourslves".[45] Even though this statement certainly makes sense, it is important to point out that much of this security is due to the part criticism has played in their tradition. In part, the Latin American critic's insecurity comes from the fact that each time a specific area is approached, the researcher becomes a pioneer in that area. Although in some areas lots of projects and studies are being carried out, they are often partial and theoretically limited. In Latin American theatre, for instance, the problem is serious for there are no really comprehensive studies. Thus, to study Latin American theatre is a risky business.

Fernández Retamar and others recognise this and when Retamar refers to the literary history of Latin America (that is still to be written), he says that it should be done "with scientific criteria, the absence of which constitutes a heavy difficult for our work". He adds further that the work yet to be done consists of "capturing the true formal characteristics of our works, including the conceptual function of these characteristics, for which the lesson of Della Volpe is of much use".[46]

This book attempts to rise to this challenge of the search for a theory and methodology for Latin American theatre. However, unlike most of the above proposals, I believe that much of the European theoretical and methodological work is applicable and useful for the task at hand. Latin American theatre is one of the most neglected and least studied areas of Latin American literature and due to its complexity, it is impossible to study without some theory to serve as guide and method in describing and explaining the texts. In this area where so little is defined, I could summarise my attitude by quoting Günter Müller: "How can tragedy (or any other genre) be defined before knowing on what works the definition should be based? And how do we know what works should be the basis of the definition before defining tragedy?"[47] The answer is simple: the only way of approaching contemporary Latin American theatre is to begin with a theoretical model that would serve as a point of reference when approaching the object, which would be recognised from the general properties of theatre. This should be accompanied by a method that provides a description and explanation. In this way, the formulation of systems of theatre production (and in some cases sub-systems) might be organized into periods. This does not mean that theory and method are immutable and mechanical; on the contrary, they serve as a point of reference that evolves with the actual object. The study of a corpus of works guided by theory will help us understand these works. In the next few pages, I will present the methodological and theoretical basis indispensable to theatre history.

IV. THEORETICAL PROPOSAL

A) *Formal Level*

If the model is to be coherent, what should first be formulated is our understanding of theatre history or literary history in general. Doing history is not simply a matter of reconstructing the past. It is also: a) describing literary *evolution*, showing how forms change; b) explaining literary evolution: why, where, and when the change occurs. At the basis of this understanding of literary history is the notion of *change/rupture/variability*. But why study change and what changes? With respect to change, history is only understandable if the events that have occurred are described and explained in relation to their context and to what came before and after. History is simply the projection of the synchronic axis into the diachronic axis, or the intersection of these two axes. The diachronic axis is made up of a series of synchronic views, of 'slices of time' that are projected onto the diachronic axis. This axis accounts for the historic process; in it, the historicity of the phenomena (literary, political, etc.) is manifest and this axis allows for a comprehensive and retrospective view of the cultural phenomena. In this approach to history, the study of 'synchrony' and of the various synchronies that make up the synchronic axis is essential. This is where the methods of literary science should be used, for they are the basis for the formulation of synchronies. Furthermore, neither the synchronic axis nor the diachronic dynamic is a static entity.[48] The diachronic axis is a product of the synchronies which are conditioned by diachronic facts. If it is true that every synchrony is itself a system and that, as such, synchronies produce and constitute the diachrony, then it is also true that diachronic facts influence the synchrony. In a relevant study, Eugenio Coseriu points out that "the 'diachronic fact' is in reality the product of a synchronic fact and that the 'change' and the 'reorganization of the system' are not two phenomena, but rather one phenomenon".[49] This is another way of looking at the problem, that is, as history producing the present, as diachrony producing synchronies. In my opinion, however, there is a dialectic, for any change in the synchronic system involving the transformation or reorganization of a system creates change in the diachronic axis. Saussure argues that synchrony, and not diachrony, forms a system.[50] As Coseriu has pointed out, however, "it is not fitting to speak of 'system' and 'movement' - as of opposite things - but only of 'system *in movement*'".[51] In my view, the diachronic axis consists of the projection of a series of expressive systems because cultural series in the theatre function synchronically and are composed diachronically. Furthermore, the dynamism of the system is evident in its analysis and description. To do this is to do history, for "the description of a historical object is a moment of its history".[52] In this way, *to describe* is to present the object in a given moment of its process.

In formulating the relationships that exist between synchrony and diachrony, we often use the concept of *system*. A system may be understood as the ensemble of rules and components that unify a series of correlated objects. In the case of literature and literary production, the system is not permanent. It is always changing within certain periods of time. When we speak of a system, we are also referring to the concept of model, that is, the abstract and theoretical description of a structure and how it works.[53] Within a system, a model might be formulated. That is, the system allows us to articulate abstract generic properties of the objects to make a generic model - and this has nothing to do with formulating 'genre'.[54] As for genre, we will not discuss this old and tired problem and will only make a few comments on its relevance to our discussion.

In his magnificent book on this point as well as in the article "The Life and Death of Literary Forms", Alastair Fowler provides an interesting version of genre and the nature of generic change. He articulates the similarities and differences between genre and mode: "By genre I mean a better defined and more external type than mode. Genres each have their own formal structures, whereas modes depend less explicitly on [the situation] ...".[55] The main difference is the following: whereas genre is strictly regulated by its historical moment and is therefore frankly historical, mode is the variation of genre into a new form that can also become a genre determined by another historical moment but nevertheless originating from the first genre. Further on, Fowler proposes three phases which make up the process of *change* or evolution/transformation of a genre. In the first phase, a given historic genre is determined; in the second, a secondary version of the genre develops; and in the third, this secondary form is used in a completely new way, inverting the former genre. The relationship between genre and mode is dialectical. In other words, genres *generate* modes and modes generate new genres.[56] In this sense, a mode is more closely related to and dependent upon the enunciating mode which varies within a given genre, thus forming new genres. Tzvetan Todorov has presented a similar concept. For the French critic, "a new genre is always the transformation of one or several old genres: by inversion, by displacement, by combination".[57] Genres, then, are abstract systems that are transformed internally. That is, genre operates on an abstract structural level, but the way these structures materialize differs in the course of history. Thus, since genre is not static or unchanging, perhaps the study of dramatic genre should be with reference to the various diachronic forms that materialize in the process. What is immutable in genre are the basic components; for example in theatre, such things as dialogue, the diegetic structure (act/stage) and the dramatic situation remain while the way these components are organised and performed changes. Genres, as Todorov has stated, are *classes of texts* that have properties in common at a moment in time or through time.[58] This is how the production and perception of texts occur in relation to a *norm* that is simply the code of the discursive properties. The very notion of genre as a class of texts is fundamental. This means that any attempt at doing, in this case, a history of theatre requires a systematization of the notions of text, DT and PT. This was done in chapter II.

The notion of genre is certainly of heuristic value and of use in historical research, for genre is based on *generic* structures that are manifestations of an enunciative attitude.[59] The establishment of a system of generic structures organised into classes of text is useful for explaining and observing genres that exist simultaneously (in a few cases) or that persist or reappear in the historical process. One could argue, then, that genre and system are homogeneous, when in fact they are separate realities. The dramatic genre, if we accept such a notion, is articulated in history in different ways and these different *types* of articulation make up systems included *within* the notion of 'dramatic text'. The term system is preferable since genre is historical and, therefore, theoretical.[60] Also, this system is made up of *texts* that change the system when they change.

Explicit in the notions synchrony/diachrony, system/model and text/type are the notions evolution/change. When we argue that history consists of systems, and that each synchrony is a system from which a model emerges originating from the texts (which are types of enunciation), we are describing the *process of change* or of evolution. The process of change is considered not from an axiological point of view but, rather, as a process, since forms change and are transformed instead of actually evolving. The objective of literary history is to explain, at an analytical level, *how and why* systems change as well as to identify what it is that allows us to say that there is a formal change (or changes) in a dramatic structure. On the other hand, the notion of change connotes mutation, rupture and deconstruction: it suggests the substitution of one system for another. In its broad sense, change signifies the alteration of certain systemic elements causing the emergence of a sub-system (or sub-systems) but not a completely new or *ex novo* one.

At this point we must question how a system or series of systems emerges. If a history of theatre is to be done (for example, my project of doing a Latin American history of theatre from 1900 to the present), then a series of synchronic slices has to be formulated and then projected into the diachronic axis. But, where does one make these cuts? Theoretically, this can be done at any point, since a concise description and empirical examination will always provide data. These data will have to be classified according to methodological criteria which at the first, structural level organizes the common properties of the texts. The end result forces us to change the diachronic axis, both retrospectively and prospectively. This arrangement allows for interrelationships to be articulated between the diachronic systems. If one wishes to work scientifically, this is the only practical way of proceeding. One must momentarily abandon all predetermined labels. For example, some critics speak of the *chico criollo* genre in Argentina, but either no one establishes its generic structure or properties or they do it too quickly.[61] Our approach has the virtue of being able to invalidate or reject previous classifications by means of reliable methodological criteria. The formulation of synchronic systems also eases the problem of establishing sub-systems within the overall system, since a period often has a variety of generic forms or combinations that have to be described. This is particularly important when discussing Latin American theatre because its forms come from other cultures and are rarely 'pure'. In this regard, one has to proceed carefully so as not to fall prey to inadequate reductionist or other methods that attempt to force the object into an adapted or pre-conceived model. The approach we have proposed also allows us to identify what is authentic in Latin America; it allows the researcher to examine forms coming from a given country's dramaturgical tradition and practice and to separate these from forms of external origin.[62]

Another very important thing the synchronic slices reveal are the texts that cause the mutation of an expressive form, or what Jauss has called "epoch-making moments".[63] These texts undergo a radical transformation which consists of the institution (or restoration) of a new genre or even of a totally new form of expression. Beginning with these texts, which then become the model once they are canonized, a period is born in which this form lives out its potential and exhausts all of its possibilities, and then a new form of expression emerges. For example, when the so-called theatre of the absurd emerged, it did so *ex novo* and it took some time before it was accepted by the public as a new form. During the 1960s, this form spread throughout Europe and America. The structure of these texts and their use of language 'glue' its meaning to the signifier, and a unified signified and meaning evolved. The theatre of the absurd had a profound effect on theatre, but it is also the product of a whole series of experiments that began with the *isms* of the early twentieth century. A study of the theatre of the absurd would have to include previous developments in theatre in order to be able to say how this system relates to what came before and after. Moreover, other types of theatre existed at the same time - the 'thesis' type of theatre by Jean-Paul Sartre as well as certain contemporary forms of Spanish or English theatre, to name just a few.

These are the ruptures that should be studied, for they provide foci around which major changes occur. In Latin America this is far from clear, first, because such studies have not yet been done (except for Juan Villegas' recent work) and, second, because the theatre production of the many countries that make up the continent is far from uniform. There is, in fact, a substantial variation of aesthetic and formal interests within Latin American theatre. One can still say, however, that in countries like Mexico, Argentina, Chile and Uruguay, there is talk of experimental movements or of ruptures that would have occurred in the 1930s. For example, in the introduction to his book *Teatro chileno contemporáneo*, Julio Durán points out that *La viuda de Apablaza* marks the end of a period; he does this - and this is valid - from a purely thematic point of view and does not refer to the play's formal properties.[64]

A problem directly related to our task that is rarely alluded to is the selection of a corpus. How does one select? Generally, in literary history a corpus is selected on the basis of the authors' status or reputation. In other words, texts chosen for study tend to be by well-known writers. The problem with this approach is that usually nothing is discussed other than the authors' names, the content of their work and the cultural atmosphere of the time. Generally, there is no discussion of the problems alluded to here; nor is an explanation of change or evolution facilitated. We could add that these histories are quite anecdotal and subjective and lack scientific rigour. It matters little that these histories are grouped according to period, authors or literary currents: the selection really happens according to author and not on the merits of the text. This way of doing things does not lend any service to literary history and even less to the comprehension of change and evolution in the historical process of literary forms. A history should also include secondary writers that have contributed to the development and establishment of a form. This problem was already presented more than a century ago by the Russian Formalists, but few theorists followed their advice.

Throughout this book, we have seen that this neglect of corpus by the specialists is a recurrent theme. A few interesting points have been made by István Söter who suggests that selection should be done on the basis of the aesthetic and historical importance of texts.[65] For Rita Schober, the problem of selecting a corpus is subordinate to that of periodization.[66] Although she does not elaborate on either of the two problems, the suggestion is valid, depending on how one considers or interprets her position. If periodizing means establishing a system or set of synchronic systems projected onto the diachronic axis to represent history, then this implies that a selection comprising the periods or formulation of the period has already been done. But how is this established in the first place?[67]

The reading of a large number of texts is inevitable, for there is no other way of establishing systems. This reading, however, could be guided by different ideas: a) the selection should include texts that have ruptured with or radically transformed the system, thus establishing another system in the process. These texts could serve as points of reference for the periods. Of course, other works would be grouped in and thus constitute each period; b) considering texts that point to a new form of expression and thus a new system implies that the old system has ceased to exist (or exists vestigially); therefore, a retrospective analysis of the period is required to bring to light the works that initiated this change and that would therefore also constitute the final works of the old system. In this way, the entire system could be established; c) one could also work prospectively, that is, beginning with a text that creates a new system and then proceeding to describe the basis of this new system and its subsequent weakening until another rupture comes along. Thus, the *selection* is done functionally as it relates to the system, and examples of these functions should be *inscribed* in the writing of the history.

In the early stages before writing, the establishment of these systems could be determined by a rather large group of texts that would help in its formulation, and then texts/authors fulfilling the functional roles within the system could be chosen. These could be determined on the basis of texts marking a new point, thus establishing a new system. Texts that standardize and extend the system (turn it into *a canon*) should then be chosen. Finally, texts that exhaust the system until a new one appears should also be included (this does not mean the texts from previous systems cease to exist, only that they mark the rupture). In this perspective, texts pertinent to the system are included as opposed to only well-known texts or texts accessible to the critics who emphasize them too much.

This theoretical view is concerned with the purely *formal*, internal level of the dramatic text; it would describe the systems and their changes at certain specific moments of the historical process. Such a view would explain how and what constitutes a system but not why it changes. This occurs at the contextual level.

B) *Contextual Level*

The answer to the question of why signifying systems change is found in the extra-literary terrain. The analysis of the historical and cultural context (social context) is fundamental in contextualizing the production of texts and other cultural objects. Thus, one has to study the relationships existing between literary systems - in our case, dramatic texts - and the society that produces them. Although views differ, most agree that the social context (SC) plays a central role in understanding the literary text and that it can also explain many of the formal and thematic changes in literary systems.

Latin American criticism has always been hampered by our literature's strong links with the SC, that is, with the political, cultural, social and economic life of a given moment.[68] Of course, this does not necessarily mean that in order to understand our literature one has to fall into a sort of Victorian historicism in which the genre, life of the author, etc., is studied. Rather, it means establishing the extent of the social context's impact on the literary work. Nor does it mean that mechanical relationships between infrastructure and superstructure should be articulated, where this or that infrastructural change would correspond to some superstructural change.[69] Tynianov's opinion is close to my own on this point: literature should not be considered as an autonomous reality as it relates to society; to the contrary, it is an integral and dynamic part of the SC.[70]

Every literary text is related to (or correlates to) the SC by means of the language which is shared by all of its producers and receivers. At this point it is important to emphasize the semantic dimension of any verbal act. What interests us here is meaning, for the emergence of a new form often foreshadows a problematic that needs to be expressed differently. New realities and/or conflicts can not always be expressed in existing forms. Good examples are found in Brecht's epic theatre and in the theatre of the absurd. This explains why a text has to be located in its historic moment and why we must know the extra-literary factors that certainly play a central role in the text's production.

The text is a cultural manifestation and a social product, by the simple fact that an author does not work in a vacuum but is both a part of and surrounded by the SC he or she shares with the readers/spectators and is affected by the general atmosphere of this context. In this way, every text necessarily includes or foreshadows a current *social practice*. There is a dialectic between the internal and external changes of literary texts. Form and content do not change as a consequence of isolated intra- or extra-literary facts, since literary production is part of social life and art often foreshadows real changes in society in general. There is no doubt that it is difficult to establish the true nature of this dialectic.[71] Nevertheless, its study is the only way of explaining how, where and when a given literary text appears.

It is important, therefore, to establish extra-literary criteria to account for or explain this change. If we begin with the presupposition that every text expresses and reveals society at a given moment, then the following criteria might help in the analysis: a) the general cultural situation; b) the political situation; c) the class the artist comes from and the composition of the audience. By general cultural situation we refer to the cultural forms adopted from other cultures - and this is especially important in Latin America. For example, the adoption of naturalism in Latin America is a fact, and it can be proven in the theatre production of Florencio Sánchez.[72] It is also important to ask what it is that was adopted from European naturalism. This form was incorporated simply because the dramatic vanguard was influenced by the Latin American novel which was already applying this aesthetic (which is also a structure), and it is also possible this was simply a necessary contextual evolution. At such a level it is important to untangle what comes from outside and is adopted/adapted and is part of the theatre tradition of a country. For example, one of the forms that developed the most in the nineteenth century was the one-act farce and its influence was felt for a long time from the so-called Río de Plata theatre. Of importance as well are the respective periods of renovation, for example, in the theatre of Chile, Argentina, Mexico and Uruguay. During these periods, works from the European Vanguard were incorporated and this certainly had an impact on national production in these countries and on authors trying to abandon old and antiquated naturalist forms that had reached a point of exhaustion. There is yet another point: in many Latin American countries, one-act farces are still being produced even though their historic moment is long over. Old and new forms co-exist simultaneously, and this can only be explained by using the third criteria.

The socio-political situation has always played a central role in Latin American theatre. No one can ignore the political reality of the Latin American continent: dictatorships, repression, censure, self-censure, etc. The producer's attitude toward the theatre text differs according to his or her situation. What is key here is that political changes bring with them formal and especially content changes, as in, for example, contemporary Chilean theatre.[73] The theatre from before the coup d'état in 1973 and today's theatre are quite different, and not simply on the level of message or type of message, but also in the way this message is received in a new horizon of expectations. Thus, one can say that the circulation and manner of interpreting messages is influenced and determined by their historical moment. That is, it is never possible to say exactly what one wants in the form and at the time one desires. In a very perceptive article, Hayden White writes: "In a given period and place in history, the system of encodation and decodation permits the transmission of certain *kinds of messages regarding the context* and not others ...".[74]

Finally, the class of the producer plays an important role, for his or her production is directed toward a certain type of audience. This is where the *social formation* and the discursive position are important. They function within what Noé Jitrik calls *the field of the production of texts*,[75] or areas of textual production. There is a close relationship between textual production and ideology and for this reason textual changes should be compared to the ideological component which not only sets the tone of the text's meaning but can also affect choices of textual expression. On this point, Noé Jitrik and Hernan Vidal say the following:

> All textual production is governed by an ideology which, in its turn, is a tributary of a broader theory which defines a certain manner of considering the social production; said ideology may be implicit - or hidden - or explicit -assumed or discussed or destroyed - and from there one writes, or better still, in it one finds the 'techniques' appropriate for finishing the work.[76]

Thus we can talk of texts that *reproduce* the dominant ideology while other texts *produce* new forms that try to confront and expose the dominant ideology. This distinction provides two criteria for analyzing two general forms in Latin America. This does not mean that this process is automatic; it is, however, unavoidable.

The opinion of the audience on the receiving end of this form/content is important, for a dramatic/performance text is always directed toward a well-defined group. Expectations, or *the horizon of expectations*, vary with each group. At this point it is important to integrate some aspects of reception theory as elaborated in chapter IV, for keeping the text-performance-public relationship in mind will facilitate the task of doing theatre history. This relationship between text and public is a dialectic one: a change in the horizon of expectation can occur in two ways. The production of a text in a new form of expression can introduce a new horizon of expectation to which the spectator is unaccustomed. As this new form becomes more widespread and well-known, the spectator eventually adopts (or fails to do so, in some cases) a new horizon of expectation. But it is also possible that a form of expression reaches such a point of exhaustion that the producer of the new form is simply satisfying what is demanded of him or her by an audience expecting a new horizon of expectation.

If these two levels are properly formulated, then it will be possible to produce the first history of contemporary Latin American theatre founded on rigorous scientific principles. In the next few pages, I will discuss some of the methodological points that need to be applied if our theory is to be used.

V. METHODOLOGY

I will not attempt a detailed explanation of this methodology since it is still in its development stages. Rather, I will point out some analytical tools that might be useful in formulating the synchronic and diachronic axes at both the formal and the contextual level.

At the level of formal analysis, the following model could be proposed:

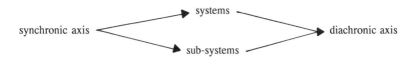

This model shows how a given synchrony is made up of systems and subsystems which are projected into the diachronic axis and in this way constitute the process of change and history. As for explaining the heterogeneity of theatre production and vestiges of past practices, further systematic formulations are required if I hope to be comprehensive and scientific. This is why I propose the following types of system: a) the supersystem; b) the macrosystem; and c) the microsystem.

The *supersystem* is a comprehensive one, for example the *modern* or *renaissance* system. In the case of Latin America, two supersystems could be formulated: the modern system, from the beginning to the middle of the twentieth century, and the contemporary system that would go up to the present. Within these two supersystems are *macrosystems*, the internal divisions of the supersystem. The macrosystem can be further divided into microsystems which would reveal the different types of text and theatre production within the macrosystem, for example 'experimental', 'epic', or 'popular' theatre.

We should now consider the analytical tools required to formulate these systems. On the formal level, two elements should be outlined: first, the structural and second, the stylistic. The structural element should give an account of how a given series of dramatic texts becomes articulated as well as of the language used in the texts. To do so, the types of texts and how they *occur* need to be formulated. Type could be considered the name of a class of texts that, from a certain point of view (in this case, stylistic and structural) is 'equivalent' to the concrete texts which are part of this class of texts, and the actual texts are occurrences of this type. The 'equivalence' or 'identity' is not made with reference to all the constituents or structural and stylistic properties, only to the *dominant* ones in these texts. Thus, one can argue that certain texts (occurrences) are of the same type if they contain a given number of common properties that allow them to be identified as belonging to the same class. Every text having these properties would be a member of the same class while other texts would not, and this would help to formulate other systems and microsystems.[77] Thus, the analytical process is a classification based on *definition*; that is, the enumeration of textual properties has to occur if texts are to become members of that group. The classification provides heuristic means by which to formulate systems. The description and explanation of *types* and their *occurrence* would help in explaining change, but only when the rules of a system have been clearly defined.

In the case of theatre, both the structure and style of a class of texts have to be linked to the sort of theatre convention being used, for convention determines structural forms and stylistic modes. At the same time, theatre convention can be linked to theatre genre, keeping in mind that genre is really a 'general type' and thus should be considered according to the concepts we have just formulated.[78]

The first stage of this work, then, is the formulation of these textual properties that will be part of a vast corpus which will then be reduced to the manifestations of systems at a given moment, and which will also have to be connected to the social context. The second stage is extremely important, for it contains the text's response to the audience, the producer's reactions to the social context. The following might serve as a guide to this analytical process:

- a) description of the social context (political, cultural, etc.) to contextualize texts from a given historical moment;
- b) the formulation of how the society of the producers and the audience (class structure) is composed, for producers belonging to different social strata will produce works aimed at a public sharing his or her class position;
- c) the formulation of the horizon of expectation the text has provided and that the audience expects. This will help in observing changes in the horizon of expectation, changes that often affect the formal level.

All these factors that are part of the social context are determined by the *production context* (PC), that is, the context that determines the production of a certain type of message or text at a given moment. The PC produces or is produced by a *reception context* (RC) that appears in a concrete manner in the horizon of expectation. For example, the PC can be composed of political changes, international events, the economy, etc., that somehow affect and determine the producer to produce certain messages. But this same PC also affects and determines the RC. This process can be represented in the following diagram:

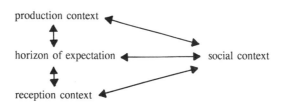

The PC produces a horizon of expectation and the RC claims or receives the horizon, which is shared with the general SC. Naturally, we begin with the premise that first and foremost, every cultural production is social. This is why it is indispensable to contextualize and link production to the dual articulation we have been discussing, since every cultural manifestation *expresses* various problems and realities of a given moment. I am not trying to involve some sort of reflexive theory here, only the real and concrete fact that every producer is a *historical agent* writing for a real audience and inscribed in a reality that is both political and ideological. No text is innocent, least of all those of Latin American theatre.

How, then, does one integrate the formal and contextual levels? One could begin from the contextual level so as to localize texts of a given moment and then proceed to classify these texts (and their properties). Once the different classes of texts making up a system were established (macro, micro), one could then study the relationship between these systems and their social context.

No doubt, this methodological process (as with the theoretical) will have to be tested simply by seeing how well it works when applied. Only results will prove its value.

ENDNOTES
CHAPTER VI

1. One must not forget that the very concept of *literary history* is relatively recent, and in fact, is a product of Modernity, which began in the eighteenth century. At that time the concept was defined, invoking the active participation of poetics in the debate. For more information on the old way of doing history, see "Toward a New History of Literary Studies", *Profession 84*, (1984), 16-23, by Herbert Lindenberg; "De l'évolution littéraire", by Juri Tynianov in *Théorie de la littérature*, texts by the Russian Formalists collected, presented, and translated by Tzvetan Todorov, preface by Roman Jakobson (Paris: Editions socials, 1965), pp. 120-137; "La théorie de la 'méthode formelle'", by Boris Eikhenbaum, *Ibid*, pp. 31-75.

2. The Russian Formalists were the first to define and approach the literary object. Boris Eikhenbaum claimed that: "We have posited and we still posit as a fundamental affirmation that the object of literary science must be the study of the specific particularities of literary objects which distinguish them from all other subject matter, and this independently of the fact that, by their secondary characteristics, this matter may serve as a pretext and a right to use it in the other sciences as an auxiliary object". Later he adds the well-known definition by Roman Jakobson: "The object of literary science is not literature, but rather 'literariness' (*'literaturnost'*), that is to say that which makes a given work a literary work". "La théorie de la 'méthode formelle'", in *Théorie de la littérature*, p. 37 (our translation). Later, René Wellek and Austin Warren returned to this point in their well-known book, *Theory of Literature*. The edition used here is: New revised edition (New York: Harcourt, Brace and World, 1970). See also István Söter, "The Dilemma of Literary Science", *New Literary History*, II, 1 (Autumn 1970), 85-113. The Prague School also researched this problem: Felix Vodička and O. Obelic in "La historia de la literatura" in *El mundo de las letras*, 2nd edition (Santiago, Chile: Editorial Universitaria, 1971), pp. 15-58.

3. See Juri Tynianov, "De l'évolution littéraire", p. 121.

4. *Ibid.*, p. 137 (our translation).

5. For more on the Russian Formalists, see Victor Erlich's book, *Russian Formalism: History - Doctrine* (The Hague and Paris: Mouton, 1969).

6. This is exactly what F.W. Bateson suggested in "Literary History: Non-Subject *Par Excellence*", *New Literary History*, II, 1 (Autumn 1970), 115-122.

7. Vladimir Propp, *The Morphology of the Folktale*, second edition revised and edited with a preface by Louis A. Wagner, new introduction by Alan Dundes (Austin: University of Texas Press, 1988); Gérard Genette, *Figures* (Paris: Editions du Seuil, 1966, 1969, 1972). Tzvetan Todorov, *Grammaire du Décaméron* (The Hague: Mouton, 1969); Claude Bremond, *Logique du recit* (Paris: Editions du Seuil, 1973); Marco De Marinis, *Semiotica del teatro* (Milano: Studi Bompiani, 1982); Patrice Pavis, *Problèmes de sémiologie théâtrale* (Montréal: Presses de l'Université de Québec, 1976); *Voix et images de la scène* (Lille: Presses Universitaires de Lille, 1982).

8. This problem has often been debated in the congresses of the International Association of Comparative Literature and their annals always have a section on this material. Also the journal *New Literary History* has played a central role in the last few years in trying to reconsider the place of literary history. For example, Michal Glowinski's invaluable article on this debate in this journal stated that "both the synchronic and diachronic perspectives belong to research methods whose objective is historical" and that "For historical poetics, the synchronic and diachronic aspects are inseparable". "Theoretical Foundations of Historical Poetics", *New Literary History*, VII, 2 (Winter 1976), 237 and 241, respectively.

9. For example, the excellent study by Juan Villegas, *Teoría de historia literaria y poesía lírica* (Ottawa: Girol Books, 1984) or see Mario Valdés, "Heuristic Models of Inquiry", *New Literary History*, XII, 1 (Autumn 1980), 253-267; Oldric Belic, "La periodización y sus problemas", *Revista Latino-Americana de Teoría y Crítica*, I, 2 (septiembre 1972), 17-21; Hans-Robert Jauss, "Literary History as a Challenge to Literary Theory", *New Literary History*, II, 1 (Autumn 1970), 7-37, and *Pour une esthétique de la réception*, translated from the German by Claude Maillard, preface by Jean Starobinski (Paris: Editions Gallimard, 1978); Carlos Rincón, "Sobre la crítica e historia literaria hoy en Hispanoamérica", *Casa de las Américas*, XIV, 80 (septiembre-octubre 1973), 135-147; Michel Riffaterre, "Pour une approche formelle de l'histoire littéraire", in *La production du texte* (Paris: Editions du Seuil, 1979), pp. 89-112.

10. An exemplary case is provided by Herbert Lindenberg, who maintains that "the new history has developed out of a contemporary - one might almost say postmodernist - critical paradigm. Unlike the older history, which often remained unreflective about the model of historical change it was using, the new history is aware that models do not exist in nature, that they function as frameworks within which to observe and interpret phenomena that seem important but that stand outside the area of inquiry investigated by the older history". "Toward a New History in Literary Study", *Profession 84*, (1984), 18-19.

11. "Pour une approche formelle de l'histoire littéraire", p. 89 (our translations).

12. *Ibid.*, p. 89.

13. *Ibid.*, p. 97.

14. What is clear is Riffaterre's view of the linguistics of change: "As always, when a structure is affected the modification of a single component brings about the modification of the entire system." *Ibid.*, p. 95 (our translation). This is something that remains to be proven in the area of literary texts, for to take a linguistic model without considering the fact that texts do not function exactly like speech results in mechanical applications that are irrelevant to the object being studied.

15. *Ibid.*, p. 98 (our translation).

16. *Ibid.*, p. 98.

17. *Ibid.*, p. 105 (our translation). See also Hans-George Ruprecht, *Theaterpublikum um Textauffassung* (Bern: Herbert Lang; Frankfurt am Main/München: Peter Lang, 1976).

18. "Literary History as a Challenge to Literary Theory", 9.

19. *Ibid.*, p. 10.

20. *Ibid.*, p. 17.

21. Quoted by Jauss. *Ibid.*, p. 20.

22. *Ibid.*, p. 23.

23. *Ibid.*, p. 26. Jauss adds further on that "the literary past can only return when a new reception has brought it into the present again - whether it be that a different aesthetic attitude has intentionally taken up the past, or that a new phase of literary evaluation has expectedly illuminated past works". *Ibid.*, pp. 26-27.

24. *Ibid.*, p. 27.

25. *Ibid.*, p. 29. Roman Jakobson says something similar on this point: "Synchronic description considers not only the literary production of a given period, but also that part of the literary tradition which has remained alive or has been resurrected in the period in question.... If it is to be truly comprehensive, historical poetics, like the history of language, must be conceived of as a superstructure, built on a series of successive synchronic descriptions". *Essais de linguistique générale* (Paris: Editions du Seuil, 1963), p. 212 (our translation).

26. Villegas began his study *Teoría de historia literaria y poesía lírica* in the same way as this one, and it is significant that many of our viewpoints converge, especially since our sources are so similar.

27. *Ibid.*, p. 9 (our translation).

28. *Ibid.*, p. 12 (our translation).

29. For example, doing history using generations, currents, eras, etc., does not solve the main problem of explaining how and why a given system of texts evolves. The chronological sequence, inherent to these approaches, can not easily explain this fact.

30. *Teoría de historia literaria y poesía lírica*, p. 20 (our translation).

31. Although he rejects much of the generation 'theory', he retains the notion of *group*, which, in my opinion, has similar problems to those of the generation theory, which in fact, should not really be considered as literary theory at all, let alone historical theory.

32. Pedro Henríquez Ureña, *Las corrientes literarias in América Hispánica* (Mexico: Fondo de Cultura Económica, 1949); Max Henríquez Ureña, *Breve historia del modernismo*, 2nd edition (Mexico: Fondo de Cultura Económica, 1978); Fernando Alegría, *Historia de la novela hispanoamericana*, 4th edition (Mexico: Ediciones de Andrea, 1974); Enrique Anderson Imbert, *Historia de la literatura hispanoamericana*. Vol. I and II, 2nd edition (Mexico: Fondo de Cultura Económica, 1970); José Juan Arrom, *Esquema generacional de las letras hispanoamericanas*, 2nd edition (Bogota: Instituto Caro y Cuervo, 1977); Luis Alberto Sánchez, *Proceso y contenido de la novela Hispano-Americana*, 2nd edition (Madrid: Editorial Gredos, 1968); *Historia comparada de las literaturas americanas*, 4 vols. (Buenos Aires: Editorial Losada, 1973, 1973, 1974 and 1976, respectively); Cedomil Goic, *Historia de la novela hispanoamericana* (Valparaíso: Ediciones Universitarias, 1972); Jean Franco, *Historia de la literatura hispanoamericana* (Barcelona: Editorial Ariel, 1975).

33. *Esquema generacional de las letras hispanoamericanas*, p. 244 (our translation).

34. This is exactly what Jauss criticizes in saying that conventional historical methods "are only the collected and classified past and therefore not history at all, but pseudo-history. Anyone who considers such literary data as history confuses the eventful character of a work of art with that of historical matter-of-factness". "Literary History as a Challenge to Literary Theory", 10.

35. See the criticism by Carlos Rincón on the generational method: "Sobre crítica e historia de la literatura hoy en Latinoamérica". See also Juan Villegas, *Teoría de historia literaria y poesía lírica*, pp. 25-37, and Raimundo Lida, "Períodos y generaciones en historia literaria", in *Letras Hispánicas* (Mexico: Fondo de Cultura Económica, 1958).

36. "La periodización y sus problemas", 18 (our translation).

37. *Ibid.*, p. 18 (our translation). Nevertheless, he also adds that: "In order to reveal and describe literary evolution, one must use exclusively literary criteria; in order to explain it, it will be necessary to resort to extra-literary factors". *Ibid.*, p. 20 (our translation).

38. In an interesting article, Rita Schober argues that what has to be done is "to detect the specific proceedings, that is, formal, which are capable of expressing a new content which is itself determined by the changes which the subject and the esthetic object have undergone". "Périodization et historiographie littéraire", *Romanistica Pragensia*, 5 (1968), 22, (our translation). See also Claudio Guillén, "Second Thoughts on Literary Periods" in *Literature as System: Essays Toward the Theory of Literary History* (Princeton, New Jersey: Princeton University Press, 1971), pp. 420-469; Oscar Tacca, *La historia literaria* (Madrid: Editorial Gredos, 1968), pp. 96-104; José A. Portuondo, *La historia de las generaciones* (Cuba: Editorial Letras Cubanas, 1981).

39. "Algunos problemas teóricos de la literatura hispanoamericana", *Revista de crítica literaria latinoamericana*, Año 1, 1 (1975), 21 (our translation). When referring to Russian Formalist and Marxist theory, Jaime Labastida claims that "On the contrary, the correct method seems to be the one which will unite, but without eclecticism, that which is most valuable from both tendencies or attempted solutions". "Alejo Carpentier: realidad y conocimiento estético", *Casa de las Américas*, 87 (noviembre-diciembre 1975), 24 (our translation).

40. See the work of Fernández Retamar and Jaime Labastida cited above.

41. "La palabra, esa nueva Cartuja", *El escritor latinoameriocano y la revolución posible* (Bs. As: Editorial Alfa Argentina, 1974), p. 52 (our translation).

42. Fernández Retamar refers to the small amount of theoretical work that exists on Latin American literature as 'colonized' in "Algunos problemas teóricos de la literatura hispanoamericana", 27.

43. For a systematic approach to Latin American theatre, see Fernando de Toro, *Brecht en el teatro hispanoamericano contemporáneo* (Buenos Aires: Editorial Galerna, 1987). The urgency and need referred to is obvious if you consider our *Bibliografía del teatro hispanoamericano contemporáneo (1900-1980)*, 2 vols. (Frankfurt: Vervuert Verlag, 1985). The first volume lists published dramatic works and amounts to 473 pages. The second volume lists critical work and amounts to only 226 pages. The lack of balance is obvious.

44. "La crítica teatral y América Latina", in *Hacia una Crítica Literaria Latinoamericana* (Buenos Aires: Fernando García Cambeiro, 1976), p. 27 (our translation).

45. "Algunos problemas teóricos de la literatura hispanoamericana", p. 27 (our translation).

46. *Ibid.*, p. 29 (our translation). Examples of researchers of Latin American literature concerned with the problem of literary history, besides those already mentioned, include Juan Villegas, who, it should be mentioned in passing, was consulted for this study. His excellent article is: "El discurso teatral y el discurso crítico: El caso de Chile", *Anales de la Universidad de Chile*, quinta serie, 5 (agosto 1984), 316-336. There is also a collective project of which I am a part that has been underway for several years on a history of contemporary Latin American theatre (1500-present). This project is being funded by a grant from the Social Sciences and Humanities Research Council of Canada.

47. "Bermerkungen zur Gattungspoetik", *Philosophischer Anzeiger*, III (1928), 136 (our translation).

48. F. de Saussure considered that the synchronic axis "is a relation between simultaneous elements, the other [the diachronic] the substitution of one element for another in time, an event". *Course in General Linguistics* (London: Fontana, 1974), p. 174.

49. *Sincronía, diacronía e historia* (Madrid: Editorial Gredos, 1978), p. 260 (our translation).

50. *Course in General Linguistics* (London: Fontana, 1974), p. 182.

51. *Sincronía, diacronía e historia* (Madrid: Editorial Gredos, 1978), p. 272 (our translation).

52. *Ibid.*, p. 279-280 (our translation).

53. Adrián Marino points out that this is why the system is never deformed or equalized, nor does it ever level out; rather, the dominant elements of the system necessarily stand out. "Idée littéraire, structure, modèle", *Degrés*, quatrième année, 10 (printemps 1975-76), c3. See also, Claudio Guillén, *Literature as System. Essays Toward the Theory of Literary History*, pp. 375-419.

54. We should say, however, that a genre is an abstraction that occurs beginning with a series of works that define the category of, for example, tragedy, comedy, etc., or that fall within a category that is then named. It is very interesting to note what Boris Tomachevśky has said on the topic: "The characteristics of the genre, that is to say, the proceedings which organize the composition of the work, are the dominant proceedings; in other words, all the other proceedings necessary for the creation of the artistic whole submit to them. The dominant proceeding is called *la dominante*. The ensemble of *dominantes* represents the element which authorizes the formation of a genre". "Thématique", in *Théorie de la littérature*, texts by the Russian Formalists collected, presented, and translated by Tzvetan Todorov, preface by Roman Jakobson (Paris: Editions du Seuil, 1965), p. 303 (our translation). See also the interesting and in many respects, definitive article on the concepts of tragedy, tragicomedy, and comedy by A. de Toro, "Observaciones para una definición de los términos 'tragoedia', 'comoedia' y 'tragicocomedia' en los dramas de honor de Calderón", in *Texto-Mensaje-Recipiente* (Tübingen: Gunter Narr Verlag, 1988), pp. 101-132. And also, Wellek and Warren, "Literary Genres" in *Theory of Literature*, pp. 226-237 and F. Vodička and O. Obelic, "Los géneros literarios", pp. 98-122.

55. *New Literary History*, II, 2 (Winter 1971), 202. In his book, *Kinds of Literature: An Introduction to the History of Genres and Modes* (Cambridge, Mass.: Harvard University Press, 1982), he adds: "Although genre terms are notoriously inconsistent, they exhibit at least one regularity. The terms for kinds, perhaps in keeping with their obvious external embodiment, can always be put in noun form ('epigram'; 'epic'), whereas modal terms tend to be adjectival", p. 106.

56. *Ibid.*, pp. 212-214.

57. "L'origine des genres", in *Les genres du discours* (Paris: Editions du Seuil, 1978), p. 47 (our translation).

58. *Ibid.*, p. 47.

59. See Dieter Hanik, "Fonction heuristique et valeur d'explication de l'idée de genre", *Oeuvres et Critiques*, II, 2 (1977-78), 27-38. He formulates five notions of genre: 1) the notion of the specific *Techné* of an author, as expressed in his writings (for example, the *Examens* by Corneille); 2) the notion of genre that explains the norms and procedures of a specific *Techné*, for example, *L'Art de Dictier et de fere chançons* by Eustache Deschamps and the many poetics of the sixteenth and seventeenth century; 3) analysis and description of classes, the categories of which derive from philosophy, for example, material, form, etc., and according to analytic procedures (inductive, deductive, etc.); 4) elaboration of second grade typologies, for example, Epic, Lyrical, Drama; 5) the *a priori* acceptance of a generic model that would serve as a norm (model) for any similar attempt. *Ibid.*, pp. 29-30.

60. See T. Todorov, "L'origine des genres", p. 48. On the difference between historical genres and theoretical genres, see Christine Brooke-Rose, "Historical Genres/Theoretical Genres: A Discussion of Todorov on the Fantastic", *New Literary History*, VIII, 1 (Autumn 1976), 145-158.

61. This is the case in the book by Susana Marco, Abel Posadas, Marta Speroni and Griselda Vignolo, *Teoría del género chico criollo* (Buenos Aires: Eudeba, 1974) as well as the book by Eva Gollouscio, *Etude sur le 'cocoliche' scénique et édition annotée de "Mateo" d'Armando Discépolo* (Toulouse: Institut d'Etudes Hispaniques et Hispano-Américaines, Université Toulouse-Le-Mirail, 1979); and the studies by Loreto Valenzuela, "La Novela Comica", *Apuntes*, 92 (septiembre 1984), 3-56; "Teatro y sociedad chilena en la mitad del siglo XX: El Melodrama", *Apuntes*, 91 (noviembre 1983), 7-78. These studies are certainly valuable and highly informative. Nevertheless, if all of this research were to be systematized according to a theoretical model and, more importantly, in a rigorous manner, the results would then be definitive.

62. In this regard, the above cited works are significant, especially those by the research group from the Universidad Católica de Chile, which includes Loreto Valenzuela, Consuelo Morel, Giselle Munizaga and others.

63. "Literary History as a Challenge to Literary Theory", 27-28 and 31, respectively. See also, Claudio Guillén, "On the Object of Literary Change", in *Literature as System: Essays Toward the Theory of Literary History*, pp. 470-510.

64. *Teatro chileno contemporáneo* (Madrid: Aguilar, 1970), pp. 14-15.

65. "The Dilemma of Literary Science", 97.

66. "Périodization et historiographie littéraire", 23.

67. F.W. Bateson places the problem of selection before anything else because, according to him, history "cannot be the history of all the books ever written, a process of selection must be a necessary preliminary. And if the selection is not to be merely conventional or mechanical, a critical reading is the first necessity". "Literary History: A Non-Subject *Par Excellence*", 119.

68. Several decades ago, Alfonso Reyes said with respect to the formalist approach that it "could not lead to a complete judgement and comprehension. If we do not take into account certain social, historical, biographical or psychological factors, we will not arrive at a just valuation". "Fragmento sobre la interpretación social de las letras iberoamericanas", in *Marginalia*, primera serie (México 1952), p. 154 (our translation).

69. See the excellent book and article by Pierre V. Zima on this topic: *Pour une sociologie du texte littéraire* (Paris: Union Générale d'Editions, 1978), and "Towards sociological semiotics", in *Texte et idéologie/Text and Ideology, Symposium* (Ottawa: Carlton Universtiy, 1986).

70. Tynianov says on this subject: "The study of literary *evolution* does not reject the dominant signification of the principal social factors, on the contrary, it is only within this framework that the signification may be elucidated in its totality". "De l'évolution littéraire", p. 137 (our translation).

71. I do not agree with Oldrich Belic "that no one today would be capable of outlining exactly the role of immanent factors in relation to the role of extraliterary impulses". "La periodización y sus problemas", 20 (our translation). This is the challenge of literary history where formal changes and the relationship these have to social life and the changes occurring there need to be explained.

72. Regarding this subject, see the study by Enrique Giordano, *La teatralización de la obra dramática: De Florencio Sánchez a Roberto Arlt* (Mexico: La Red de Jonás PREMIO EDITORA, 1982).

73. See our article, "El teatro chileno: ruptura y renovación. Perspectiva semiológica de los fenómenos de producción y recepción en los ultimos dos años", *Conjunto*, 70 (October-December 1986) and the same article in *Le théâtre sous la contrainte*. Aix-en-Provence: Université de Provence, 1988, 237-248, and the above noted articles (note 62) by Maria de la Luz Hurtado, Carlos Ochsenius, Loreto Valenzuela.

74. "The Problem of Change in Literary History", *New Literary History*, VII, 1 (Autumn 1975), 107. He also adds, "Changes in the code, finally, can be conceived to be reflective of changes in the historiconatural context in which a given language game is being played", *Ibid.*, p. 107.

75. *Producción literaria y producción social* (Buenos Aires: Editorial Sudamericana, 1975), p. 52 (our translation). See Hernan Vidal's book as well: *Literatura hispanoamericana e ideología: surgimiento y crisis* (Buenos Aires: Ediciones Hispamérica, 1976).

76. *Ibid.*, p. 55 (our translation).

77. On the problem of models, see Adrian Marino's article: "Idée littéraire, structure, modèle", *Degrés*, quatrième année, 10 (Spring 1975-76), c-c24.

78. On the problematic of type and occurrence, refer to Teun A. Van Dijk, *Text and Context: Explorations in Semantics and Pragmatics of Discourse* (London: Longmans 1977), pp. 298-319.

BIBLIOGRAPHY

Alegría, Fernando. *Historia de la novela hispanoamericana*. México: Ediciones de Andrea, 1974.
Alter, Jean. "From Text to Performance." *Poetics Today*, II, 3 (Spring 1981), 113-139.
Alter, Jean. "El discurso cómico y la referencia." *Dispositio*, XIII, 33-35 (1988), 81-90.
Alter, Jean. *A Socio-Semiotic Theory of Theatre*. Philadelphia: University of Pennsylvania Press, 1990.
Anderson Imbert, Enrique. *Historia de la literatura hispanoamericana*. Vol. I. Second edition, revised and supplemented. México: Fondo de Cultura Económica, 1970.
Anderson Imbert, Enrique. *Historia de la literatura hispanoamericana*. Vol. II. Second edition. México: Fondo de Cultura Económica, 1970.
Angenot, Marc. *Glossaire pratique de la critique contemporaine*. Québec: Editions Hurtubise HMH, 1979.
Angenot, Marc. "L'intertextualité: enquête sur l'émergence et la diffusion d'un champ notionnel". *Revue des sciences humaines*, LX, 189 (janvier-mars 1983), 121-135.
Angenot, Marc. "Intertextualité, interdiscursivité, discours social". *Texte*, 2 (1983), 101-112.
Angenot, Marc. "Présupposé, topos, idéologème". *Etudes françaises*, XIII, 1-2 (1977), 11-34.
Anspach, Silvia Simone. "La especificidad no específica del lenguaje teatral: la postmodernidad y el actor en Brasil". In *De la Colonia a la Postmodernidad: Teoría teatral y Crítica sobre teatro Latinoamericano*. Edited by Peter Roster and Mario Rojas. Buenos Aires and Ottawa: Editorial Galerna and IITCTL, 1992, pp. 177-186.
Anspach, Silvia Simone. "Gerald Thomas: o de Carmenes, filtros e mortes". In *Hacia una nueva crítica y un nuevo teatro latinoamericano*. Frankfurt am Main: Vervuert Verlag, 1993, pp. 103-114.
Arrom, José Juan. *Esquema generacional de las letras hispanoamericanas*. Second edition. Bogotá: Instituto Caro y Cuervo, 1977.
Artaud, Antonin. *The Theatre and its Double*. Translated from the French by Mary Caroline Richards. New York: Grove Press, 1958.
Aslan, Odette. *El actor en el siglo XX. Evolución de la técnica*. Translated by J. Giner. Prologue by X. Fábregas. Barcelona: Editorial Gustavo Gile, 1979.

D'Aubignac, François Hédelin. *La pratique du théâtre*. Nachdruck der dreibändigen Ausgabe Amsterdam 1715 mit einer einleitenden Abhandlung von Hans-Jörg Neuschäfer. Genève: Slatkine Reprints, 1971.

Austin, John L. *How to Do Things with Words*. Second edition. Cambridge, Massachusetts: Harvard University Press, 1975.

Azparren, Leonardo. "Nuevo teatro venezolano". In *De la Colonia a la Postmodernidad: Teoría teatral y Crítica sobre teatro Latinoamericano*. Edited by Peter Roster and Mario Rojas. Buenos Aires and Ottawa: Editorial Galerna and IITCTL, 1992, pp. 77-88.

Bablet, Denis. *Svoboda*. Lausanne: Editions L'Age d'Homme, 1970.

Bablet, Denis. *T. Kantor. Les voies de la création théâtrale*. Vol. XI. Paris: Editions du Centre National de la Recherche Scientifique, 1983.

Banhanou, Anne-Françoise, et. al.. *Vitez: toutes les mises en scène*. Paris: Jean-Cyrville Godefroy, 1981.

Barba, Eugenio. *Alla ricerca del teatro perduto*. Padova: Marsilio, 1965.

Barba, Eugenio. *Beyond the Floating Islands*. Translated by Judy Barba, Richard Fowler, Jerrold C. Rodesch, and Saul Shapiro. New York: Performing Arts Journal, 1986.

Barba, Eugenio. "El caballo de plata". *Escénica* (1986). Special edition. Introduction and synthesis of the seminar on the theory and practice of dance-theatre. Under the direction of Patricia Cardona.

Barba, Eugenio. "El camino del rechazo". *Maldoror*, 22 (1983), 35-44.

Barba, Eugenio. *La canoa de papel*. México: Grupo Editorial Gaceta, 1992.

Barba, Eugenio. *The Dilated Body*. Followed by *The Gospel According to Oxyrhincus*. Rome: Ziami Libri, 1985.

Barba, Eugenio. "Introducião à antropologia teatral". *INACEN*, Ano II, 2o série (1986), 2-3.

Barba, Eugenio. "Más allá de las islas flotantes". *Maldoror*, 22 (1983), 11-20.

Barba, Eugenio. *Más allá de las islas flotantes*. México: Fripo y Doral, Editors, 1987.

Barba, Eugenio. "Notas sobre antropología teatral y técnicas de la representación e historiografía". *Espacio*, Año 4, 8 (octubre 1990), 55-60.

Barba, Eugenio. "Teatro e revolução". *INACEN*, Ano II, 2o série (1987), 2-20.

Barba, Eugenio. "La tercer orilla del río". *Espacio*, Año 2, 4 (julio 1988), 15-24.

Barba, Eugenio and Nicola Savarese. *Anatomía del actor*. Translated by Bruno Bert. Edited by Edgar Ceballos. México: Grupo Editorial Gaceta, 1988.

Barba, Eugenio and Nicola Savarese. *Anatomie de l'acteur*. Translated by Eliane Deschamps-Pria. Rome: Zeami Libri, 1985.

Barthes, Roland. "L'effet de réel". *Communications*, 11 (1968), 84-89.

Barthes, Roland. *Essais critiques*. Paris: Editions du Seuil, 1964.

Barthes, Roland. "Introduction à l'analyse structurale des récits". *Communications*, 8 (1966), 1-27.

Barthes, Roland. *Sur Racine*. Paris: Editions du Seuil, 1963.

Barthes, Roland. "Texte (Théorie du)". In *Encyclopedia Universalis*. Vol. 15. Paris: Encyclopedia Universalis, Editeur, 1968, pp. 1013-1017.
Bateson, F.W. "Literary History: Non-Subject *Par Excellence*". *New Literary History*, II, 1 (Autumn 1970), 115-122.
Beck, Julian. *The Life of the Theatre*. New Foreword by Judith Malina. New York: Limelight Editions, 1986.
Beckerman, Bernard. *Dynamics of Drama*. New York: Knopf, 1970.
Beckett, Samuel. *Waiting for Godot*. New York: Grove Press, 1954.
Belic, Oldric. "La periodización y sus problemas". *Revista Latino-Americana de Teoría y Crítica*, I, 2 (septiembre 1972), 17-21.
Bellemin-Noël, Jean. *Le texte et l'avant-texte*. Paris: Librairie Larousse, 1972.
Benedetti, Mario. "La palabra, esa nueva Cartuja". In *El escritor latinoamericano y la revolución posible*. Bs. As.: Editorial Alfa Argentina, 1974, pp. 51-60.
Benedetti, Robert. *The Actor at Work*. New York: Performing Arts Journal, 1990.
Benhanou, Anne-Françoise, *et al. Vitez: toutes les mises en scène*. Paris: Jean-Cyrville Godefroy, 1981.
Benveniste, Emile. *Problèmes de linguistique générale, I*. Paris: Editions Gallimard, 1966.
Benveniste, Emile. *Problèmes de linguistique générale, II*. Paris: Editions Gallimard, 1974.
Berlyne, D.E. and Joyce Ditkofsky. "Effects of Novelty and Oddity on Visual Selective Attention". *British Journal of Psychology*, 67 (1976), 175-180.
Berthoud, Anne Claude. "Aller et venir: verbes de déplacement soumis à des contraintes déictiques, topologiques, interactives et situationnelles". *Degrés*, Onzième année, 35-36 (automne-hiver 1983), d-d16.
Bettetini, Gianfranco. *Produzione del senso e messa in scena*. Milano: Studi Bompiani, 1975.
Billaz, André. "Le point de vue de la réception: prestiges et problèmes d'une perspective". *Revue des sciences humaines*, LX, 189 (janvier-mars 1983), 21-36.
Biner, Pierre. *Le living theatre*. Lausanne: Editions L'Age d'Homme, 1968.
Blau, Herbert. *Take up the Bodies: Theatre at the Vanishing Point*. Urbana, Chicago and London: University of Illinois Press, 1982.
Boal, Augusto. *Jeux pour acteurs et non-acteurs*. Paris: François Maspero, 1980.
Boal, Augusto. *Stop! C'est magique*. Paris: Hachette, 1980.
Boal, Augusto. *Théâtre de l'opprimé*. Paris: François Maspero, 1977.
Bogatyrev, Petr. "Forms and Functions of Folk Theatre". In *Semiotics of Art. Prague School Contributions*. Ladislav Matejka and Irwin R. Titunik, Editors. Cambridge, Massachusetts and London, England: The MIT Press, 1976, pp. 51-56.
Bogatyrev, Petr. "Semiotics of Folk Theatre". In *Semiotics of Art. Prague School Contributions*. Edited by Ladislav Matejka and Irwin R. Titunik. Cambridge, Massachusetts and London, England: The MIT Press, 1976, pp. 32-50.
Bogatyrev, Petr. "Les signes du théâtre". *Poétique*, 8 (1971), 517-530.
Bond, Edward. *Save*. London: Eyre Methuen, 1977.

Bonomi, Andrea. *Universi di discorso*. Milano: Feltrinelli, 1979.
Borie, Monique, Martine de Rougement and Jacques Scherer. *Esthétique théâtrale. Textes de Platon à Brecht*. Paris: Editions C.D.U. et Sedes, réunis, 1982.
Bourdieu, Pierre. *Ce que parler veut dire*. Paris: Librairie Arthème Fayard, 1982.
Brandt, Per Aage. "Conditions d'un concept du référent". *Degrés*, Première année, 3 (juillet 1983), g-g15.
Braun, Edward. *The Director and the Stage*. London: Methuen, 1982.
Braun, Edward. *The Theatre of Meyerhold. Revolution on the Modern Stage*. London: Methuen, 1979.
Brecht, Bertolt. *The Days of the Commune*. London: Eyre Methuen, 1978.
Brecht, Bertolt. *Mother Courage and her Children*. London: Eyre Methuen, 1962.
Bremond, Claude. *Logique du récit*. Paris: Editions du Seuil, 1973.
Brisset, Annie. *Sociocritique de la traduction*. Montréal: Le Préambule, 1990.
Brook, Peter. *The Empty Space*. Reprint. Harmondsworth, Middlesex, England: Penguin Books, 1972.
Brook-Rose, Christine. "Historical Genres/Theoretical Genres: A Discussion of Todorov on the Fantastic". *New Literary History*, VIII, 145 (Autumn 1976), 145-158.
Bürger, Peter. "La réception: problèmes de recherche". *Oeuvres et Critiques*, II, 2 (1978), 5-18.
Butor, Michel. *Essais sur le roman*. Paris: Editions Gallimard, 1975.
Cameron, J.M. "Problems of Literary History". *New Literary History*, I, 2 (Fall 1969), 7-12.
Campeanu, Pavel. "Un rôle secondaire: le spectateur". In *Sémiologie de la représentation*. Edited by André Helbo. Editions Complexe, 1975, pp. 96-111.
Canevacci, Massimo. "Antropología dialógica y alteridad teatral". In *De la Colonia a la Postmodernidad: Teoría teatral y Crítica sobre teatro Latinoamericano*. Edited by Peter Roster and Mario Rojas. Buenos Aires and Ottawa: Editorial Galerna and IITCTL, 1992, pp. 39-50.
Canevacci, Massimo. "Corpi, simboli e segni nella cultura visuale". *Problemi del Socialismo*, 11 (1988), 123-136.
Carlson, Marvin. *Places of Performance. The Semiotics of Theatre Architecture*. Ithaca, New York: Cornell University Press, 1989.
Carlson, Marvin. *Theatre Semiotics*. Bloomington and Indianapolis: Indiana University Press, 1990.
Carnap, Rudolf. *Meaning and Necessity*. Second edition. Chicago and London: The University of Chicago Press, 1956.
Chaikin, Joseph. *The Presence of the Actor*. Toronto: Collier MacMillan Canada, sixth printing, 1987.
Chappell, Fred. "Six Propositions about Literature and History". *New Literary History*, I, 3 (Spring 1970), 513-522.
Conein, Bernard, Jean Jacques Coutrine, Françoise Gadet, Jean Marie Marandin and Michel Pêcheux. *Matérialités discursives*. Lille: Presses Universitaires de Lille, 1981.

Copfermann, Emile. *La mise en crise théâtrale*. Paris: François Maspero, 1972.
Coppieters, Frank. "Performance and Perception". *Poetics Today*, II, 3 (Spring 1981), 35-48.
Cortius, Jan Brandt. "Literary History and the Study of Literature". *New Literary History*, II, 1 (Autumn 1970), 65-71.
Corvin, Michel. "Approche sémiologique d'un texte dramatique: *La parodie* d'Arthur Adamov". *Littérature*, 9 (février 1973), 86-100.
Corvin, Michel. "La redondance du signe dans le fonctionnement théâtral". *Degrés*, Sixième année, 13 (printemps 1980), c-c23.
Coseriu, Eugenio. *Sincronía, diacronía e historia*. Madrid: Editorial Gredos, 1978.
Courdesses, Louis. "Blum et Thorez en mai 1936: analyse d'énoncés". *Langue française*, 9 (février 1971), 22-33.
Craig, Edward Gordon. *El Arte del Teatro*. Translated by M. Margherita Pavía. Introduction and Notes by Edgar Ceballos. México, D.F.: Grupo Editorial Gaceta, 1987.
Craig, Edward Gordon. *On the Art of The Theatre*. New York and London: Heinemann Educational Books, 1980.
Craig, Edward Gordon. *The Theatre Advancing*. New York: Arno Press, 1979.
Culler, Jonathan. *The Pursuit of Signs: Semiotics, Literature, Deconstruction*. Ithaca, New York: Cornell University Press, 1981.
Culler, Jonathan. *Structuralist Poetics: Structuralism, Linguistics and the Study of Literature*. London: Routledge and Kegan Paul, 1975.
Dällenbach, Lucien. "Intertexte et autotexte". *Poétique*, VII, 25 (1976), 282-296.
Deldime, Roger and Jeanne Pigeon. "Réflextion épistémologique sur la mémoire, prémisse de l'élaboration du dispositif expérimental d'une enquête psychosociale". Conference paper presented to the First World Congress on Theatre Sociology, Rome, June 26-28, 1986.
De Marinis, Marco. "El actor italiano: elementos para un modelo". *Dispositio*, XIII, 33-35 (1988), 129-146.
De Marinis, Marco. *Capire il teatro*. Firenze: La casa Usher, 1988.
De Marinis, Marco. "Cognitive Processes in Performance Comprehension: Frames Theory and Theatrical Competence". In *Altro Polo. Performance. From Process tp Product*. Edited by Tim Fitzpatrick. Sydney: University of Sydney, 1989.
De Marinis, Marco. "Dallo spettatore modello allo spettatore reale: processi cognitive della ricezione teatrale". *Versus*, 52-53 (gennaio-maggio 1989), 81-98.
De Marinis, Marco. "L'esperienza dello spettatore. Fondamenti per una semiotica della ricezione teatrale". *Documenti di Lavoro*, Università de Urbino, 138-139, Serie F, (novembre-decembre 1984), 1-36.
De Marinis, Marco. "La investigación empírica del espectador: hacia una sociosemiótica de la recepción teatral". *Semiosis*, 19 (July-December 1987), 139-154.
De Marinis, Marco. *Il nuovo teatro: 1947-1970*. Milano: Bompiani, 1987.
De Marinis, Marco. "L'Odin Teatret di Eugenio Barba". In *Il nuovo teatro*. Milano: Bompiani, 1987, pp. 181-204.

De Marinis, Marco. "Problemas de semiótica teatral: la relación espectáculo-espectador". *Gestos*, 1 (avril 1986), 11-24.

De Marinis, Marco. "Problemi di analisi testuale dello spettacolo: codici spettacolari e convenzioni teatrali". In *La semiotica e il doppio teatrale*. Giulio Ferroni, Editor. Napoli: Liguori Editore, 1981, pp. 219-238.

De Marinis, Marco. "La recherche empirique sur la réception théâtrale: De la sociologie à la sémiotique". 1985. Mimeograph.

De Marinis, Marco. *Semiotica del teatro*. Milano: Studi Bompiani, 1982.

De Marinis, Marco. *The Semiotics of Performance*. Translated by Aine O'Healy. Bloomington and Indianapolis: Indiana University Press, 1993.

De Marinis, Marco. "Sociologie du théâtre: un réexamen et une proposition". *Congrès Mondial de Sociologie du Théâtre*. Edited by Roger Deldime. Roma: Bulzoni Editore, 1988, pp. 67-82.

De Marinis, Marco. "Le spectacle comme texte". In *Sémiologie et théâtre*. Lyon: Université de Lyon II, CERTEC, 1980, pp. 195-258.

De Marinis, Marco. "Theatrical Comprehension: A Socio-Semiotic Approach". *Theatre*, XV, 1 (Winter 1985), 12-17.

De Marinis, Marco. "Toward a Cognitive Semiotic of Theatrical Emotions". *Versus*, 41 (maggio-agosto 1985), 5-20.

De Marinis, Marco. "Vers une pragmatique de la communication théâtrale". *Versus*, 30 (settembre-dicembre 1981), 71-86.

De Marinis, Marco and Leonardo Altieri. "Il lavoro dello spettatore: un'indagine sul pubblico di teatro". In *Sociologia del lavoro*. 1985. Mimeograph.

De Toro, Alfonso. "Aproximaciones semiótico-estructurales para una definición de los términos 'tragoedia', 'comoedia', y 'tragicomedia': El drama de honor y su sistema". Part I, *Gestos*, 1 (Avril 1986), 53-72.

De Toro, Alfonso. "Aproximaciones semiótico-estructurales para una definición de los términos 'tragoedia', 'comoedias', y 'tragicomedia': El drama de honor y su sistema". Part II, *Gestos*, 2 (septiembre 1986), 47-64.

De Toro, Alfonso. "Aproximaciones semiótico-estructurales para una definición de los términos 'tragoedia', 'comoedia', y 'tragicomedia': El drama de honor y su sistema". *Semiosis*, 19 (July-December 1987), 213-238.

De Toro, Alfonso. "¿Cambio de paradigma? El 'Nuevo' teatro latinoamericano o la constitución de la post-modernidad espectacular". In *Hacia una nueva crítica y un nuevo teatro latinoamericano*. Alfonso de Toro and Fernando de Toro, Editors. Frankfurt am Main: Vervuert Verlag, 1993, pp. 27-46.

De Toro, Alfonso. "Entre el teatro kinésico y el teatro deconstruccionista: Eduardo Pavlovsky". *La Escena Latinoamericana*, 7 (diciembre 1991), 1-3.

De Toro, Alfonso. "Hacia un modelo para el teatro postmoderno". In *Semiótica y Teatro Latinoamericano*. Edited by Fernando de Toro. Buenos Aires and Ottawa: Editorial Galerna and IITCTL, 1990, pp. 4-23.

De Toro, Alfonso. "De la imagen al texto dramático". *La Escena Latinoamericana*, 3 (diciembre 1989), 43-45.

De Toro, Alfonso. "Observaciones para una definición de los términos 'tragoedia', 'comoedia', y 'Tragicomedia', en los dramas del honor de Calderón". In *Hacia Calderón*. Archivum Calderonianum. Edited by Hans Flasche. Stuttgart: Franz Steiner Verlag Wiesbaden GMBH, 1985, pp. 17-53.

De Toro, Alfonso. "Observaciones para una definición de los términos 'tragoedia', 'comoedia', y 'tragicomedia', en los dramas del honor de Calderón". In *Texto-Mensaje-Recipiente*. Tübingen: Gunter Narr Verlag, 1988, pp. 101-132.

De Toro, Alfonso. "Osvaldo Pellettieri y el neo-sainete". *La Escena Latinoamericana*, 3 (diciembre 1989), 53-54.

De Toro, Alfonso. "Postmodernidad en cuatro dramaturgos latinoamericanos". In *De la Colonia a la Postmodernidad: Teoría teatral y Crítica sobre teatro Latinoamericano*. Edited by Peter Roster and Mario Rojas. Buenos Aires and Ottawa: Editorial Galerna and IITCTL, 1992, 157-176.

De Toro, Alfonso. "Semiois teatral postmoderna: intento de un modelo". *Gestos*, Año 5, 9 (Avril 1989), 23-52.

De Toro, Alfonso. "Sistema semiótico-estructural del drama de honor en Lope de Vega y Calderón de la Barca". *Revista Canadiense de Estudios Hispánicos*, IX, 2 (Winter 1985), 181-202.

De Toro, Alfonso. "Sistema semiótico-estructural del drama del honor en Lope de Vega y Calderón de la Barca". In *Texto-Mensaje-Recipiente*. Tübingen: Gunter Narr Verlag, 1988, pp. 81-100.

De Toro, Alfonso. *Texto, Mensaje, Recipiente*. Buenos Aires: Editorial Galerna, 1990.

De Toro, Alfonso. "'Tragoedia', 'comoedia' y 'tragicomedia' española en los siglos XVI y XVII". *Semiosis*, 19 (julio-diciembre 1987), 239-260.

De Toro, Alfonso. "Y el mundo vendrá (Eduardo Rovner)". *La Escena Latinoamericana*, 3 (diciembre 1989), 62-64.

De Toro, Alfonso. *Die Zeitstruktur im Gegenwartsroman*. Tübingen: Gunter Narr Verlag, 1986.

De Toro, Alfonso, Editor. *Texte-Kontexte-Strukturen*. Beiträge zur französischen, spanischen und hispanoamerikanischen Literatur. Festschrift zum 60. Geburtstag von Karl Alfred Blüher. Edited by Alfonso de Toro. Tübingen: Gunter Narr Verlag, 1987.

De Toro, Alfonso and Fernando de Toro, Editors. *Hacia una nueva crítica y un nuevo teatro latinoamericano*. Theorie und Praxis des Theaters/Teoría y Práctica del Teatro. Frankfurt am Main: Vervuert Verlag, 1993.

De Toro, Fernando. "Análisis actancial de *Pirámide 178* de Máximo Aviles Blonda". *Revista Iberoamericana*, 142 (enero-marzo 1988), 271-287.

De Toro, Fernando. "La articulación del discurso en los textos de Griselda Gambaro". *Espacio*, Año 4, 6-7 (avril 1990), 35-38.

De Toro, Fernando. *Brecht en el teatro hispanoamericano contemporáneo*. Buenos Aires: Editorial Galerna, 1987.

De Toro, Fernando. *Brecht en el teatro hispanoamericano contemporáneo*. Ottawa: Girol Books, 1984.

De Toro, Fernando. "Brecht und Lateinamerika". In *Theater in Lateinamerika*. Edited by Heidrun Adler. Berlin: Reimer Verlag, 1991, pp. 89-104.

De Toro, Fernando. "Chejoviana: una nueva forma de escritura teatral". *Repertorio*, 7-8 (enero 1989), 88-91.

De Toro, Fernando. "Desde Stanislavsky a Barba: modernidad y postmodernidad o la epistemología del trabajo del actor en el siglo XX". In *Semiótica y teatro latinoamericano*. Edited by Fernando de Toro. Buenos Aires and Ottawa: Editorial Galerna and IITCTL, 1990.

De Toro, Fernando. "El espacio escénico y la integración del espectador como observador participante". *Primer Acto*, 3, 5 (avril 1989), 57-62.

De Toro, Fernando. "Estructuras de convergencia en el teatro del Siglo de Oro". In *Texte-Kontexte-Strukturen*. Beiträge zur französischen, spanischen und hispanoamerikanischen Literatur. Festschrift zum 60. Geburstag von Karl Alfred Blüher. Edited by Alfonso de Toro. Tübingen: Gunter Narr Verlag, 1987, pp. 265-282.

De Toro, Fernando. "Griselda Gambaro o la desarticulación semiótica del lenguaje". In *Poder, deseo y marginalización: aproximaciones a la obra de Griselda Gambaro*. Edited by Nora Mazziotti. Buenos Aires: Editorial Punto Sur, 1988, pp. 41-54.

De Toro, Fernando. "La identidad actoral en el Tercer Teatro". *La Escena Latinoamericana*, 6 (mayo 1991), 32-44.

De Toro, Fernando. "Ideología y teatro épico en *Santa Juana de América*". *Latin American Theatre Review*, XIV, 1 (Fall 1980), 55-64.

De Toro, Fernando. "Objeto y práctica de la semiología teatral: El espectáculo". *Espacio*, Año 2, 4 (julio 1988), 57-62.

De Toro, Fernando. "El Odin Teatret y Latinoamérica". *Latin American Theatre Review*, 21-22 (Fall 1988), 91-97.

De Toro, Fernando. "Post-Modern theatricality: Simulation, palimpsest, and rhizoma". *Gestos*, Año 8, 16 (Noviembre 1993), 23-50.

De Toro, Fernando. "Prometeo encadenado según Alberto Kurapel". *La Escena Latinoamericana*, 1 (avril 1989), 55-57.

De Toro, Fernando. "La referencialidad especular del discurso en Griselda Gambaro". In *Teatro argentino de los '60: Polémica, continuidad y ruptura*. Edited by O. Pellettieri. Buenos Aires: Ediciones Corregidor, 1989, pp. 183-198.

De Toro, Fernando. "Reflexiones para la historia de la literatura y una historia del teatro hispanoamericano". *Gestos*, 1 (Avril 1986), 101-120.

De Toro, Fernando. "La semiosis teatral". *Cuadernos de Investigación Teatral*, 23 (1987). Centro Latinoamericano de Creación e Investigación teatral. 38 pgs.

De Toro, Fernando. "La semiosis teatral". *Gestos*, Año 2, 4 (noviembre 1987), 47-64.

De Toro, Fernando. "Semiótica y recepción: teoría y práctica de la recepción teatral". *Dispositio*, XIII, 33-35 (1988), 91-114.

De Toro, Fernando. "¿Teatralidad o teatralidades? Hacia una definición nocional". *Espacio,* Año 2, 3 (septiembre 1987), 7-14.

De Toro, Fernando. "El teatro en Chile: ruptura y renovación. Perspectiva semiológica de los fenómenos de producción y recepción en los últimos doce años". *Conjunto*, 68 (avril-junio 1986), 23-32.
De Toro, Fernando. "El teatro en Chile: ruptura y renovación. Perspectiva semiológica de los fenómenos de producción y recepción en los últimos doce años". In *Le théâtre sous la contrainte*. Aix-en-Provence: Université de Provence, 1986, pp. 237-248.
De Toro, Fernando. "El teatro épico hispanoamericano: estructuras de convergencia". *Iberoamericana*, XIX-XX, 2-3 (1983), 69-85.
De Toro, Fernando. "El teatro latinoamericano actual: modernidad y tradición". In *Hacia una nueva crítica y un nuevo teatro latinoamericano*. Frankfurt am Main: Vervuert Verlag, 1993, pp. 9-11.
De Toro, Fernando. "Text, Dramatic Text, Performance Text". *Degrés*, Seizième année, 56 (hiver 1988), g-g10.
De Toro, Fernando. "Text, Reception, Ideology". In *Texte et ideologie/Text and Ideology*. Edited by A. W. Halsall and R. B. Rutland. Ottawa: Carleton University Press, 1988, pp. 105-114.
De Toro, Fernando. "Texto, texto dramático, texto espectacular". *Actes*, IV (1987), 295-307.
De Toro, Fernando. "Texto, texto dramático, texto espectacular". *Semiosis*, 19 (julio-diciembre 1987), 101-128.
De Toro, Fernando. "Theatre and Film: A Semiotic Approach to their Specificity". In *Theatre and Television*. Amsterdam: International Theatre Bookshop, 1988, pp. 179-196.
De Toro, Fernando. "Theatricality or theatricalities? Toward a Notional Definition". *Theater Three*, 6 (Spring 1989), 12-3.
De Toro, Fernando. "Toward a New Theatrology". *The Canadian Journal of Drama and Theatre*, 1, 2 (1991), 47-58.
De Toro, Fernando. "Toward a Socio-Semiotics of the Theatre". *Semiotica*, 72. 1-2 (1988), 37-70. Also in *Congrès Mondial de Sociologie du Théâtre*. Selected Papers. Edited by Roger Deldime. Roma: Bulzoni Editore, 1988, pp. 83-121.
De Toro, Fernando. "Towards a Specification of Theatre Discourse". *The American Journal of Semiotics*, VII, 3 (1990), 75-90.
De Toro, Fernando. "Toward a Specification of Theatre Discourse". *Versus*, 54 settembre-dicembre (1989), 3-20.
De Toro, Fernando. "Vers un théâtre multimédia". *Jeu*, 44 (1987), 116-123.
De Toro, Fernando, Editor. *Reflexiones sobre teatro latinoamericano del siglo veinte*. Buenos Aires and Kiel: Editorial Galerna and Lemcke Verlag, 1989.
De Toro, Fernando, Editor. *Semiótica y Teatro Latinoamericano*. Buenos Aires and Ottawa: Editorial Galerna and IITCTL, 1990.
De Toro, Fernando and Alfonso de Toro, Editors. *Hacia una nueva crítica y un nuevo teatro latinoamericano*. Frankfurt am Main: Vervuert Verlag, 1993.
De Toro, Fernando and Peter Roster. *Bibliografía del teatro hispanoamericano contemporáneo (1900-1980)*. 2 Vols. Frankfurt am Main: Vervuert Verlag, 1985.

Diderot, Denis. *Paradoxe sur le comédien*. Précedés des *Entretiens sur le Fils naturel*. Chronology and preface by Raymond Laubreaux. Paris: Flammarion, Editeur, 1981.

Diderot, Denis. *Textos para una estética literaria*. Selection, Translation, Prologue and Notes by Kurt Jung and Zaida Jung. Santiago, Chile: Editorial Universitaria, 1971.

Díez Borque, José María and Luciano García Lorenzo, Editors. *Semiología del teatro*. Barcelona: Editorial Planeta, 1975.

Dinu, Mihai. "The Algebra of Scenic Situations". In *Semiotics of Drama and Theatre*. Edited by Herta Schmidt and Aloysius Van Kesteren. The Hague: John Benjamins, 1984, pp. 67-92.

Dragún, Osvaldo. *Heroica de Buenos Aires*. Buenos Aires: Editorial Astral, 1967.

Dubois, Jacques. "Sociologie des textes littéraires". *La pensée*, 215 (octobre 1980), 82-94.

Dubois, J., M. Giacomo, L. Guespin, C. and J.B. Marcelesi and J.P. Mével. *Dictionnaire de linguistique*. Paris: Librairie Larousse, 1973.

Duchet, Claude. "Pour une socio-critique ou variations sur un incipit". *Littérature*, 1 (février 1971), 5-14.

Ducrot, Oswald. "Analyses pragmatiques". *Communications*, 32 (1980), 11-60.

Ducrot, Oswald. "Les indéfinis et l'énonciation". *Langages*, 17 (1970), 91-111.

Ducrot, Oswald. "Présupposés et sous-entendus". *Langue française*, 4 (février 1969), 30-43.

Ducrot, Oswald. "Structuralisme, énonciation et sémantique". *Poétique*, 33 (février 1978), 107-128.

Ducrot, Oswald and Tzvetan Todorov. *Dictionnaire encyclopédique des sciences du langage*. Paris: Editions du Seuil, 1972.

Ducrot, Oswald and Tzvetan Todorov. *Diccionario enciclopédico de las ciencias del lenguaje*. Translated from the Spanish by Enrique Pezzoni. México: Siglo Veintiuno Editores, 1974.

Durán Cerda, Julio. *Teatro chileno contemporáneo*. Madrid: Aguilar, 1970.

Durand, Régis, Editor. *La relation théâtrale*. Lille: Presses Universitaires de Lille, 1980.

Eagleton, Terry. *Literary Theory: An Introduction*. Minneapolis: University of Minnesota Press, 1983.

Eco, Umberto. "Elementos preteatrales de una semiótica del teatro". In *Semiología del teatro*. Texts selected by José María Díez Borque and Luciano García Lorenzo. Barcelona: Editorial Planeta, 1975, pp. 93-102.

Eco, Umberto. "Pour une reformulation du concept de signe iconique: Les modes de production sémiotique". *Communications*, 9 (1978), 141-191.

Eco, Umberto. *The Role of the Reader*. Bloomington, Indiana: Indiana University Press, 1984.

Eco, Umberto. "El signo teatral". *Semiosis*, 19 (July-December 1987), 129-138.

Eco, Umberto. "Sémiologie des messages visuels". *Communications*, 15 (1970), 11-51.

Eco, Umberto. "Semiotics of Theatrical Performance". *The Drama Review*, XXI, 1 (March 1977), 107-117.
Eco, Umberto. *A Theory of Semiotics*. Bloomington and London: Indiana University Press, 1976.
Eco, Umberto. *Travels in Hyperreality*. Translated from the Italian by William Weaver. Orlando, Florida: Harcourt Brace Jovanovich, 1986.
Eikhenbaum, Boris. "La théorie de la 'méthode formelle'". In *Théorie de la littérature*. Texts by the Russian Formalists collected, presented and translated by Tzvetan Todorov. Preface by Roman Jakobson. Paris: Editions du Seuil, 1965, pp. 31-75.
Elam, Keir. "I mondi possibili del dramma". In *La semiotica e il doppio teatrale*. Giulio Ferroni, Editor. Napoli: Liguori Editore, 1981, pp. 83-94.
Elam, Keir. "Much Ado About Speech Acts: Atti, fatti, effetti e affetti nella rapresentazione drammatica". *Versus*, 41 (maggio-agosto 1985), 49-58.
Elam, Keir. *The Semiotics of Theatre and Drama*. London and New York: Methuen, 1980.
Elam, Keir. "Text Appeal and the Analysis Paralysis: Towards a Processual Poetics of Dramatic Production". In *Altro Polo. Performance: from Product to Process*. Edited by tim Fitzpatrick. Sydney: University of Sydney, 1989, pp. 1-27.
Erlich, Victor. *Russian Formalism: History - Doctrine*. The Hague and Paris: Mouton, 1969.
Ertel, Evelyne. "Eléments pour une sémiologie du théâtre". *Travail théâtral*, 28-29 (1977), 121-150.
Ertel, Evelyne. "Vers une analyse sémiologique de la représentation". *Travail théâtral*, 32-33 (1979), 164-172.
Eysenck, M.W. *Attention and Arousal. Cognition and Performance*. Berlin, Heidelberg, New York: Springer Verlag, 1982.
Fang, Mei Lang. *My Life on the Stage and The Enchanter from the Pear Garden by S.M. Eisenstein*. Holstebro: ISTA, 1986.
Fernández Retamar, Roberto. "Algunos problemas teóricos de la literatura hispanoamericana". *Revista de crítica literaria latinoamericana*, Año 1, 1 (1975), 7-38.
Ferroni, Giulio, Editor. *La semiotica e il doppio teatrale*. Napoli: Liguori Editore, 1981.
Fischer-Lichte, Erika. "El cambio en los códigos teatrales: hacia una semiótica de la puesta en escena intercultural". *Gestos*, Año 4, 8 (Noviembre 1989), 11-32.
Fischer-Lichte, Erika. "The Dramatic Dialogue - Oral or Literary Communication"? In *Semiotics of Drama and Theatre*. Edited by Herta Schmidt and Aloysius Van Kesteren. The Hague: John Benjamins Publishing Company, 1984, pp. 137-173.
Fischer-Lichte, Erika. "Hacia una comprensión del teatro. Algunas perspectivas de la semiótica del teatro". *Dispositio*, XIII, 33-35 (1988), 29-50.
Fischer-Lichte, Erika. *The Semiotics of Theatre*. Translated by Jeremy Gaines and Doris L. Jones. Bloomington and Indianapolis: Indiana University Press, 1992.

Fischer-Lichte, Erika. *Semiotik des Theaters*. Die Aufführung als Text. Band 3. Tübingen: Gunter Narr Verlag, 1983.
Fischer-Lichte, Erika. *Semiotik des Theaters*. Das System der Theatralischen Zeichen. Band 1. Tübingen: Gunter Narr Verlag, 1983.
Fischer-Lichte, Erika. *Semiotik des Theaters*. Vom "künstlichen" zum "natürlichen" Zeichen Theater des Barock und der Aufklärung. Band 2. Tübingen: Gunter Narr Verlag, 1983.
Fischer-Lichte, Erika. "Theatrical Code. An Approach to the Problem". *Kodikas/Code*, Vol. II. Supplement, 8 (1982), 46-62.
Fischer-Lichte, Erika. "Wandel theatralischer Kodes: Zur Semiotik der interkulturellen Inszenierung". *Zeitschrift für Semiotik*, Band 11, Heft 1 (1989), 63-86.
Fitzpatrick, Tim. "Análisis de textos dramáticos y de espectáculos: hacia un modelo teórico". *Semiosis*, 19 (July-December 1987), 191-212.
Fitzpatrick, Tim. "The Dialectics of Space-Time: Dramaturgical and Directorial Strategies for Performance and Fictional World". In *Altro Polo. Performance: from Product to Process*. Edited by Tim Fitzpatrick. Sydney: University of Sydney, 1989, pp. 49-112.
Fitzpatrick, Tim. "Models of Visual and Auditory Interaction in Performance". *Gestos*, Año 5, 9 (Avril 1990), 9-22.
Fitzpatrick, Tim. "Playscript Analysis, Performance Analysis: Towards a Theoretical Model". *Gestos*, 2 (noviembre 1986), 13-28.
Fitzpatrick, Tim, Editor. *Altro Polo. Performance: from Product to Process*. Sydney: University of Sydney, 1989.
Folch, Jean-Marie. "Sémiologie visuelle et status sémiotiques des éléments visuels du discours théâtral". *Sixième année*, 13 (Spring 1978), e-e13.
Folch, Jean-Marie. "Sémiotique d'un discours plastique non figurative". *Communications*, 34 (1981), 135-158.
Foster, David William. *The Argentine Teatro Independiente, 1930-1955*. York, South Carolina: Spanish Literature Publishing Company, 1986.
Fowler, Alastair. *Kinds of Literature: An Introduction to the History of Genres and Modes*. Cambridge, Massachusetts: Harvard University Press, 1982.
Fowler, Alastair. "The Life and Death of Literary Forms". *New Literary History*, II, 2 (Winter 1971), 39-55.
Fowler, Richard. "Grotowski and Barba: A Canadian Perspective". *Canadian Theatre Review*, 32 (1981), 44-51.
Franco, Jean. *Historia de la literatura hispanoamericana*. Barcelona: Editorial Ariel, 1975.
Frege, Gottlob. *Écrits logiques et philosophiques*. Translation and introduction by Claude Imbert. Paris: Editions du Seuil, 1971.
Freund, Elizabeth. *The Return of the Reader. Reader-Response Criticism*. London and New York: Methuen, 1987.
Frow, John. *Marxism and Literary History*. Cambridge, Massachusetts: Harvard University Press, 1986.

Gardin, Jean-Claude. *Les analyses de discours*. Neuchâtel, Switzerland: Delachau et Niestlé, S.A., 1974.
Genette, Gérard. *Figures I*. Paris: Editions du Seuil, 1966.
Genette, Gérard. *Figures II*. Paris: Editions du Seuil, 1969.
Genette, Gérard. *Figures III*. Paris: Editions du Seuil, 1972.
Genette, Gérard. "Genres, «types», modes". *Poétique*, 32 (novembre 1977), 389-421.
Genette, Gérard. *Introduction à l'architexte*. Editions du Seuil, 1979.
Giacchè, Piergiorgio. "Antropologia culturale e cultura teatrale. Note per un aggiornamento dell'approccio socio-antropologico al teatro". *Teatro e Storia*, Anno III, 5, 1 (aprile, 1988), 23-50.
Giordano, Enrique. *La teatralización de la obra dramática: De Florencio Sánchez a Roberto Arlt*. México: La Red de Jonás. PREMIDA Editora, 1982.
Girard, Gilles, Réal Ouellet and Claude Rigault. *L'Univers du théâtre*. Paris: Presses Universitaires de France, 1978.
Glowinski, Michal. "Theoretical Foundations of Historical Poetics". *New Literary History*, VII, 2 (Winter 1976), 237-245.
Goic, Cedomil. *Historia de la novela hispanoamericana*. Valparaíso: Ediciones Universitarias, 1972.
Goldstein, Leon J. "Literary History as History". *New Literary History*, VIII, 2 (Winter 1977), 321-333.
Gollouscio, Eva. *Etude sur le "cocoliche" scénique et édition annotée de "Mateo" d'Armando Discépolo*. Toulouse: Institut d'Etudes Hispaniques et Hispano-Américaines. Université de Toulouse-Le Mirail, 1979.
Gómez, José Angel. "The Appearance of Television on the Scene: a Reflection on the Historiography of Theatrical Art". In *Theatre and Television*. Amsterdam: International Theatre Bookshop, 1988, pp. 215-219.
Gourdon, Anne-Marie. *Théâtre, Public, Perception*. Paris: Editions Centre National de la Recherche Scientifique, 1982.
Gourdon, Anne-Marie. *Formation du comédian. Les voies de la création théâtrale*. Vol. IX. Paris: Editions Centre National de la Recherche Scientifique, 1981.
Greimas, Algirdas Julien. "Les actants, les acteurs et les figures". In *Sémiotique narrative et textuelle*. Paris: Librairie Larousse, 1973, pp. 161-176.
Greimas, Algirdas Julien. *Sémantique structurale*. Paris: Librairie Larousse, 1966.
Greimas, Algirdas Julien. *Du sens*. Paris: Editions du Seuil, 1970.
Gropius, Walter, Editor. *The Theatre of the Bauhaus*. Introduction by Walter Gropius. Translated by Arthur S. Wensinger. Middletown, Connecticut: Wesleyan University Press, 1961.
Grotowski, Jerzy. *Towards a Poor Theatre*. New York: Simon and Schuster, 1968.
Guerrero, Eduardo. "Espacio y poética en Ramón Griffero. Análisis de su trilogía: *Historias de un galpón abandonado, Cinema Uroppia y 99 la morgue*". In *Hacia una nueva crítica y un nuevo teatro latinoamericano*. Frankfurt am Main: Vervuert Verlag, 1993, pp. 127-137.
Guespin, Louis. "Problématique des travaux sur le discours politique". *Langages*, 23 (septembre 1971), 3-24.

Guespin, Louis. "Types de discours ou fonctionnements discursifs"? *Langages*, 11 (mars 1976), 3-12.
Guillén, Claudio. *Literature as System: Essays Toward the Theory of Literary History*. Princeton, New Jersey: Princeton University Press, 1971.
Guimbretière, André. "Approche du référent". *Degrés*, première année, 3 (juillet 1973), f-f7.
Guinsburg, Jocó. "O teatro no gesto". *Polímica*, 2 (1980), 47-50.
Guinsburg, Jocó, J. Teixeira Coelho Netto and Reni Chaves Cardoso, Editors. *Semiologia do teatro*. Sao Paulo: Editora Perspectiva, 1978.
Hamon, Philippe. "Un discours contraint". *Poétique*, 16 (1973), 411-445.
Hamon, Philippe. "Pour un statut sémiologique du personnage". *Littérature*, 6 (mai 1972), 86-100.
Hamon, Philippe. "Qu'est-ce que une description"? *Poétique*, 12 (1972), 465-485.
Hamon, Philippe. "Texte et idéologie: pour une poétique de la norme". *Poétique*, 49 (février 1982), 105-125.
Hanik, Dieter. "Fonction heuristique et valeur d'explication de l'idée de genre". *Oeuvres et Critiques*, II, 2 (1977-78), 27-38.
Helbo, André. "Approches de la réception. Quelques problèmes". *Versus*, 41 (maggio-agosto 1985), 41-48.
Helbo, André. "Le code théâtral". In *Sémiologie de la représentation*. Edited by André Helbo. Bruxelles: Editions Complexe, 1975, pp. 12-27.
Helbo, André. "Construir la coherencia. El espectáculo teatral". *Gestos*, 2 (septiembre 1986), 29-38.
Helbo, André. "Le discours théâtral: une sémantique de la relation". In *La relation théâtrale*. Texts compiled by Régis Durand. Lille: Presses Universitaires de Lille, 1980, pp. 97-106.
Helbo, André. "Evidences et strategies de l'analyse théâtrale". In *Semiotics of Drama and Theatre*. Edited by Herta Schmidt and Aloysius Van Kesteren. The Hague: John Benjamins, 1984, pp. 93-101.
Helbo, André. *Les mots et les gestes*. Lille: Presses Universitaires de Lille, 1983.
Helbo, André. "Pour un proprium de la représentation théâtrale". In *Sémiologie de la representation*. Edited by André Helbo. Bruxelles: Editions Complexe, 1975, pp. 62-72.
Helbo, André. "Problèmes d'une rhétorique scénique". *Kodikas/Code*, II, Supplement, 8 (1982), 95-107.
Helbo, André. "Regards sur la pratique théâtrale". *Kodikas/Code*, VII, 1-2 (1984), 4-9.
Helbo, André. "Les sciences du spectacle". In *Théâtre. Modes d'approche*. Edited by André Helbo, J. Dines Johansen, Patrice Pavis and Anne Ubersfeld. Bruxelles: Editions Labor, 1987, pp. 11-32.
Helbo, André. "The Semiology of Theatre or: Communication Swamped". *Poetics Today*, II, 3 (Spring 1981), 105-111.
Helbo, André. "Semiótica y recepción: Teorías y práctica de la recepción teatral". *Dispositio*, XIII, 33-35 (1988), 91-114.

Helbo, André. *Theory of Performing Arts*. Amsterdam and Philadephia: John Benjamins, 1987.
Helbo, André, Editor. *Sémiologie de la représentation*. Bruxelles: Editions Complexe, 1975.
Helbo, André, J. Dines Johansen, Patrice Pavis and Anne Ubersfeld, Editors. *Théâtre. Modes d'approche*. Bruxelles: Editions Labor, 1987.
Henríquez Ureña, Max. *Breve historia del modernismo*. Second printing. México: Fondo de Cultura Económica, 1978.
Henríquez Ureña, Pedro. *Las corrientes literarias en la América Hispánica*. Third printing. 1949; México: Fondo de Cultura Económica, 1969.
Hernadi, Paul. "Entertaining Commitments: A Reception Theory of Literary Genres". *Poetics*, 10 (1981), 195-211.
Hernadi, Paul. *Teoría de los géneros literarios*. Edited by Antoni Bosch. Barcelona, 1978.
Hess-Lüttich, Ernest W.B. "Dramatic Discourse". In *Discourse and Literature. New Approaches to the Analysis of Literary Genres*. Edited by Teun A. Van Dijk. Amsterdam and Philadelphia: John Benjamins, 1985, pp. 199-214.
Hess-Lüttich, Ernest W.B., Editor. *Multimedial Communication. Theatre Semiotics*. Vol. II. Tübingen: Gunter Narr Verlag, 1982.
Hodge, Robert. *Literature as Discourse*. Baltimore and London: The Johns Hopkins University Press, 1990.
Holub, Robert C. *Reception Theory*. London and New York: Methuen, 1984.
Honzl, Jindrich. "Dynamics of the Sign in the Theatre". In *Semiotics of Art. Prague School Contributions*. Edited by Ladislav Matejka and Erwin R. Titunik. Cambridge, Massachusetts and London, England: The MIT Press, 1976, pp. 74-93.
Honzl, Jindrich. "The Hierarchy of Dramatic Devices". In *Semiotics of Art. Prague School Contributions*. Edited by Ladislav Matejka and Irwin R. Titunik. Cambridge, Massachusetts and London, England: The MIT Press, 1976, pp. 118-127.
Honzl, Jindrich. "La mobilité du signe théâtral". *Travail théâtral*, 4 (1971), 5-20.
Hoogendoorn, Wiebe. "Notes on deixis and simultaneity in theatre performance". *Degrés*, Dixième année, 30 (printemps 1982), e-e6.
Hornby, R. *Script into Performance: A Structuralist View of Play Production*. Austin: University of Texas Press, 1977.
Hubert, J.D. "Random Reflections on Literary History and Textual Criticism". *New Literary Criticism*, II, 1 (Autumn 1970), 163-171.
Husserl, Edmund. *Logical Investigations*. Vol. II, Investigation I. Expression and Meaning. Translated by J.N. Findlay. New York: Humanities Press, 1970.
Ingarden, Roman. *The Cognition of the Literary Work of Art*. Translated by Ruth Ann Crowley and Kenneth R. Olson. Evanston: Northwestern University Press, 1973.
Ingarden, Roman. "Les fonctions du langage au théâtre". *Poétique*, 8 (1971), 531-538.

Ingarden, Roman. *The Literary Work of Art*. Translated with an introduction by George G. Grabowicz. Evanston: Northwestern University Press, 1973.
Ionesco, Eugène. *Notas contranotas*. Buenos Aires: Editorial Losada, 1965.
Ionesco, Eugène. *Notes and counter notes*. Translation from the French by Donald Watson. London: Calder, 1964.
Ionesco, Eugène. *Notes contre-notes*. Paris: Editions Gallimard, 1966.
Iser, Wolfgang. *The Act of Reading: A Theory of Aesthetic Response*. Baltimore and London: The John Hopkins University Press, 1978.
Iser, Wolfgang. "Aspect génériques de la réception". *Poétique*, 39 (1979), 253-362.
Iser, Wolfgang. *The Implied Reader*. Baltimore and London: The Johns Hopkins University Press, 1974.
Iser, Wolfgang. *Der Implizite Leser: Kommunikationsformen des Romans von Bunyan bis Beckett*. München: Wilhelm Fink Verlag, 1972.
Iser, Wolfgang. "The Reading Process: A Phenomenological Approach". *New Literary History*, III, 2 (Winter 1972), 279-299.
Jakobson, Roman. *Essais de linguistique générale*. Paris: Editions de Minuit, 1963.
Janik, Dieter. "Fonction heuristique et valeur d'explication de l'idée de genre". *Oeuvres et Critiques*, II, 2 (1977-78), 27-38.
Jansen, Steen. "Esquisse d'une théorie de la forme dramatique". *Langages*, 12 (décembre 1968), 71-93.
Jansen, Steen. "Le role de l'espace scénique dans la lecture du texte dramatique". In *Semiotics of Drama and Theatre*. Edited by Herta Schmidt and Aloysius Van Kesteren. Amsterdam and Philadelphia: John Benjamins, 1984, pp. 254-289.
Jansen, Steen. "Qu'est-ce qu'une situation dramatique"? *Orbis Litterarum*, XXVIII (1973), 235-292.
Jaques-Dalcroze, E. *Coordination et disordination des mouvements corporels*. Paris: Editions Musicales, 1935.
Jaumain, Michel. "Approches méthodologiques de l'audience théâtrale". *Cahiers théâtre Louvin*, 49 (1983). [entire issue].
Jauss, Hans-Robert. *Äesthetische Erfahrung und literarische Hermeneutik I*. München: Wilhelm Fink Verlag, 1977.
Jauss, Hans-Robert. "Estética de la recepción y comunicación literaria". *Espacio*, Año 3, 5 (avril 1989), 21-32.
Jauss, Hans-Robert. "Literary History as a Challenge to Literary Theory". *New Literary History*, II, 1 (Autumn 1970), 7-37.
Jauss, Hans-Robert. *Pour une esthétique de la réception*. Translated from the German by Claude Maillard. Preface by Jean Starobinski. Paris: Editions Gallimard, 1978.
Jauss, Hans-Robert. *Toward an Aesthetic of Reception*. Translated from the German by Timothy Bahti. Introduction by Paul de Man. Minneapolis: University of Minnesota Press.
Jitrik, Noé. *Producción literaria y producción social*. Buenos Aires: Editorial Sudamericana, 1975.

Kahn, Robert and Charles Cannell. *The Dynamics of Interviewing*. New York: Wiley, 1957.
Kaisergruber, Danielle. "Lecture/mise en scène/théâtre". *Pratique*, 15-16 (juillet 1977), 20-33.
Kaisergruber, Danielle and David Kaisergruber. "Théorie des significations". *Dialectiques*, 3 (1973), 3-19.
Kantor, Tadeusz. *Le théâtre de la mort*. Texts compiled and presented by Denis Bablet. Lausanne: Editions L'Age d'Homme, 1977.
Karl, Frederick R. *Modern and Modernism: The Sovereignty of the Artists 1885-1925*. New York: Atheneum, 1988.
Kernan, Alvin B. "The Idea of Literature". *New Literary History*, V, 1 (Autumn 1973), 31-40.
Kowalewicz, Kazimierz. "Small steps towards the spectator". *Degrés*, Seizième année, 56 (Winter 1988), c-c16.
Kowzan, Tadeusz. "Le signe au théâtre". *Diogène*, 61 (1968), 59-90.
Kristeva, Julia. "Problèmes de la structuration du texte". In *Théorie d'Ensemble*. Paris: Editions du Seuil, 1968, 297-316.
Kristeva, Julia. "La productivité dite texte". *Communications*, 11 (1968), 59-83.
Kristeva, Julia. *Semiotikè*. Paris: Editions du Seuil, 1969.
Kristeva, Julia. "Le sujet en procès". *Tel Quel*, 52 (1972), 12-30.
Kristeva, Julia. "Le sujet en procès". *Tel Quel*, 53 (1973), 17-38.
Kristeva, Julia, Jean-Claude Milner and Nicolas Ruwet, Editors. *Langue, discours, société. Pour Emile Benveniste*. Paris: Editions du Seuil, 1975.
Krysinski, Wladimir. "El cuerpo en cuanto signo y su significado en el teatro moderno: De Evreïnoff y Craig a Artaud y Grotowski". *Revista Canadiense de Estudios Hispánicos*, VII, 1 (Fall 1982), 19-38.
Krysinski, Wladimir. "La manipulación referencial en el drama moderno". *Gestos*, Año 4, 7 (Avril 1989), 9-32.
Krysinski, Waldimir. *Le paradigme inquiet. Pirandello et le champ de la modernité*. Montréal: Le Préambule, 1989.
Krysinski, Wladimir. "Semiotics Modalities of the Body in Modern Theatre". *Poetics Today*, II, 3 (Spring 1981), 141-161.
Kurapel, Alberto. "Nuevas direcciones en la escritura dramática y la puesta en escena latinoamericana". In *De la Colonia a la Postmodernidad: Teoría teatral y Crítica sobre teatro Latinoamericano*. Edited by Peter Roster and Mario Rojas. Buenos Aires and Ottawa: Editorial Galerna and IITCTL, 1992, pp. 339-348.
Labastida, Jaime. "Alejo Carpentier: realidad y conocimiento estético". *Casa de las Américas*, 87 (noviembre-diciembre 1975), 21-34.
Larthomas, Pierre. *Le langage dramatique*. Paris: Presses Universitaires de France, 1972.
Lewis, C.I. "The Modes of Meaning". In *Semantics and the Philosophy of Language*. Edited by Leonard Linsky. Champaign: University of Illinois Press, 1969, pp. 50-55.

Lida, Raimundo. "Períodos y generaciones en historia literaria". In *Letras Hispánicas*. México: Fondo de Cultura Económica, 1958, pp. 25-46.

Lindenberg, Herbert. "Toward a New History in Literary Studies". *Profession 84*, (1984), 16-23.

Linsky, Leonard, Editor. *Semantics and the Philosophy of Language*. Champaign: University of Illinois Press, 1969.

Lista, Giovanni, Editor. *Théâtre futuriste italien*. 2 vols. Lausanne: Editions L'Age d'Homme, 1976.

Lizárraga, Andrés. *Santa Juana de América*. La Habana, Cuba: Casa de las Américas, 1975.

Lodge, David. "Historicism and Literary History: Mapping the Modern Period". *New Literary History*, X, 3 (Spring 1979), 547-556.

Loriggio, Francesco. "The Anthropology in/of Fiction: Novels about Voyages". In *Literary Anthropology*. Edited by Fernando Poyatos. Amsterdam and Philadelphia: John Benjamins, 1988, pp. 305-326.

Loriggio, Francesco. "Apuntes sobre antropología teatral". In *De la Colonia a la Postmodernidad: Teoría teatral y Crítica sobre teatro Latinoamericano*. Edited by Peter Roster and Mario Rojas. Buenos Aires and Ottawa: Editorial Galerna and IITCTL, 1992, pp. 19-38.

Lotman, Yury M. "The Text and the Structure of Its Audience". *New Literary History*, XIV, 1 (Autumn 1982), 81-88.

Lyons, John. *Semantics 2*. London, New York, Melbourne and Cambridge: Cambridge University Press, 1979.

Maldidier, Denise, Claudine Normand and Régine Robin. "Discours et idéologie: quelques bases pour une recherche". *Langue française*, 15 (septembre 1972), 116-142.

Marco, Susana, Abel Posadas, Marta Speroni and Griselda Vignolo. *Teoría del género chico criollo*. Buenos Aires: Eudeba, 1974.

Marino, Adrian. "Idée littéraire, structure, modèle". *Degrés*, quatrième année, 10 (printemps 1975-1976), c-c24.

Marras, Sergio. *Macías*. Santiago, Chile: Las Ediciones del Ornitorrinco, 1984.

Martin, Jacky. "Ostension et communication théâtrale". *Littérature*, 53 (1984), 119-126.

Matejka, Ladislav and Erwin R. Titunik, Editors. *Semiotics of Art. Prague School Contributions*. Cambridge, Massachussets/London, England: The MIT Press, 1976.

Mayer, Rudolf A. M. "Social Determination of Sign Competence in the Theatre as Communication System". In *Congrès Mondial de Sociologie du Théâtre*. Selected Papers. Edited by Roger Deldime. Roma: Bulzoni Editore, 1988, pp. 131-140.

Meyerhold, Vsevolod. *El Actor sobre la escena. Diccionario de práctica teatral*. Edited with an introduction and notes by Edgar Ceballos. México, D.F.: Grupo Editorial Gaceta, 1986.

Meyerhold, Vsevolod. *Ecrits sur le Théâtre.* Vol. I. 1891-1917. Translated with a preface and notes by Béatrice Picon-Villon. Lausanne: La Cité L'Age d'Homme, 1973.
Meyerhold, Vsevolod. *Ecrits sur le Théâtre.* Vol. II. 1917-1929. Translated with a preface and notes by Béatrice Picon-Villon. Lausanne: La Cité L'Age d'Homme, 1973.
Meyerhold, Vsevolod. *Ecrits sur le Théâtre.* Vol. III. 1930-1936. Translated with a preface and notes by Béatrice Picon-Villon. Lausanne: La Cité L'Age d'Homme, 1973.
Meyerhold, Vsevolod. *Meyerhold on Theatre.* Translated and edited with a critical commentary by Edward Braun. London and New York: Eyre Methuen and Hill and Wang, 1969.
Michaud, Eric. *Théâtre au Bauhaus.* Lausanne: Editions L'Age d'Homme, 1978.
Milaré, Sebastiao. "Macunaima e o teatro brasileiro contemporaneo". In *De la Colonia a la Postmodernidad: Teoría teatral y Crítica sobre teatro Latinoamericano.* Edited by Peter Roster and Mario Rojas. Buenos Aires and Ottawa: Editorial Galerna and IITCTL, 1992, pp. 89-102.
Miller, Arthur. *Death of a Salesman.* New York: The Viking Press, 1972.
Minervini, Cosimo. *Sémiotique de la réception théâtrale.* Tesis de licenciatura. Universidad de Boloña, 1983. (Mimeograph).
Mnouchkine, Ariane, et al. "Différent le Théâtre du Soleil". *Travail Théâtral.* Special issue (février 1976).
Morris, Charles. "Foundations of the Theory of Signs". In *Foundations of the Unity of Science.* Vol. I, Nos. 1-10. Third printing. Chicago and London: The University of Chicago Press, 1971.
Mounier, Katherine. "Deux créations collectives du Théâtre du Soleil: *1793* et *L'age d'or*". In *Les voies de la création théâtrale.* Vol. V. Paris: Editions du Centre National de Recherche Scientifique, 1977, pp. 121-278.
Mounin, Georges. *Introduction à la sémiologie.* Paris: Editions de Minuit, 1970.
Mukařovský, Jan. *Aesthetic Function, Norm and Value as Social Facts.* Translated by Mark E. Suino. Ann Arbor: University of Michigan Press, 1970.
Mukařovský, Jan. "Littérature et sémiologie". *Poétique*, 3 (1970), 386-398.
Mukařovský, Jan. *Structure, Sign, and Function.* Translated and edited by John Burbank and Peter Steiner. New Haven and London: Yale University Press, 1978.
Mukařovský, Jan. *Word and Verbal Art.* Translated and edited by John Burbank and Peter Steiner. Foreword by René Wellek. New Haven and London: Yale University Press, 1977.
Müller, Günter. "Bermerkungen zur Gattungspoetik". *Philosophischer Anzeiger*, III (1928), 129-147.
Muntenau, Romul. "Acte critique et histoire littéraire". *Cahiers Roumains d'études littéraires*, 4 (1976), 51-55.
Nattiez, J.J. "Pour une définition de la sémiologie". *Langages*, 35 (mars 1974), 3-21.

Naumann, Manfred. "Literary Production and Reception". *New Literary History*, VIII, 1 (Autumn 1976), 108-126.
O'Casey, Sean. *Purple Dust*. London: MacMillan London, 1980.
Ochsenius, Carlos. *Transformaciones del Teatro Chileno en la Década del '70*. Santiago, Chile: CENECA, 1980.
O'Neill, Eugene. *The Straw*. New York: Vintage Books, 1951.
Ogden, C.K. and I.A. Richards. *The Meaning of Meaning*. New York: Harcourt, Brace and World, 1923.
Osinski, Zbigniew. *Grotowski and His Laboratory*. New York: Performing Arts Journal, 1986.
Parret, Herman. "L'énonciation en tant que déictisation et modalisation". *Langages*, 70 (juin 1983), 83-98.
Passow, Wilfried. "The Analysis of Theatrical Performance". *Poetics Today*, II, 3 (Spring 1981), 237-254.
Pavis, Patrice. "Del texto a la escena: un parto difícil". *Semiosis*, 19 (July-December 1987), 173-190.
Pavis, Patrice. *Diccionario del Teatro*. Translated by Fernando de Toro. Barcelona: Ediciones Paidos, 1984.
Pavis, Patrice. *Dictionnaire du théâtre*. Paris: Editions Sociales, 1980.
Pavis, Patrice. *Dictionnaire du théâtre*. Paris: Editions Sociales, 1987.
Pavis, Patrice. *Languages of the Stage*. New York: Performing Arts Journal Publications, 1982.
Pavis, Patrice. *Marivaux à l'épreuve de la scène*. Paris: Publications de La Sorbonne, 1985.
Pavis, Patrice. "Per un'estetica della ricezione teatrale. Variazioni su alcune relazioni". In *La semiotica e il doppio teatrale*. Edited by Giulio Ferroni. Napoli: Liguori Editore, 1981, pp. 187-218.
Pavis, Patrice. "Pour une esthétique de la réception théâtrale". In *La relation théâtrale*. Texts compiled by Régis Durand. Lille: Presses Universitaires de Lille, 1980, pp. 27-54.
Pavis, Patrice. *Problèmes de sémiologie théâtrale*. Montréal: Presses de l'Université de Québec, 1976.
Pavis, Patrice. "Production et réception au théatre: la concrétisation du texte dramatique et spectaculaire". *Revue des sciences humaines*, LX, 189 (janvier-mars 1983), 51-88.
Pavis, Patrice. "La réception du texte dramatique et spectaculaire: les processus de fictionnalisation et idéologisation". *Versus*, 41 (maggio-agosto 1985), 69-94.
Pavis, Patrice. "Réflextions sur la notation de la représentation théâtrale". In *Voix et images de la scène*. Lille: Presses Universitaires de Lille, 1982.
Pavis, Patrice. "Représentation, mise en scène, mise en signe". *The Canadian Journal of Research in Semiotics*, IV, 1 (Fall 1976), 63-86.
Pavis, Patrice. "El teatro y los medios de comunicación: especificidad e interferencia". *Gestos*, 1 (avril 1986), 25-52.
Pavis, Patrice. *Le théatre au croisement des cultures*. Paris: Corti, 1990.

Pavis, Patrice. "Du texte à la mise en scène: l'histoire traversée". *Kodikas/Code*, VII, 1-2 (1984), 24-41.
Pavis, Patrice. "Théorie du théâtre et sémiologie: sphère de l'objet et sphère de l'homme". *Semiotica*, XVI, 1 (1976), 45-86.
Pavis, Patrice. "Vers une sociocritique du théâtre"? In *Voix et images de la scène. Pour une sémiologie de la réception*. New edition revised and expanded. Lille: Presses Universitaires de Lille, 1985, pp. 309-316.
Pavis, Patrice. *Voix et images de la scène*. Lille: Presses Universitaires de Lille, 1982.
Pavis, Patrice. *Voix et images de la scène. Pour une sémiologie de la réception*. New edition revised and expanded. Lille: Presses Universitaires de Lille, 1985.
Paz, Marta Lena. "La crítica teatral y América Latina". In *Hacia una Crítica Literaria Latinoamericana*. Buenos Aires: Fernando García Cambeiro, 1976, pp. 213-226.
Pêcheux, Michel. "L'étrange miroir de l'analyse de discours". *Langages*, 62 (June 1981), 5-8.
Pêcheux, Michel. *Les vérités de La Palice*. Paris: François Maspero, 1975.
Peirce, Charles S. *La ciencia de la semiótica*. Buenos Aires: Ediciones Nueva Visión, 1974.
Peirce, Charles S. *Collected Papers of Charles Sanders Peirce*. Volume I. *Principles of Philosophy*. Edited by Charles Hartshorne and Paul Weiss. Cambridge: Harvard University Press, 1931.
Peirce, Charles S. *Collected Papers of Charles Sanders Peirce*. Volume II. *Elements of Logic*. Edited by Charles Hartshorne and Paul Weiss. Cambridge: Harvard University Press, 1932.
Peirce, Charles S. *Collected Papers of Charles Sanders Peirce*. Volume V. *Pragmatism and Pragmaticism*. Edited by Charles Hartshorne and Paul Weiss. Cambridge: Harvard University Press, 1934.
Peirce, Charles S. *Ecrits sur le signe*. Collected, Translated and Commented by Gérard Deledalle. Paris: Editions du Seuil, 1978.
Pelc, Jerzy. "Some Methodological Problems in Literary History". *New Literary History*, VII, 1 (Autumn 1975), 89-96.
Pellettieri, Osvaldo. *Cien años de teatro argentino: Del Moreira a Teatro Abierto*. Buenos Aires and Ottawa: Editorial Galerna and IITCTL, 1990.
Pellettieri, Osvaldo. "Los modelos del teatro popular argentino de las primeras décadas del siglo y su productividad en el sistema teatral abierto en los sesenta". In *De la Colonia a la Postmodernidad: Teoría teatral y Crítica sobre teatro Latinoamericano*. Edited by Peter Roster and Mario Rojas. Buenos Aires and Ottawa: Editorial Galerna and IITCTL, 1992, pp. 119-134.
Pellettieri, Osvaldo. "Postales argentinas: cambio y tradición en el sistema teatral argentino". In *Hacia una nueva crítica y un nuevo teatro latinoamericano*. Frankfurt am Main: Vervuert Verlag, 1993, pp. 59-75.

Perales, Rosalina. "Nuevas escenificaciones en el teatro puertoriqueño". In *De la Colonia a la Postmodernidad: Teoría teatral y Crítica sobre teatro Latinoamericano*. Peter Roster and Mario Rojas, Editors. Buenos Aires and Ottawa: Editorial Galerna and IITCTL, 1992, pp. 161-170.

Perales, Rosalina. "Teatro de fricción o Las nuevas correintes del teatro puertorriqueño". In *Reflexiones sobre el teatro latinoamericano del siglo XX*. Edited by Fernando de Toro. Buenos Aires and Kiel: Editorial Galerna and Lemcke Verlag, 1989, pp. 73-82.

Perales, Rosalina. *Teatro Hispanoamericano, 1967-1987*. Vol. I. México: Grupo Editorial Gaceta, 1989.

Perales, Rosalina. *Teatro Hispanoamericano, 1967-1987*. Vol. II. México: Grupo Editorial Gaceta, 1993.

Pinter, Harold. *The Caretaker*. London: Eyre Methuen, 1979.

Piscator, Erwin. *Le théâtre politique*. French text by Arthur Adamov with the collaboration of Claude Sebisch. Paris: L'Arche Editeur, 1962.

Portillo, Rafael y Jesús Casado. *Diccionario inglés-español/español-inglés de teatral*. Madrid: Editorial Fundamentos, 1986.

Portis, Winner, Irene and Thomas G. Winner. "The Semiotics of Cultural Texts". *Semiotica*, XVIII, 2 (1976), 101-156.

Portuondo, José A. *La historia de las generaciones*. Cuba: Editorial Letras Cubanas, 1981.

Pradier, Jean-Marie. "Le public et son corps: de quelques données paradoxales de la communication théâtrale". *Degrés*, Seizième année, 56 (hiver 1988), b-b20.

Procházka, Miroslav. "On the Nature of Dramatic Text". In *Semiotics of Drama and Theatre*. Edited by Herta Schmidt and Aloysius Van Kesteren. The Hague: John Benjamins, 1984, pp. 102-126.

Propp, Vladimir. *Morphologie du conte*. Translated by Marguerite Derrida, Tzvetan Todorov and Claude Kahn. Paris: Editions du Seuil, 1970.

Propp, Vladimir. *Morphology of the Folktale*. First edition translated by Laurence Scott with an introduction by Svatava Pirkova-Jakobson. Second edition revised and edited with a preface by Louis A. Wagner. New introduction by Alan Dundes. Austin: University of Texas Press, 1988.

Quadri, Franco. "Eugenio Barba". In *Invenzione di un teatro diverso*. Torino: Giulio Einaudi Editore, 1984, pp. 43-104.

Radrigán, Juan. "Hechos consumados". In *Teatro de Juan Radrigán. 11 obras*. Santiago, Chile and Minnesota: CENECA and University of Minnesota, 1984.

Raillon, Jean-Claude. "La fonction de représentation". *Degrés*, Première année, 3 (juillet 1973), e-e21.

Rastier, François. "Un concept dans le discours des études littéraire". *Littérature*, 7 (1972), 185-221.

Recanati, François. "Qu'est-ce qu'un acte locutionnaire"? *Communications*, 32 (1980), 190-215.

Rector, Mônica and Aluizio R. Trinta. *Comunicacão não-verbal. A gestualidade Brasileira*. São Paulo: Petropolis, Vozes, 1985.

Reiss, Timothy J. "Peirce, Frege, la verité, le tiers inclus et le champ pratiqué". *Langages*, 58 (1980), 103-127.
Rey, Alain. "Référence et littérature". *Degrés*, Première année, 3 (juillet 1973), h-h8.
Reyes, Alfonso. "Fragmento sobre la interpretación social de las letras iberoamericanas". In *Marginalia*. Primera serie. México: 1952, pp. 154-159.
Ricoeur, Paul. "The Model of the Text: Meaningful Action Considered as a Text". *New Literary History*, I, 1 (Autumn 1973), 91-117.
Ricoeur, Paul. "Qu'est-ce qu'un texte"? In *Hermeneutik und Dialektik*. Tübingen: J.C. Mohr, 1970, pp. 181-200.
Riffaterre, Michel. "Pour une approche formelle de l'histoire littéraire". In *La production du texte*. Paris: Editions du Seuil, 1979, pp. 89-112.
Rincón, Carlos. "Sobre crítica e historia literaria hoy en Hispanoamérica". *Casa de las Américas*, XIV, 80 (septiembre-octubre 1973), 135-147.
Robbe-Grillet, Alain. *Pour un nouveau roman*. Paris: Editions Gallimard, 1963.
Robin, Regine. *Histoire et linguistique*. Paris: Librairie Armand Colin, 1973.
Roster, Peter and Mario Rojas, Editors. *De la Colonia a la Postmodernidad: Teoría teatral y Crítica sobre teatro Latinoamericano*. Buenos Aires and Ottawa: Editorial Galerna and IITCTL, 1992.
Rozik, Eli. *The Language of the Theatre*. Glasgow: University of Glasgow, 1992.
Rozik, Eli. "On The Apparent Double Reference of Theatrical Texts". *Degrés*, Seiziéme année, 56 (hiver 1988), f-f20.
Rueckert, William. "Literary Criticism and History: The Endless Dialectic". *New Literary History*, VI, 3 (Spring 1975), 491-512.
Ruffini, Franco. "Anthropologie". In *Théâtre. Modes D'Approche*. Edited by André Helbo, J. Dines Johansen, Patrice Pavis and Anne Ubersfeld. Bruxelles: Editions Labor, 1987, pp. 91-112.
Ruffini, Franco. "L'attore e il dramma. Saggio teorico di antropologia teatrale". *Teatro e Storia*, Anno III, 5, 2 (ottobre 1988), 177-250.
Ruffini, Franco. "Le milieu-scène: pré-expression, énergie, présence". *Bouffonneries*, 15-16 (1986), 33-61.
Ruffini, Franco. "Pour une sémiologie concrète de l'acteur". *Degrés*, Dixième année, 30 (printemps 1982), b-b11.
Ruffini, Franco y Ferdinando Taviani. "Antropología teatral". *Gestos*, Año 3, 5 (Avril 1988), 9-32.
Runes, Dagobert D., Editor. *Dictionary of Philosophy*. New Jersey: Littlefield, Adams, 1962.
Ruprecht, Hans-George. "Intertextuality". *Intertextuality*. Edited by Heinrich F. Plett. Berlin and New York: Walter de Gruyter, 1991.
Ruprecht, Hans-George. "Intertextualité". *Texte*, 2 (1983), 13-22.
Ruprecht, Hans-George. *Theaterpublikum und Textauffassung*. Bern: Herbert Lang - Frankfurt am Main und München: Peter Herbert, 1976.
Rutten, Frans. "Sur les notions de texte et de lecture dans une théorie de la réception". *Revue des sciences humaines*, XLIX, 177 (janvier-mars 1980), 67-83.

Ryan, Marie-Laure. "Toward a Competence Theory of Genre". *Poetics*, 8 (1979), 307-337.
Saison, Maryvonne. "Les objets dans la création théâtrale". *Revue de metaphysique et morale*, LXXIX, 1 (janvier-mars 1974), 253-268.
Salvat, Ricard. *El teatro como texto, como espectáculo*. Barcelona: Montesinos, 1983.
Sánchez, Luis Alberto. *Historia comparada de las literaturas americanas*. 4 vols. Buenos Aires: Editorial Losada, 1973, 1974 and 1976.
Sánchez, Luis Alberto. *Proceso y contenido de la novela hispanoamericana*. Second edition, revised. Madrid: Editorial Gredos, 1968.
Saraiva, A.J. "Message et littérature". *Poétique*, 17 (1974), 1-13.
Saussure, Ferdinand de. *Course in General Linguistics*. Edited by Charles Bally and Albert Sechehaye in collaboration with Albert Riedlinger. Translated, with an Introduction and Notes by Wade Baskin. New York: McGraw-Hill, 1966.
Savarese, Nicola. *Il teatro al di la' del mare*. Lodi: G.E.L., 1988.
Schachter, Stanley. "The Interaction of Cognitive and Physiological Determinants of Emotional States". In *Anxiety and Behavior*. Edited by C. Spielberger. New York: Academic Press, 1966, pp. 193-224.
Schachter, Stanley and J.E. Singer. "Cognitive, Social and Physiological Determinants of Emotional State". *Psychological Review*, LXIX, 5, (September 1962), 379-399.
Schechner, Richard. *Between Theatre and Anthropology*. Philadelphia: University of Pennsylvania Press, 1985.
Schlemmer, Oskar. *Théâtre et abstraction*. Translated, with a preface and notes by Eric Michaud. Lausanne: Editions L'Age d'Homme, 1978.
Schmidt, Herta and Aloysius Van Kesteren, Editors. *Semiotics of Drama and Theatre*. Amsterdam and Philadelphia: John Benjamins, 1984.
Schober, Rita. "Périodisation et historiographie littéraire". *Romanistica Pragensia*, 5 (1968), 13-24.
Schober, Rita. "Réception et historicité de la littérature". *Revue des sciences humaines*, LX, 189 (janvier-mars 1983), 7-20.
Schoenmakers, Henry. "The Tacit Majority in the Theatre". *Kodikas/Code*, II, Supplement, 8 (1982), 108-155.
Schoenmakers, Henry and Ed Tan. "'Good guy bad guy' effects in Political Theatre". In *Semiotics of Drama and Theatre*. Edited by Herta Schmidt and Aloysius Van Kesteren. Amsterdam and Philadelphia: John Benjamins, 1984, pp. 467-508.
Segre, Cesare. "Narratology and Theatre". *Poetics Today*, II, 3 (Spring 1983), 95-104.
Sehers, Rien T. "A propos de la nécesité de la collaboration entre la sémiologie et l'esthétique de la réception". *Degrés*, huitième année, 24-25 (hiver 1980-1981), h-h14.
Serpieri, Alessandro, et. al. *Come comunica il teatro: dal texto alla scena*. Milano: Il Formichiere, 1978.

Serpieri, Alessandro, Keir Elam, Paola Gulli Publiatti, Tomaso Kemeny and Romana Rutelli. "Toward a Segmentation of the Dramatic Text". *Poetics Today*, II, 3 (Spring 1981), 163-200.
Shakespeare, William. *The Tragedy of Hamlet, Prince of Denmark*. In *The Riverside Shakespeare*. Boston: Houghton Mifflin Company, 1974.
Shevtsova, Maria. "Notes Towards The Sociology of Performance". In *Congrès Mondial de Sociologie du Théâtre*. Selected Papers. Edited by Roger Deldime. Roma: Bulzoni Editore, 1988, pp. 175-198.
Sieveking, Alejandro. *Tres tristes tigres*. Santiago, Chile: Editorial Universitaria, 1974.
Simonin-Grumbach, Jenny. "Pour une typologie des discours". In *Langue, discours, société. Pour Emile Benveniste*. Under the direction of Julia Kristeva, Jean-Claude Milner and Nicolas Ruwet. Paris: Editions du Seuil, 1975, pp. 85-121.
Skinne, Quentin. "Hermeneutics and the Role of History". *New Literary History*, VII, 1 (Autumn 1975), 209-232.
Sötér, István. "The Dilemma of Literary Science". *New Literary History*, II, 1 (Autumn 1970), 85-113.
Souriau, Etienne. *Les deux cent mille situations dramatiques*. Paris: Flammarion, Editeur, 1950.
Stanislavsky, Konstantin. *An Actor Prepares*. Translated by Elizabeth Reynolds Hapgood. London: Geoffrey Bles, 1937.
Stanislavsky, Konstantin. *Building a Character*. Translated by Elizabeth Reynolds Hapgood. New York: Theatre Arts Books, 1949.
Stanislavsky, Konstantin. *Creating a Role*. Translated by Elizabeth Reynolds Hapgood. New York: Theatre Arts Books, 1961.
Steinmetz, Horst. "Réception et interprétation". In *Théorie de la littérature*. Edited by A. Kibédi Varga. Paris: Picard, 1981, pp. 193-209.
Stempel, Wolf-Dieter. "Aspects génériques de la réception". *Poétique*, 39 (1979), 353-362.
Stierle, Karlheinz. "Réception et fiction". *Poétique*, 39 (septembre 1979), 300-320.
Strasberg, Lee. *Strasberg at the Actors Studio*. Tape-recorded sessions. Robert H. Hethom, Editor. New York: Viking Press, 1965.
Strasberg, Lee. *Le travail à l'Actors Studio*. Collected and presented by Robert H. Hethmon. Translated by Dominique Minot. Paris: Editions Gallimard, 1969.
Strawsom, P.F. "Phrase et acte de parole". *Langages*, 17 (mars 1970), 20-33.
Styan. J.L. *Modern Drama in Theory and Practice 1. Realism and Naturalism*. Vol. I. Cambridge: Cambridge University Press, 1983.
Styan, J.L. *Modern Drama in Theory and Practice 2. Symbolism, Surrealism and the Absurd*. Vol. II. Cambridge: Cambridge University Press, 1983.
Styan, J.L. *Modern Drama in Theory and Practice 3. Expressionism and Epic Theatre*. Vol. III. Cambridge: Cambridge University Press, 1983.
Suleiman, Susan R., Editor. *The Reader in the Text: Essays on Audience and Interpretation*. Princeton, New Jersey: Princeton University Press, 1980.

Suvin, Darko. "Per una teoria dell'analisi agenziale". *Versus*, 30 (settembre-dicembre 1981), 87-109.
Szondi, Peter. *Theory of the Modern Drama*. Edited and translated by Michael Hays. Foreword by Jochen Schulte-Sasse. Minneapolis: University of Minnesota Press, 1987.
Tacca, Oscar. *La historia literaria*. Madrid: Editorial Gredos, 1968.
Taïrov, Alexandre. *Le Théâtre libéré*. Laussane: La Cité L'Age d'Homme, 1974.
Tan, Ed. "Cognitive Process in Reception". *Kodikas/Code*, II, Supplement, 8 (1982), 156-203.
Taviani, Ferdinando. "L'énergie de l'acteur comme premisse". *Bouffonneries*, 15-16 (1986) 23-33.
Théâtre du Soleil. "Différent le Théâtre du Soleil". *Travail théâtral*, special edition, (février 1976).
Tindemans, Carlos. "Coherence and Focality. A Contribution to the Analysability of the Theatre Discourse". In *Semiotics of Drama and Theatre*. Edited by Herta Schmidt and Aloysius Van Kesteren. Amsterdam and Philadelphia: John Benjamins, 1984, pp. 128-134.
Todorov, Tzvetan. *Les genres du discours*. Paris: Editions du Seuil, 1978.
Todorov, Tzvetan. *Grammaire du Décaméron*. The Hague: Mouton, 1969.
Todorov, Tzvetan. *Littérature et signification*. Paris: Librairie Larousse, 1967.
Todorov, Tzvetan. "L'origine des genres". In *Les genres du discours*. Paris: Editions du Seuil, 1978, pp. 44-60.
Todorov, Tzvetan, ed. *Théorie de la littérature*. Texts by the Russian Formalists collected, presented and translated by Tzvetan Todorov. Preface by Roman Jakobson. Paris: Editions du Seuil, 1965.
Tomachevsky, Boris. "Thématique". In *Théorie de la littérature*. Texts by the Russian Formalists collected, presented and translated by Tzvetan Todorov. Preface by Roman Jakobson. Paris: Editions du Seuil, 1965, pp. 263-308.
Tompkins, Jane P., Editor. *Reader-Response Criticism: From Formalism to Post-Structuralism*. Baltimore and London: The Johns Hopkins University Press, 1980.
Tordera, Antonio. "Aspects sociaux et asociaux de l'essence du théâtre". In *Congrès Mondial de Sociologie du Théâtre*. Selected Papers. Edited by Roger Deldime. Roma: Bulzoni Editore, 1988, pp. 153-174.
Tordera, Antonio. "Aspectos sociales y asociales de la esencia del teatro". *Gestos*, Año 2, 3 (Avril 1987), 11-28.
Turner, Victor. *From Ritual to Theatre*. New York: Performing Arts Journal, 1982.
Turner, Victor. *The Anthropology of Performance*. Preface by Richard Schechner. New York: Performing Arts Journal, 1986.
Tynianov, Juri. "De l'évolution littéraire". In *Théorie de la littérature*. Texts by the Russian Formalists collected, presented and translated by Tzvetan Todorov. Preface by Roman Jakobson. Paris: Editions du Seuil, 1965, pp. 120-135.
Ubersfeld, Anne. *L'école du spectateur. Lire le théâtre 2*. Paris: Editions Sociales, 1981.

Ubersfeld, Anne. "Le lieu du discours". *Pratiques*, 15/16 (juillet 1977), 10-19.
Ubersfeld, Anne. *Lire le théâtre*. Paris: Editions Sociales, 1977.
Ubersfeld, Anne. *Lire le théâtre*. Postscript to the fourth edition. Paris: Editions Sociales, 1982.
Ubersfeld, Anne. "Notes sur la dénégation théâtrale". In *La relation théâtrale*. Texts compiled by Régis Durand. Lille: Presses Universitaires de Lille, 1980, pp. 11-25.
Ubersfeld, Anne. *Semiótica teatral*. Madrid: Catédra and Universidad de Murcia, 1989.
Ubersfeld, Anne. "Sur le signe théâtral et son référent". *Travail théâtral*, 31 (avril-juin 1978), 120-123.
Vaïs, Michel. *L'écrivain scénique*. Montréal: Les Presses de l'Université du Québec, 1978.
Valdés, Mario J. "Heuristic Models of Inquiry". *New Literary History*, XII, 1 (Autumn 1980), 253-267.
Valenzuela, José Luis. "Barba y nuestro teatro débil". *Espacio*, Año 3, 5 (avril 1989), 13-20.
Valenzuela, José Luis. "La ética de las máscaras". *Espacio*, Año 2, 2 (avril 1987), 53-56.
Valenzuela, Loreto. "La Novela Cómica". *Apuntes*, 92 (septiembre 1984), 3-56.
Valenzuela, Loreto. "Teatro y sociedad chilena en la mitad del siglo XX: El Melodrama". *Apuntes*, 91 (noviembre 1983), 7-78.
Vallauri, Carlo. "Per una sistemetizazione teorica della sociologia del teatro come scienza operativa". In *Congrès Mondial de Sociologie du Théâtre*. Selected Papers. Edited by Roger Deldime. Rome: Bulzoni Editore, 1988, pp. 315-324.
Van Dijk, Teun A. *Text and Context: Explorations in Semantics and Pragmatics of Discourse*. London: Longmans, 1977.
Van Kesteren, Aloysius. "Theatre and Drama Research: An Analytical proposition". In *Semiotics of Drama and Theatre*. Edited by Herta Schmidt and Aloysius Van Kesteren. Amsterdam and Philadelphia: John Benjamins, 1984, 16-99.
Van Kesteren, Aloysius. "Theatre, Video and Incompetence". *Kodikas/Code*, II, Supplement, 8 (1982), 204-321.
Van Kesteren, Aloysius and Herta Schmidt, Editors. *Semiotics of Drama and Theatre*. Amsterdam and Philadelphia: John Benjamins Publishing Company, 1985.
Van Zoest, Aart. "Interprétation et sémiotique". In *Théorie de la littérature*. Edited by A. Kibédi Varga. Paris: Picard, 1981, pp. 240-255.
Veinstein, André. *La mise en scène théâtrale et sa condition esthétique*. Paris: Flammarion, Editeur, 1955.
Veltrusky, Jiři. "Basic Features of Dramatic Dialogue". In *Semiotics of Art. Prague School Contributions*. Edited by Ladislav Matejka and Irwin R. Titunik. Cambridge, Massachusetts and London, England: The MIT Press, 1976, pp. 128-133.

Veltrusky, Jiři. "Construction of Semantic Contexts". In *Semiotics of Art. Prague School Contributions*. Edited by Ladislav Matejka and Irwin R. Titunik. Cambridge, Massachusetts and London, England: The MIT Press, 1976, pp. 134-144.

Veltrusky, Jiři. "Cualidades sonoras del texto y la actuación del actor". *Gestos*, Año 4, 8 (Noviembre 1989), 33-48.

Veltrusky, Jiři. *El drama como literatura*. Translated by Milena Grass. Buenos Aires and Ottawa: Editorial Galerna and IITCTL, 1990.

Veltrusky, Jiři. "Dramatic Text as a Component of Theatre". In *Semiotics of Art. Prague School Contributions*. Edited by Ladislav Matjka and Erwin R. Titunik. Cambridge, Massachusetts and London, England: The MIT Press, 1976, pp. 94-117.

Veltrusky, Jiři. "The Prague School Theory of Theatre". *Poetics Today*, II, 3 (Spring 1981), 225-235.

Veron, Eliseo. "Pertinence (idéologique) du 'code'". *Degrés*. Deuxième année, 7-8 (juillet-octobre 1974), b-b13.

Vidal, Hernán. *Literatura hispanoamericana e ideología: surgimiento y crisis*. Buenos Aires: Ediciones Hispamérica, 1976.

Viëtor, Karl. "L'histoire des genres littéraires". *Poétique*, 32 (novembre 1977), 490-506.

Villegas, Juan. "De canonización y recanonización: la historia del teatro latinoamericano". In *De la Colonia a la Postmodernidad: Teoría teatral y Crítica sobre teatro Latinoamericano*. Edited by Peter Roster and Mario Rojas. Buenos Aires and Ottawa: Editorial Galerna and IITCTL, 1992, pp. 99-106.

Villegas, Juan. "El discurso teatral y el discurso crítico: El caso de Chile". *Anales de la Universidad de Chile*. Quinta serie, 5 (agosto 1984), 316-336.

Villegas, Juan. "La especificidad del discurso crítico sobre el teatro hispanoamericano". *Gestos*, 2 (Noviembre 1986), 57-74.

Villegas, Juan. "Historia del teatro hispanoamericano: tipos de discursos críticos y discursos teatrales". *Dispositio*, XIII, 33-35 (1988), 147-160.

Villegas, Juan. "La historicidad del discurso crítico metateatral". In *Reflexiones sobre el teatro latinoamericano del siglo XX*. Edited by Fernando de Toro. Buenos Aires and Kiel: Editorial Galerna and Lemcke Verlag, 1989, pp. 1-6.

Villegas, Juan. *Ideología y discurso crítico sobre el teatro de España y América Latina*. Minneapolis, Minnesota: The Prisma Institute, 1988.

Villegas, Juan. *Interpretación y análisis del texto dramático*. Ottawa: Girol Books, 1982.

Villegas, Juan. *Nueva interpretación y análisis del texto dramático*. Second edition, revised and expanded. Ottawa: Girol Books, 1991.

Villegas, Juan. *Teoría de historia literaria y poesía lírica*. Ottawa: Girol Books, 1984.

Vitez, Antoine and Emile Copfermann. *De Chaillot à Chaillot*. Paris: Hachette, 1981.

Vodička, Felix. "Historia de la repercusión de la obra literaria". In *Lingüística formal y crítica literaria*. Madrid: Plaza Mayor, 1970, pp. 47-62
Vodička, Felix and O. Obelic. *El mundo de las letras*. Second edition. Santiago, Chile: Editorial Universitaria, 1971.
Vodička, Felix. *Die Struktur der literarischen Entwicklung*. Translated by Christian Tuschinsky, Peter Richter and Frank Boldt. München: Wilhelm Fink Verlag, 1976.
Vološinov, V.N. *Marxism and the Philosophy of Language*. Translated by Ladislav Matejka and I.R. Titunik. Cambridge, Massachusetts and London, England: Harvard University Press, 1986.
Warning, Reiner. "Pour une pragmatique du discours fictionnel". *Poétique*, 39 (septembre 1979), 321-337.
Weimann, Robert. "French Structuralism and Literary History: Some Critiques and Reconsiderations". *New Literary History*, IV, 3 (Spring 1970), 437-469.
Weinrich, Harald. "Les temps et les personnes". *Poétique*, 39 (septembre 1979), 338-352.
Wellek, René and Austin Warren. *Theory of Literature*. New revised edition. New York: Harcourt, Brace and World, 1970.
White, Hayden. "The Problem of Change in Literary History". *New Literary History*, VII, 1 (Autumn 1975), 97-111.
Wittgenstein, Ludwig. *Philosophical Investigations*. Second edition. Translated by G.E.M. Anscombe. Oxford: Blackwell, 1958.
Wittig, Susan. "Toward a Semiotic Theory of the Drama". *Educational Theatre Journal*, 26 (1974), 441-454.
Wolff, Egon. *Alamos en la azotea*. In *Teatro chileno contemporáneo*. Santiago, Chile: Editorial Andrés Bello, 1982, pp. 127-184. [Includes: *El tony chico* by Luis Alberto Heiremans, pp. 11-82 and *El árbol Pepe* by Fernando Debesa, pp. 83-126].
Wolff, Egon. *Flores de papel*. Ottawa: Girol Books, 1979, pp. 149-222. [Includes: *Invitación a la muerte* by Xavier Villaurrutia, 11-88; *Los siameses* by Griseld Gambaro, 93-144].
Wolff, Egon. *Los invasores*. In *El teatro hispanoamericano contemporáneo*. Second edition. Edited by Carlos Solórzano. México: Fondo de Cultura Económica, 1975, pp. 126-192. [Includes: *Sempronio* by Agustín Cuzzani, pp. 17-63; *Ida y Vuelta* by Mario Benedetti, pp. 64-125; *El fabricante de deudas* by Sebastián Salazar Bondy, pp. 193-262; *La muerte no entrará en Palacio* by René Marqués, pp. 310-417].
Worton, Michael and Judith Still, Editors. *Intertextuality: Theories and Practices*. Manchester and New York: Manchester University Press, 1990.
Zima, Pierre V. *Pour une sociologie du texte littéraire*. Paris: Union Générale d'Editions, 1978.
Zima, Pierre V. "Towards Sociological Semiotics". In *Texte et idéologie/Text and Ideology*. Colloquium at Carleton University, Ottawa, April 1986. (Mimeograph).

Books and Special Issue Journals Devoted to Theatre Semiotics and Theatre Theory

Altro Polo. Performance: from Product to Process. Edited by Tim Fitzpatrick. Sydney: University of Sydney, 1989.
Analyse sémiologique du spectacle théâtral. Studies Directed and Presented by Tadeuz Kowzan. Lyon: Centre d'Etudes et de Recherches Théâtrales, Université Lyon II, 1976.
Como comunica il teatro: dal testo alla scena. Edited by Alessandro Serpieri. Milano: Il Formichiere, 1978.
La comunicazione teatrale. Edited by Massimo Canevacci and Alfonso de Toro. Roma: Edizioni Seam, 1993.
La critica teatrale. In *Quaderni di teatro*, II, 5 (1979).
Estudios sobre el drama y el teatro hispanoamericano. *Revista Canadiense de Estudios Hispánicos*, VII, 1 (Fall 1982). Under the direction of J. Varela and R. Young.
Hacia una nueva crítica y un nuevo teatro latinoamericano. Edited by Alfonso de Toro and Fernando de Toro. Frankfurt am Main: Vervuert Verlag, 1993.
Inszernierung von Welt: Semiotik des Theaters. *Zeitschrift für Semiotik.* Band 11, Heft 1 (1989).
Multimedial Communication. In *Theatre Semiotics.* Vol. II. Edited by Ernest W.B. Hess-Lüttich. Tübingen: Gunter Narr Verlag, 1982.
1er Congrès Mondial de Sociologie du Théâtre. Edited by Roger Deldime. Roma: Bulzoni Editore, 1988.
La relation théâtrale. Texts compiled by Régis Durand. Lille: Presses Universitaires de Lille, 1980.
La scène. *Littérature*, 9 (février 1973).
Semiología del teatro. Texts Selected by José María Díez Borque and Luciano García Lorenzo. Barcelona: Editorial Planeta, 1975.
Semiología del teatro. Edited by Fernando de Toro. *Semiosis*, 19 (julio-diciembre 1987).
Semiologia do teatro. Organized by J. Guinsburg, J. Teixeira Coehlo Netto and Reni Chaves Cardoso. São Paulo: Editora Perspectiva, 1978.
Sémiologie de la représentation. Edited by André Helbo. Bruxelles: Editions Complexe, 1975.
Sémiologie du spectacle. Edited by André Helbo. *Degrés*, Dixième année, 30 (Spring 1982).
Sémiologie et théâtre. Lyon: Centre d'études et de recherches théâtrales, Université Lyon II, Organon 80, 1980.

Semiotica della ricezione teatrale. Edited by Marco De Marinis. *Versus*, 41 (maggio-agosto 1985).
Semiotica del teatro. Edited by Manuel Angel Vázquez Medel. *Discurso*, 1, 1987.
Semiótica del teatro. Edited by Mario Rojas. *Dispositio*, XIII, 33-35 (Fall 1988).
La semiotica e il doppio teatrale. Edited by Giulio Ferroni. Napoli: Liguori Editore, 1981.
Semiótica y Teatro Latinoamericano. Edited by Alfonso de Toro and Fernando de Toro. Buenos Aires and Ottawa: Editorial Galerna and IITCTL, 1990.
Semiotics of Art. Prague School Contributions. Edited by Ladislav Matejka and Irwin R. Titunik. Cambridge, Massachusetts and London, England: The MIT Press, 1976.
Semiotics of Drama and Theatre. Edited by Herta Schmidt and Aloysius Van Kesteren. The Hague: John Benjamins, 1984.
Le spectacle au pluriel. Edited by Paul Delsemme and André Helbo. *Kodikas/Code*, VII, 1-2 (1984).
Spectacle et communication. Edited by André Helbo. *Degrés*, Seizième année, 56 (hiver 1988).
Teatro e communicazione gestuale. Edited by Umberto Eco. *Versus*, 22 (1979).
Teatro e semiotica. Edited by Umberto Eco. *Versus*, 21 (1978).
Théâtre and Television. Edited by Robert L. Erenstein. Amsterdam: International Theatre Bookshop, 1988.
Théâtre et sémiologie. Edited by André Helbo. *Degrés*, 13 (1978).
Le théâtre et ses réceptions. *Revue des sciences humaines*, LX, 189 (janvier-mars 1983).
Théâtre. Modes d'approche. Edited by André Helbo, J. Dines Johansen, Patrice Pavis and Anne Ubersfeld, Editors. Bruxelles: Eidtions Labor, 1987.
Le théâtre sous la contrainte. Edited by R. Thierceli. Aix-en-Provence: Université de Provence.